Greeks and Romans Bearing Gifts

Greeks and Romans Bearing Gifts

How the Ancients Inspired the Founding Fathers

Carl J. Richard

ROWMAN & LITTLEFIELD PUBLISHERS, INC.
Lanham • Boulder • New York • Toronto • Plymouth, UK

ROWMAN & LITTLEFIELD PUBLISHERS, INC.

Published in the United States of America
by Rowman & Littlefield Publishers, Inc.
A wholly owned subsidary of The Rowman & Littlefield Publishing Group, Inc.
4501 Forbes Boulevard, Suite 200, Lanham, Maryland 20706
www.rowmanlittlefield.com

Estover Road, Plymouth PL6 7PY, United Kingdom

British Library Cataloguing in Publication Information Available

Library of Congress Cataloging-in-Publication Data
Richard, Carl J.
 Greeks and Romans bearing gifts : how the ancients inspired the Founding Fathers /
Carl J. Richard.
   p. cm.
 Includes bibliographical references and index.
 ISBN-13: 978-0-7425-5623-2 (cloth : alk. paper)
 ISBN-10: 0-7425-5623-9 (cloth : alk. paper)
 1. Political science—United States—History—18th century. 2. Political science—
Greece—History. 3. Political science—Rome—History. 4. Philosophy, American—18th
century. 5. Founding Fathers of the United States. 6. Civilization, Classical. I. Title.
 JA84.U5R484 2008
 320.0973'09033—dc22

                                                                         2007039018

Printed in the United States of America

⊗™ The paper used in this publication meets the minimum requirements of
American National Standard for Information Sciences—Permanence of Paper
for Printed Library Materials, ANSI/NISO Z39.48-1992.

For Paul Conkin, my beloved mentor

~

Contents

~

Preface

When researching my first book, *The Founders and the Classics: Greece, Rome, and the American Enlightenment* (1994), I was struck by the ancient historians' remarkable skill as storytellers, by the profound impact of their stories on the Founding Fathers, and by most modern Americans' lack of familiarity with many of these influential stories. Though my book was received favorably by both academic and popular reviewers, even many highly educated readers confided that they struggled with it due to a lack of knowledge concerning many of the ancients to whom I alluded. This is understandable since modern schools, in stark contrast to their eighteenth-century forebears, spend little time teaching students about classical history and mythology.

Our stories are not the founders' stories, and, ironically, the founders themselves are partly responsible for this fact. In their successful quest to match the deeds of the ancients (their own heroes, whom they first encountered in the tales of the ancient historians while still children), the founders became our heroes, the source of so many of our own national stories. Thus, the founders drove the ancients from their pedestals and occupied their places. While Washington spoke of Cincinnatus and the plow, we speak of Washington and the cherry tree. But, however understandable the modern public's lack of familiarity with some of the tales of Greece and Rome, it is an unfortunate situation, for in neglecting these stories we neglect an important part of our own heritage. After all, these were the tales that inspired the founders to rebel against the mother country and to establish a republic they hoped would one day rival those of Greece and Rome.

It is my hope, therefore, that this volume will be useful to general readers who have an interest in the Founding Fathers, in ancient history, or in both. It is not a monograph intended for specialists. Its purpose is not to extend the frontiers of knowledge but rather to reintroduce Americans to a lost part of their heritage in a way that I hope will be both informative and entertaining. The story of the founders' relationship with the ancients is itself a good story.

To refer to the historians of Greece and Rome as storytellers is not an insult, nor is it meant to imply that they wrote pure fiction. On the contrary, most modern historians consider these early practitioners of their craft reliable in general, if not in all particulars, and consider their works of inestimable value, the loss of which would leave our knowledge of the ancient world incomparably poorer. Indeed, most modern historians marvel at the degree of accuracy attained by many of their ancient counterparts, considering the enormous difficulties that confronted them. Of course, each classical historian possessed biases related to his gender (all were male), economic class (nearly all were aristocrats), culture, and personal background that readers must always take into consideration. But modern historians, while benefiting enormously from advances in the accessibility of information, are no freer of bias than their ancient counterparts. Therefore, when I call the ancient historians master storytellers, I intend it as a compliment—and most of them would have interpreted it as such, since they considered the writing of history an art as well as a science.

No one possesses more influence than a master storyteller. The love of stories seems to be an innate human trait, present in all cultures. Every teacher knows that students are far more apt to remember a story than to remember any other information. The better the tale and the more vividly it is told, the more humans want to believe it and the more apt they are to internalize whatever lesson it imparts. (Most stories do impart a lesson, however subtly, by their very structure, and most readers and listeners are not pleased with tales they feel have not imparted one, considering such stories a waste of their time.) For this reason, it has been said that those who control a society's stories control the society. Every nation has its own stories, tales that tend to exalt the motherland. Jesus taught mostly through parables. Indeed, Bible stories written more than two millennia ago still fascinate Jews, Christians, and some nonbelievers as well. Filmmakers constitute today's most influential storytellers, though novelists, playwrights, and songwriters still contribute stories to the popular consciousness.

The Founding Fathers' favorite storytellers were the historians of Greece and Rome. From these master storytellers the founders learned valuable lessons—

personal, social, and political—that influenced both the birth and the course of the United States.

In the first chapter I will discuss the ancient historians and orators the founders admired, detailing the historical context in which each wrote and what each sought to accomplish. In the second I will describe the unique political system and culture of Sparta and discuss the founders' love-hate relationship with this, their favorite Greek republic. In the ensuing chapters I will summarize the various eras of Greek and Roman history, drawing heavily on the founders' favorite storytellers, and identify the central lesson the founders learned from each period. There were, of course, many other lessons that individual founders learned from the ancients, some of which conflicted with one another, but I have chosen to focus on the most important political lessons the founders learned, since these were the lessons that most shaped their decisions as statesmen.

I would like to thank Rowman & Littlefield Publishers for allowing me to reproduce material from my own previous book, *Twelve Greeks and Romans Who Changed the World* (2002), throughout this volume. I would also like to express my gratitude to my friend and colleague Caroline Winterer, one of the leading experts on the classical tradition in America, for her sage advice. Additionally, I would like to thank my editor, Susan McEachern, for her unfailing enthusiasm and wisdom. As always, I would like to thank my precious wife, Debbie, my other half, for her unceasing prayers and support.

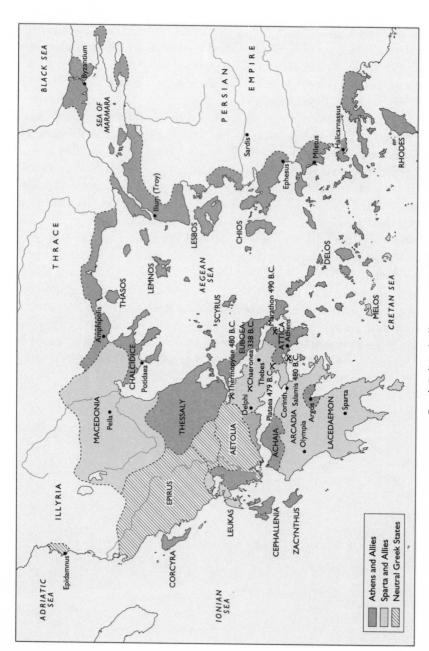

Greek Political Alliances, 431 BC

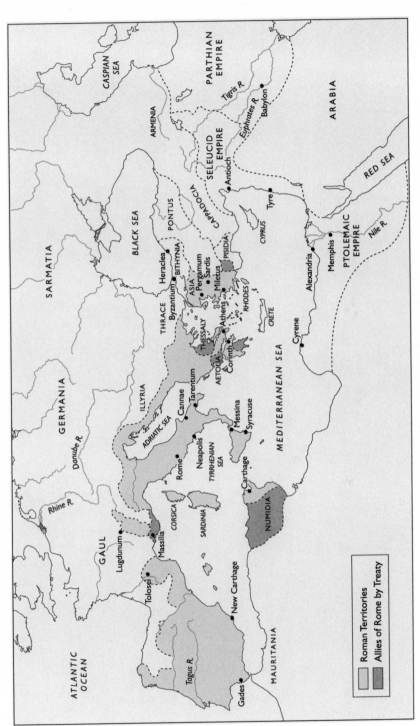

The Roman World, 133 BC

Roman Territories
Allies of Rome by Treaty

CHAPTER ONE

⁓

The Storytellers and the Founders

The Greek and Roman historians and orators whom the Founding Fathers studied were a small, select group who possessed backgrounds and concerns that were similar to those of the founders themselves. Like the founders, these historians tended to be learned, moralistic, aristocratic males who possessed some political and military experience.

Herodotus (ca. 484–425 BC)

Justly termed the "Father of History," Herodotus of Halicarnassus (on the southwestern coast of what is now Turkey) was the first person to use the Greek term *historia* (meaning "research" or "inquiry") to refer to the study of the past. Herodotus differed from the mythologists of previous eras in several ways. First, he attributed most past events to natural causes. Although Herodotus did not banish the supernatural completely from his *Histories*, an account of the Persian Wars between the Greek republics and the Persian Empire (499–479 BC), he ascribed the most significant events to natural causes. In particular, he portrayed human behavior as the prime determinant of history. Herodotus's claim that the wisdom of the Athenian leader Themistocles and the courage of free men had won the Persian Wars contrasted sharply with the constant meddling of the gods in Homer's *Iliad* and in the other Greek poems. Herodotus even discussed those occasions when prophecies of the oracle of Delphi, the priestess through whom the god

Apollo revealed the future, proved inaccurate and when the oracle had been bribed to favor a participant in a dispute.

Second, unlike the mythologists, Herodotus based his history upon real research. Herodotus did a remarkable job of gathering evidence throughout the eastern Mediterranean world and weaving it together into a plausible narrative. His accuracy was astonishing, considering that some of the events he related had occurred centuries before his time and that he had to rely mostly on oral sources. While he did greatly exaggerate the size of the Persian army, his exaggeration was due partly to the unreliability of his Persian sources.

Third, unlike the mythologists, Herodotus always identified his sources, even when he doubted their veracity. He wrote, "For myself, my duty is to report all that is said; but I am not obliged to believe it all alike—a remark which may be understood to apply to my whole history." Indeed, after Herodotus related the popular story of a diver who swam eleven miles underwater without ascending for air, he deadpanned, "My own opinion is that on this occasion he took a boat."

Fourth, the difference between history and mythology was further expressed in the decision of Herodotus and his successors to write prose, not poetry—significantly, the same decision previously made by many of the Greek philosophers who founded Western science. Though his work was highly entertaining, Herodotus's principal purpose was to inform, only secondarily to entertain.

Exiled from Halicarnassus in 457 BC for his alleged opposition to Persian rule in that part of Asia Minor, Herodotus traveled through much of the known world—Egypt, Cyrene, Tyre, Mesopotamia, Arabia, the Black Sea, and the north Aegean—gathering material for a geographical work. He then landed at Athens, where Pericles and Sophocles befriended him. Both the city itself and Athenian stories of the Persian Wars so impressed Herodotus that he decided to change his topic of study. The first part of Herodotus's *Histories* concerned the rise of the Persian Empire, the second portion the resulting war with Greece.

Herodotus was not only the first historian but also one of the most entertaining historians who has ever written. His hilarious digressions on Near Eastern cultures, the product of a passionate curiosity and love of life, represent a gold mine of anthropological research (he has been called the first anthropologist, sociologist, and archaeologist). No subject was too small or inconsequential to evoke Herodotus's interest, none too dull for his fertile imagination to enliven. A typical example was Herodotus's discussion of the theory that Egyptian skulls were harder than Persian skulls. A true scientist, Herodotus felt compelled to test the hypothesis. So he journeyed to a battlefield where the Egyptians and Persians had recently fought and began smashing corpses over the head with rocks. He found that while Egyptian skulls could barely be cracked with huge stones, Persian skulls could be crushed using only small rocks. Having validated the hypothesis, Herodotus then developed a typically imaginative theory to explain the phenomenon. Because Egyptians shaved their heads and walked about without any head covering while the Persians wore their hair long and wrapped in a turban, the Egyptians required thicker skulls to withstand the heat of the sun. This was almost a theory of natural selection.

Another tale typical of Herodotus is that of Darius I's accession to the Persian throne. When the previous emperor, Cambyses, died without heir, the seven leading noblemen of Persia met to determine who should replace him. The seven decided to allow the gods to decide. (Ancient peoples often employed what modern humans would call "games of chance" to allow the gods to participate in important decisions.) The seven Persian aristocrats decided to ride their favorite horses to a certain spot before dawn the next day. The owner of the first horse to neigh after sunrise would become the new emperor. Darius's lowly groomsman found a way to fix the contest. Before dawn, he rubbed the genitalia of the favorite mare of his master's horse and stuffed his hands in his cloak to preserve the smell. Then, as the sun rose at the designated location, the groomsman pretended to fasten the horse's bit. The horse smelled his hands and neighed. That is how Darius became emperor of Persia, the most powerful man in the world. The story is typical of Herodotus because it demystifies an important event, attributing it to a clever human, rather than to the gods. (In reality, it was not quite as easy as all that; Darius had to win a brief but bloody civil war to secure his throne.) Herodotus is like a favorite uncle, brilliant, endearingly eccentric, and, above all, always fun.

Unfortunately, Herodotus died at the Athenian colony of Thurii in 425 BC before he had quite completed the *Histories*. Ironically, the very man who immortalized Athens at the height of its glory was barred from becoming an Athenian citizen by his friend Pericles' restrictions on naturalization.

Thucydides (ca. 460–400 BC)

Thucydides (ca. 460–400 BC), an Athenian of aristocratic lineage, has been called the "first scientific historian." By this it is meant that he was the first to remove supernatural causation from history altogether. Indeed, he was virtually alone among historians in this regard until Niccolò Machiavelli (sixteenth century). He also began the association of history with political and military affairs, an equation that dominated Western historiography until the 1960s, when Herodotean social history was resurrected (though even Herodotus felt compelled to justify his lengthy, anthropological digressions on the dubious grounds of establishing the background for his central concern, the Persian Wars). For millennia the association of history with politics and war made it the exclusive study of adult male aristocrats, leaving little place for a discussion of the lives of lower-class males, women, children, and slaves.

Thucydides began his *History of the Peloponnesian War*, his account of the momentous war between Athens and Sparta (431–404 BC), by remarking that although his work would not be as entertaining as that of some unnamed predecessor (Herodotus, of course), he hoped it would be "a possession for all time." Thucydides succeeded, penning one of the most thoughtful histories ever written. A masterpiece of concision and precision, its insights are so universal in application that it continues to be read and cited by the best historians, political scientists, and military strategists. Thucydides' distinction between the underlying and immediate causes of war still dominates that field of inquiry. His grave and intense language effectively conveys the drama of history.

Thucydides believed that history was cyclical. If one selected an important set of events that included many variables and closely investigated that historical sequence, one would find a pattern that could be used to predict future events. Although Thucydides believed that human society moved in cycles, his belief in the utility of history nevertheless implied that knowledge of the past might allow humans to break these cycles.

Thucydides believed that historians should write only about recent events, since he doubted the accuracy of oral accounts of the distant past. For this reason, some have called Thucydides a journalist rather than a historian, though in several instances he did recount the events of past centuries— largely to show that past wars had been inferior to the Peloponnesian War in size and significance.

Like Herodotus, Thucydides had a habit of creating fictitious speeches for historical figures as a means of conveying their personalities and ideas, though he assured the reader that he did his best to faithfully reflect the content, if not always the wording, of what had actually been said. While this practice, followed by nearly all ancient historians, would be considered scandalous if practiced by a historian today, it was expected by contemporary readers and, hence, was not deceptive in any sense.

In 424 BC, while serving as a *strategos*, one of the ten military and political leaders of Athens, Thucydides was ostracized for arriving too late to defend the Athenian colony of Amphipolis against a Spartan attack. Located on the northern coast of the Aegean, Amphipolis (the "city surrounded" by the looping Strymon River) was a vital source of metals and timber and an essential base for protecting grain shipments from the Black Sea region.

Thucydides' period of exile, much of it spent in the Peloponnesus, left him with plenty of time to write a history. His banishment probably increased his bitterness toward Athenian democracy, which he portrayed as the severest form of mob rule. Indeed, Thucydides bolstered an antidemocratic tradition that dominated Western literature until the rise of representative democracy in the nineteenth century. Thucydides' reverential treatment of Pericles was perhaps a way of contrasting him with the "demagogues" who succeeded him, one of whom (Cleon) played a leading role in Thucydides' ostracism.

Yet, Thucydides retained an obvious love for his former polis and displayed great pity at its suffering. Furthermore, however colored by his own experience, much of what Thucydides wrote was probably true. Some modern historians have been so infuriated that anyone would dare to criticize democracy that they have missed the opportunity to use Thucydides to learn more about the weaknesses of democracy, knowledge essential to its survival and improvement. Fortunately, most historians still acknowledge and seek to emulate the rare degree of balance in Thucydides' narrative. Although he fell short of his impossible goal of complete objectivity, Thucydides was perhaps the greatest of all the ancient historians.

Thucydides returned to Athens after the war ended, in 404 BC, but died about four years later, before he could complete his *History of the Peloponnesian War*. It ends in midsentence in the year 411 BC.

Demosthenes (384–322 BC)

Although Demosthenes was an orator and not a historian, his highly influential speeches illuminated the mid- to late fourth century BC, the period when Greece fell to Macedonian domination. The son of a sword manufacturer, Demosthenes overcame a speech impediment to become one of the greatest orators in Western history. Demosthenes began studying rhetoric in order to prosecute the inept or corrupt trustees whose mismanagement had cost him his father's estate. Able to recover only a portion of his inheritance, he turned to speech writing for litigants for his livelihood. He spent months at a time in an underground study, writing and practicing speeches before a full-length mirror, even shaving one cheek so that he would not be tempted to go out of the house and neglect his rhetorical training.

In a series of stirring speeches called the *Philippics* (351–341 BC), Demosthenes warned against the growing power of Macedon under the cunning

King Philip II, who sought to rule all of Greece. Demosthenes contrasted the apathy and corruption of Athens in the fourth century BC with the glorious Athens of the previous century, the Athens that had scorned the bribes and resisted the incursions of another set of barbarians, the Persians. Demosthenes warned of "the restless activity which is a part of Philip's very being and which will not allow him to content himself with his achievements and remain at peace." Demosthenes concluded,

> This peace that he speaks of is a peace which you are to observe towards Philip, while he does not observe it towards you. . . . If we will not fight him now in his own country we shall perhaps be obliged to do so in ours. . . . It is by deeds and actions, not by words, that a policy of encroachment must be arrested. . . . The Greeks see these things and endure them, gazing as they would at a hailstorm, each praying that it may not come their way, but no one trying to prevent it. . . . Heaven grant that the time may not come when the truth of my words will be tested with all severity.

Demosthenes' effort to save Greece from Macedonian control failed. Philip conquered Greece, and his son Alexander the Great led the Greeks in the conquest of the Persian Empire. When Alexander died without a clear heir, Athens revolted. Antipater, a Macedonian general, crushed the revolt. Demosthenes killed himself with a poison he had taken to carrying in a hollow bracelet in the event of such a desperate situation.

Modern republicans considered Demosthenes a martyr to the cause of freedom. Many centuries later, when facing down yet another cunning tyrant with ambitions of conquest and control, Winston Churchill drew solace from the example of Demosthenes.

Polybius (200–118 BC)

The Greek historian Polybius of Megalopolis (ca. 200–118 BC) chose as his subject the most important development of the Hellenistic Period, the period after Alexander the Great conquered the eastern Mediterranean and much of the Near East. That crucial development was the rise to power of a little village in Italy called Rome. Polybius's audience consisted largely of fellow Greeks who were confused by the Romans' unprecedented success in conquering the Mediterranean world. Having befriended Roman leaders while held hostage in Rome for sixteen years (as the Achaean League's cavalry officer), Polybius contended that the rise of Rome was the fated product of *Tyche* (Fortune), a vague entity similar to the Stoic World Soul or Fate.

But even Fortune must utilize secondary causes to achieve its purposes. Therefore, Polybius attributed Roman success, more specifically, to their alleged mixed government. Polybius agreed with Aristotle (fourth century BC) that the best constitution assigned approximately equal amounts of power to the three orders of society, the one, the few, and the many. He explained that only a mixed government could circumvent the cycle of discord that was the inevitable product of the three simple forms of government: monarchy (rule by the one), aristocracy (rule by the few), and democracy (rule by the many). Hence only a mixed government could provide a state with the internal harmony necessary for prosperity and for the defeat of external enemies. Polybius claimed that the cycle began when primitive man, suffering from chaos and violence, consented to be ruled by a strong and brave leader. Then, as men began to conceive of justice (by developing a habit of putting themselves in others' positions), they replaced the strong and brave leader with the just leader and chose his son to succeed him. This last move was a mistake. They expected that the son's lineage and education would lead him to emulate his father. But, having been accustomed to a special status from birth, the son did not possess any sense of duty toward the public and, soon after acquiring power, sought to distinguish himself from the rest of the people. Monarchy had deteriorated into tyranny. But when the bravest and noblest of the aristocrats (for who else would risk their lives in such an endeavor?) overturned the tyranny, the people naturally selected them to succeed the king as rulers. The result was aristocracy, "rule by the best." Unfortunately, the aristocrats' children were not "the best" but rather the most spoiled and, like the king's son, soon placed their own welfare above that of the people. Aristocracy had deteriorated into oligarchy. The oppressed people rebelled against the oligarchy and established a democracy. But the wealthy, seeking to raise themselves above the common level, soon corrupted the people with bribes and created factions. The result was the chaos and violence that always accompany mob rule. When these reached epic proportions, sentiment grew for a dictatorship. Monarchy reappeared. This cycle, Polybius contended, would repeat itself indefinitely until the society had the wisdom to balance the power of the three orders.

Polybius believed that the Roman republic was the most outstanding example of mixed government. He claimed that the Roman system of government, which had been constructed slowly through trial and error and had reached perfection at the time of the Second Punic War (218–201 BC), was the secret of Roman success. Its balance between the two consuls, the Senate, and the popular assemblies necessitated compromise, which, in turn, produced internal harmony.

As we shall see, the Roman government at this time was largely an oligarchy, in which both the two executives and the assemblies lacked the power to serve as effective counterweights to the aristocratic Senate. But it was only natural that Polybius, in his anxiety to explain a momentous development—the Roman conquest of "almost the whole of the inhabited world" (the Mediterranean basin)—should turn to a Greek theory proposed by the most respected of all philosophers, however poorly Greek theories might fit Roman realities. Indeed, Polybius's analysis was so persuasive he even convinced Roman intellectuals like Cicero that Rome possessed a mixed government and that it was the secret of Roman success.

Whatever the flaws in Polybius's approach, he was certainly correct in noting the tremendous significance of the rise of Rome. Within a few centuries this small village in central Italy had conquered much of western Europe, North Africa, and the Near East and had transmitted an amalgam of its own culture and Greek civilization throughout its vast empire.

Cicero (106–43 BC)

The classical author who contributed most to the Founding Fathers' understanding of the late Roman republic, the period of ancient history with which they were most intensely concerned, was not a historian at all. Rather, he was a statesman, political theorist, and philosopher who wrote mostly about his own era.

It was Marcus Tullius Cicero, more than anyone, who transformed the Latin language into a supple and sophisticated tool of expression. A master of Latin prose, Cicero astounded both ancients and moderns with the eloquence of his 106 orations, his 900 letters, and his numerous political and philosophical essays. Cicero's florid style, balanced clauses, and rhythmic cadences so dominated Latin prose that the highly respected rhetorician Quintilian said Cicero was "the name, not of a man, but of eloquence itself."

Cicero was the acknowledged master of each of the three types of rhetoric: deliberative, epideictic, and forensic—speeches for the Senate building, the funeral hall, and the courtroom. His rhetorical writings advocated careful attention to every aspect of public speaking—care of the throat, breath control, tone variation, carriage, expression, eyebrow movement, gestures, toga arrangement, stride, and even the production of tears. His speeches were so persuasive that, as consul, he convinced the masses to oppose debt relief and land distribution.

Like Mark Twain or Winston Churchill in later times, Cicero became so famous for his wit that the witticisms of others were often attributed to him.

Though Cicero's humor was essential in court, often distracting jurors from the legal weaknesses of a case, his biting wit earned him many enemies. When a snobbish aristocrat sneered, "Who is your father?" Cicero replied, "I can scarcely ask you the same question since your mother has made it rather difficult to answer." When the wealthy politician Crassus said that no member of his family had ever lived past sixty, then reversed himself, asking, "What could I have been thinking when I said that?" Cicero replied that he must have been attempting to elicit applause. When a young man accused of having given his father a poisoned cake said angrily that he would give Cicero "a piece of his mind," Cicero replied, "I would prefer it to a piece of your cake." When the demagogue Clodius was acquitted of adultery by a jury he had bribed, he told Cicero, who was the prosecutor, that the jury had not believed his evidence. Cicero replied, "You will find that twenty-five of them trusted in my word since they voted against you, and that the other thirty did not trust yours, since they did not vote for your acquittal until they had actually gotten your money in their hands." While tribune, Clodius later had Cicero banished and his villas destroyed.

Cicero's speeches, epistles, and essays, gathered for posthumous publication by his faithful secretary, freedman, and friend Marcus Tullius Tiro, shed more light on the stresses and strains of the late Roman republic than any other historical source. They reveal the strengths and weaknesses of the Roman aristocracy, who were cultured, proud, patriotic, intensely political, vain, and self-interested. Perhaps the greatest compliment Cicero ever received came from his nemesis, Julius Caesar, who claimed that Cicero's achievement was greater than his own: "It is better to have extended the boundaries of the Roman spirit than of the Roman Empire."

Cicero's On Duties (44 BC), written after the fall of the republic had driven him from politics, were his last musings on life, proper behavior, and the duties of public office. Cicero's ominous warning foreshadowed the downfall of many future republics:

> The armed forces stationed to attack the state are more in number than those which defend it; for it takes only a nod of the head to set in motion the reckless and the desperate—indeed of their own initiative they incite themselves against the state. The sound elements [of society] rouse themselves more slowly. . . . At the last moment [they] are stirred into belated action by the sheer urgencies of the situation.

Cicero saw the horror of tyranny not merely in its destruction of liberty but in its corruption of morals as well. He considered On Duties his manifesto and his masterpiece.

Cicero's elegant prose placed the Greek doctrines of popular sovereignty, mixed government, and natural law at the center of Western thought. Although Cicero did not explicitly discuss the theory of popular sovereignty, the belief that all political authority ultimately derived from the people, his political writings assumed that no form of government (whether monarchy, aristocracy, democracy, or mixed government) was legitimate unless the people consented to it. (Even the later edicts of the emperors were thought to have the force of law not merely because the emperor willed it but rather because the people supposedly consented to that mode of legislation.) Furthermore, like Polybius's *Histories*, Cicero's *Republic* attributed Roman success to the republic's allegedly mixed government.

A philosopher as well as a statesman and political theorist, Cicero helped popularize the crucial theory of natural law, the belief in a universal code of ethics inherent in nature that transcended time and culture and that was discernable by humans. Though possessing an eclectic mix of opinions on various philosophical issues, Cicero was largely Stoic on the question of natural law. He conceived of the universe as "one commonwealth of which both gods and men are members." Natural law was not handed down by the gods but was the glue that connected them to humans in the one great organism of the universe. Humans discerned natural law through a combination of reason and intuition. He wrote, regarding Nature and Man,

> It is true that she gave him a mind capable of receiving virtue, and implanted at birth and without instruction some small intimations of the greatest truths, and thus, as it were, laid the foundation for education and instilled into those faculties which the mind already had what may be called the germs of virtue. But of virtue itself she merely furnished the rudiments; nothing more. Therefore, it is our task (and when I say "our" I mean that it is the task of art) to supplement those mere beginnings by searching out the further developments which are implicit in them, until what we seek is fully realized.

Concerning natural law Cicero wrote,

> This law, my lords, is not a written but an innate law. We have not been taught it by the learned; we have not received it from our ancestors; we have not taken it from books; it is derived from nature and stamped in invisible characters upon our very frame. It was not conveyed by instruction but wrought into our constitution. It is the dictate of instinct. . . . There cannot be one law now, and another hereafter; but the same eternal immutable law comprehends all nations, at all times, under one common master and governor of all.

Cicero used the two analogies of sparks and seeds to clarify his position. At one point, he stated that humans were all sparks temporarily separated from the Great Flame (the World Soul), but a spark might be extinguished by a bad upbringing. On another occasion he argued that the seeds of virtue were manifested in the social nature of humans, in their "gregarious impulses." (The two analogies differed somewhat: nurturing a seed into a full-grown plant generally requires more conscious effort than keeping a flame lit.) Like most of the classical philosophers, Cicero possessed an optimistic conception of nature and, hence, of human nature, writing, "Great-heartedness and heroism, and courtesy, and justice, and generosity are far more in conformity with nature than self-indulgence. . . . Our nature impels us to seek what is morally right." Those who violated natural law were punished, not by the "penalties established by law, for these they often escape" but rather by "their own degradation." The reward of virtue was self-respect and the respect of others: "The reputation and the glory of being a good man are too precious to be sacrificed in favor of anything at all."

Cicero's philosophical treatises, written late in life as he grieved over the deaths of both his daughter Tullia and the Roman republic itself, noted the need to endure old age patiently and expressed confidence in the existence of an afterlife. He noted,

> Great deeds are not done by strength or speed or physique; they are the products of thought, and character, and judgment. And far from diminishing, such qualities actually increase with age. . . . If some god granted me the power to cancel my advanced years and return to boyhood, and wail once more in the cradle, I should firmly refuse. Now that my race is run, I have no desire to be called back from the finish to the starting point!

The marvelous nature of the human mind convinced him that it "cannot be mortal." He added, "It is only after liberation from all bodily admixture has made them pure and undefiled that souls enter upon true wisdom. . . . I look forward to meeting the personages of whom I have heard, read, and written. . . . I am leaving a hostel rather than a home. . . . As I approach death I feel like a man nearing harbor after a long voyage: I seem to be catching sight of land."

Although Cicero's philosophical ideas were hardly original—he once conceded, "I supply only the words, and I don't lack those!"—"supplying the words" is at least as crucial to the popularity of a philosophy as supplying the ideas. Indeed, in Cicero's case supplying the words involved inventing a whole new Latin vocabulary that could correspond to technical terms in

Greek philosophy. Modern republicans later deduced from Cicero's exposi-tions on the theory of natural law the concept of natural rights, which forms the basis of those bills of rights that now distinguish democratic nations from the rest of the world.

For nearly two millennia every educated European and American read Ci-cero. Indeed, Cicero's very character, or, rather, an idealized version of Ci-cero's character, became the model for future Western statesmen. Along with Demosthenes, Cicero became the symbol of the statesman who sacrifices popularity, a short-term benefit that could be purchased only by vice, for fame, an everlasting glory that could be secured only through virtue.

Sallust (86–35 BC)

Sallust (Gaius Sallustius Crispus) was one of the few ancient historians who sided with the popular party rather than with the aristocratic party. In 50 BC the censors expelled him from the Roman Senate for immorality, though the charges were probably false. Nevertheless, as proconsul of North Africa, Sal-lust plundered the province mercilessly and escaped prosecution only be-cause of an enormous bribe to Julius Caesar. He retired from politics after Caesar's death in 44 BC.

In retirement Sallust wrote *The Jugurthine War* and *Catiline's Conspiracy* concerning two episodes of the late second and first centuries BC that he de-picted as epitomizing severe moral decline in Rome. The first concerned the effort by the Numidian Jugurtha to bribe Roman senators into looking the other way while he ravished a Roman province and killed Roman citizens. According to the famous characterization of Sallust, Jugurtha declared about Rome, "Here is a city put up for sale, and its days are numbered if it finds a buyer." The second episode involved the attempt by the corrupt Catiline to seize control of the Roman government after losing his second consecutive election for the consulship, an effort thwarted by Cicero.

Sallust was the first Roman historian to state the theory of the "Punic Curse," the belief that the downfall of the Roman republic had been caused by unprecedented wealth, which was itself the product of Rome's defeat of its nemesis, Carthage, in the Punic Wars. Sallust wrote that love of money "knows no bounds and can never be satisfied: he that has not wants, and he that has wants more." Sallust's moralistic pose, ironic in light of his own be-havior in North Africa, earned him tremendous popularity, not merely in his own day but in the medieval and modern worlds as well. His epigrammatic style influenced Tacitus and several of the early Church Fathers, including Jerome and Augustine.

Livy (59 BC–AD 17)

Livy (Titus Livius) was perhaps the most popular of all Roman historians. He wrote the *History of Rome* over a period of about thirty years, beginning in 26 BC. A prose epic of 142 "books" (a classical book was roughly equivalent to one of our chapters), only thirty-five of which survive, the *History* charted the Roman past from the foundation of Rome to 9 BC.

Livy's *History* was extremely patriotic. As the historian R. H. Barrow once put it, "[In Livy] Rome is the heroine inspiring Romans to heroic deeds to fulfill her destiny. Virgil and Livy perfected the language for showing the Roman at his noblest in action and character." Livy boasted, "If any nation deserves the privilege of claiming a divine ancestry that nation is our own." Indeed, though Livy chose much the same subject matter as Polybius—the origins of the Roman Empire—he attributed Roman success more to its traditional values than to its government form. He wrote, "I hope my passion for Rome's past has not impaired by judgment; for I do honestly believe that no country has ever been greater or purer than ours or richer in good citizens and noble deeds; none has been free for so many centuries from the vices of avarice and luxury; nowhere have thrift and plain living been for so long held in such esteem."

Although those portions of the *History* that concern Livy's own time have been lost, he made it clear in other passages that, although he admired the republican age above all, he was grateful to Augustus, the first of the Roman emperors, for restoring peace and order after a full century of devastating civil wars. (In Augustan Rome praise for the republic was not only permissible but was also actually encouraged, since Augustus shrewdly pretended to have restored it.) Livy also echoed Augustus's fear of a moral decline. Livy wrote, "The might of an imperial people is beginning to work its own ruin. . . . Of late years wealth has made us greedy, and self-indulgence has brought us, through every form of sensual excess, to be, if I may so put it, in love with death both individual and collective." (A few years ago Pope John Paul II referred to the prosperous, modern West as a society "in love with death." Did he borrow this phrase from the Roman historian?) Livy referred to "the sinking of the foundations of morality as the old teaching was allowed to lapse, then the final collapse of the whole edifice, and the dark dawning of our modern day when we can neither endure our vices nor face the remedies needed to cure them." He added, "The study of history is the best medicine for a sick mind; for in history you have a record of the infinite variety of human experience plainly set out for all to see; and in that record you can find for yourself and your country both examples and warnings, fine things to take as models, base things, rotten through and through, to avoid."

Livy wrote with astonishing skill and charm in a style famously fluent and colorful. Yet most modern historians have also judged Livy's work essentially solid and dependable—aside from his first ten books on archaic Rome, which were more mythological than historical.

Plutarch (ca. AD 46–120)

The greatest biographer of antiquity, the prolific Plutarch of Chaeronea in Greece, retired from his post as a Neoplatonic philosopher in order to study Greek and Roman history. The result was the *Parallel Lives*, forty-six biographies of famous Greeks and Romans arranged in pairs for comparison (e.g., Alexander the Great is paired with Julius Caesar). Plutarch hoped to demonstrate that the Greeks had produced men as great as the greatest Romans, as well as to extract moral lessons from history.

Nevertheless, Plutarch was quite aware of the difficulties involved in uncovering historical truth. He noted, "How thickly the truth is hedged around with obstacles and how hard it is to track down by historical research. Writers who live after the events they describe find that their view of them is obscured by the lapse of time, while those who investigate the deeds and lives of their contemporaries are equally apt to corrupt and distort the truth."

Plutarch emphasized natural causes but maintained that they were the principal means the gods employed to shape events. He wrote, "Those who say that to discover the cause of a phenomenon disposes of its meaning fail to notice that the same reasoning which explains away divine portents would also dispense with the artificial symbols created by mankind. The beating of gongs, the blaze of beacons, and the shadows on sun-dials all have their particular causes, but have also been contrived to signify something else."

A classic of Greek literature, whose engaging style and numerous anecdotes never fail to sustain the reader's interest, Plutarch's *Lives* is also a mine of information for modern historians of Greece and Rome. Plutarch demonstrated an unparalleled gift for recognizing and relating the telling detail that discloses the true nature of a historical figure's character. He noted, "The most brilliant exploits often tell us nothing of the virtues or vices of the men who performed them, while on the other hand a chance remark or a joke may reveal far more of a man's character than the mere feat of winning battles. . . . It is my task to dwell upon those actions which illuminate the workings of the soul." Republican in spirit, the *Parallel Lives* was written during the tolerant rule of the emperor Trajan (AD 98–117). Plutarch also wrote the *Moralia*, a collection of more than eighty essays on issues of moral philosophy that later influenced Montaigne, Ralph Waldo Emerson, and numerous others.

Plutarch was the most influential of all the ancient historians and perhaps the most influential historian in all of Western history. He was a favorite author of the Renaissance and of the eighteenth century. Shakespeare used his biographies as the basis for *Julius Caesar* and *Antony and Cleopatra*. Nearly every home in the American colonies possessed the Bible and an English translation of Plutarch.

Tacitus (ca. AD 55–117)

Considered the greatest of the Roman historians, Tacitus (Publius Cornelius Tacitus) was the most fervent in his denunciation of the emperors. The son of an imperial representative (a procurator) stationed on the Rhine, Tacitus was a lawyer and a government official. As an official under the paranoid emperor Domitian, he was horrified, disgusted, and shamed by the emperor's ruthless reign.

Tacitus's style was concise and caustic. He was a master of dark irony and the deflating postscript. When presented with varying accounts of the emperors' motivations and behavior, he almost invariably selected the least flattering version.

In the *Annals of Rome*, a haunting, tortured history of Rome from the death of Augustus to that of Nero (AD 14–68), and in the *Histories*, the history of Rome from the death of Nero to that of Domitian (AD 68–96), Tacitus vividly depicted the degeneration of Roman morals, which he believed had begun with Tiberius. He wrote,

> Rome of old explored the utmost limits of freedom; we have plumbed the depths of slavery, robbed as we are by informers even of the right to exchange ideas in conversation. . . . Think of it. Fifteen whole years [under Domitian]— no small part of a man's life—taken from us. . . . The few of us that survive are no longer what we once were, since so many of our best years have been taken from us. . . . The worst of our torments under Domitian was to see him with his eyes fixed upon us. Every sigh was registered against us.

Underlying Tacitus's meticulous attention to detail was a sense of the malevolence of destiny, a theme reinforced by his serious treatment of divine omens and wrath. He wrote, "The gods are indifferent to our tranquility, but eager for our punishment."

Although Tacitus's heart was republican, his mind told him that Rome had become too degraded to avoid one-man rule. Consequently, his heroes tended to be people like himself, those who quietly devoted themselves to their public posts and maintained their own morality even under tyrants like Domitian. In the *Agricola*, Tacitus's eloquent biography of his revered father-in-law, Tacitus wrote, with palpable defensiveness, "Let all those whose habit is to admire acts of civil disobedience realize that great men can exist even under bad emperors, and that compliance and an unassuming demeanor, if backed by energy and hard work, can attain a pitch of glory which the majority reach, without benefiting their country, through an ostentatious and untimely death."

Tacitus's *Germania* (ca. AD 98), his discussion of the frugal, chaste, and liberty-loving culture of the Germanic tribes of western Europe, constituted an implicit attack on the corruption of imperial Rome. He wrote concerning the Germans, "They live uncorrupted by the temptations of public shows or the excitements of banquets. . . . No one in Germany finds vice amusing, or calls it 'up-to-date' to seduce and be seduced. . . . Good morality is more effective in Germany than good laws are elsewhere." Yet, though Tacitus equated the Germans with the early Romans, whom he idealized, he did not shrink from criticizing German drunkenness and quarrelsomeness. Tacitus showed great foresight in perceiving the Germanic tribes as a potential threat to Rome, and his *Germania* cast some rare light on the tribes that were to destroy the empire three centuries later.

Like many of the classical historians before him, Tacitus had the remarkable ability to combine a fervent patriotism with a willingness to explore the arguments of his nation's enemies in a fair-minded manner. Recall that it was Tacitus, the Roman imperialist, who placed in the mouth of a Briton the famous criticism of Roman imperialism: "They make a desert and call it peace."

Suetonius (ca. AD 69–140)

A former secretary of the emperor Hadrian who had been dismissed for disrespect to the empress, Suetonius (Gaius Suetonius Tranquillus) of Hippo Regius (in what is now Algeria) wrote *The Twelve Caesars* (ca. AD 121), a collection of biographies of Julius Caesar and the Julio-Claudian and Flavian dynasties. Because Suetonius loved to tell anecdotes, his work is a mine of information on the early Roman Empire. Until the Renaissance, when Plutarch came into his own, Suetonius's *Twelve Caesars* was the leading model for biographers. Though modern republicans like the Founding Fathers read *The Twelve Caesars* and mined it for negative information about the emperors, they were less inclined to praise Suetonius than they were to exalt Plutarch and Tacitus because Suetonius's tone was far less moralistic, far more detached (though somewhat gossipy), and far less bitter toward the emperors.

The Eighteenth-Century Educational System and Its Impact

The Founding Fathers encountered most of these ancient historians and orators at an early and impressionable age, in grammar school and at college. In fact, the "grammar" in "grammar school" referred to Greek and Latin grammar, not English grammar; the mother tongue was not taught in American grammar schools until after the Revolutionary War, since most eighteenth-century Americans believed that precious school time should be reserved for serious academic subjects like the classical languages, not wasted on knowledge the child could learn at home.

The founders' training in the classical languages frequently began at age eight or so, whether under the direction of public grammar schoolmasters or private tutors. Teachers concentrated on the works from which candidates for college admission were expected to recite, a list that changed little throughout the seventeenth and eighteenth centuries. Such works included the writings of Cicero, Virgil, and Homer, and the Greek New Testament. As Noah Webster put it, "The minds of youth are perpetually led to the history of Greece and Rome or to Great Britain; boys are constantly repeating the declamations of Demosthenes and Cicero or debates upon some political question in the British Parliament." Only the poorest areas lacked grammar schools.

The better teachers, such as James Madison's instructor Donald Robertson, went beyond the short list of classical authors. Robertson instructed his students in the works of Herodotus, Thucydides, Plato, Julius Caesar, Tacitus, and many others. Madison's early training was so thorough that, although he arrived at the College of New Jersey (Princeton) in 1769 only two weeks before final examinations, he passed them all. Madison later testified regarding Robertson, "All that I have been in life I owe to that man."

The college curricula were as standardized and classically based as the grammar school curricula and the college entrance examinations. Colleges typically required at least three more years of Greek and Latin. Schoolmates of Thomas Jefferson recalled that he carried his Greek grammar with him wherever he went. College students frequently joined secret societies that assigned them pseudonyms taken from ancient history. Commencement exercises often featured exhibitions in which students competed for prizes by reading Greek and Latin or by speaking Latin extemporaneously. A few possessed the wealth to obtain a classical education in Europe.

While they were students, and frequently afterward, the founders kept commonplace books, notebooks in which they copied the literary passages that most interested them. John Adams transferred sizable excerpts from Sallust's *Catiline's Conspiracy* into his Harvard commonplace book. Thereafter, he maintained a great respect for the Roman historian. In 1778, when Benjamin Franklin told the author of a Russian history that he had surpassed Sallust, Adams declared, "I thought this as good a french Compliment as the best of the Company could have made." In 1782 Adams wrote to a friend, "My boy should translate Sallust and write to his papa." In 1812, when some New Englanders, angry over the United States' approaching war with Great Britain, spoke of secession, Adams quoted Sallust, "Small communities grow great through harmony; great ones fall to pieces through discord." Madison's commonplace book cited Tacitus on the vices of the Roman emperors.

Although Alexander Hamilton's education at King's College (Columbia) was cut short by the outbreak of the Revolutionary War, which drew him into the Continental Army in January of 1776, he converted his military pay book into a commonplace book. He copied large extracts from Plutarch's lives of Theseus, Romulus, Lycurgus, and Numa Pompilius, all founders of republics. Indeed, Hamilton's sons later testified that Plutarch and Alexander Pope were Hamilton's favorite authors. Similarly, Benjamin Rush, one of the signers of the Declaration of Independence, kept a commonplace book in his adult years, a book in which he copied extracts from Tacitus's *Annals*.

Thomas Jefferson was so immersed in the classical historians that they profoundly influenced his writing style, helping to produce the clarity and concision that stand as his trademark. Jefferson used the speeches of Livy, Sallust, and Tacitus as models for oratorical writing. Well aware that nearly all the ancient historians had crafted fictitious orations for their subjects, Jefferson took care, after declaring that the best speeches were those of Scipio Africanus, Cato, and Caesar, to identify the historians (Livy and Sallust) who had really composed them. From these historians Jefferson learned the three qualities he deemed most essential to good republican oratory. These were simplicity, brevity, and rationality. In 1824 Jefferson applauded the speeches of Livy, Sallust, and Tacitus for that "sententious brevity which, using not a word to spare, leaves not a moment for the inattention of the hearer." Rationality was equally crucial to a good speech. He explained, "In a republic, whose citizens are to be led by reason and persuasion, and not by force, the art of reasoning becomes of the first importance." He claimed that the orations of Livy, Sallust, and Tacitus were models of rationality as well.

Jefferson particularly admired Tacitus. As a young man, Jefferson copied into his commonplace book the warning of Tacitus: "The more corrupt the commonwealth the more numerous the laws." In 1808 Jefferson wrote, "Tacitus I consider the first writer in the world without a single exception. His book is a compound of history and morality of which we have no other example." In 1823 Jefferson reiterated his claim that Tacitus was "the strongest writer in the world." By that time he had quoted Tacitus on the role of the historian: "This I hold to be the chief duty and office of the historian, to judge the actions of men, to the end that the good and the worthy may meet with the rewards due to eminent virtue, and that pernicious citizens may be deterred by the condemnation that waits on evil deeds at the tribunal of posterity." "History" was the ultimate judge, dispensing fame to the virtuous, infamy to the vicious.

The other founders admired Tacitus as well. Reading Tacitus as a young man in 1756, John Adams was filled with horror at the violence of the Roman emperors. John Dickinson, author of the most influential pamphlet of the Revolutionary era (*Letters from a Pennsylvania Farmer*, 1768), praised Tacitus as "that excellent historian and statesman . . . whose political reflections are so justly and universally admired." In his 1774 will the patriot Josiah Quincy left his son the works of Tacitus, Francis Bacon, Algernon Sidney, and John Locke, books he considered most apt to instill "the spirit of liberty" in a boy. He described Tacitus's historical writing as "masterly," "elegant," and "instructive." Benjamin Rush compared Tacitus's descriptions with the paintings of "the best artists." In 1813, near the end of his life, Rush praised Samuel Miller's *Memoirs of Dr. John Rogers* in the best fashion he knew: "You have given an importance to the most minute incidents in his life by your reflections upon them. In doing so, you have happily imitated the manner of Tacitus."

The founders loved the other ancient historians as well. Having read Livy in the original Latin at age fifteen, Patrick Henry made it a rule to read a translation of the historian through every year. John Dickinson was particularly fond of Memmius's declaration in Sallust's *Jugurtha*: "I shall certainly aim at the freedom handed down from my forebears; whether I am successful or not in doing so is in your control, my fellow countrymen." He used the line to begin a 1764 speech and to end his *Letters from a Pennsylvania Farmer*, which rallied the patriots against parliament's Townshend Acts. Charles Lee, the Revolutionary War general, declared, "I have ever from the first time I read Plutarch been an Enthusiastick for liberty . . . and for liberty in a republican garb." He noted regarding the tremendous influence of the ancient historians on the youth of his age, "It is natural to a young person whose chief companions are the Greek and Roman Historians and Orators to be dazzled with the splendid picture." As a young man, Benjamin Franklin relished an English translation of Plutarch's *Lives*, later recording in his autobiography, "I still think that time spent to great advantage." In 1775 Franklin wrote that, although "as yet the Muses have scarcely visited these remote Regions," he hoped that the proceedings of Congress would "furnish materials for a future Sallust." James Wilson, who is often credited with being second only to James Madison in shaping the U.S. Constitution, expressed the common reverence for Thucydides when he wrote regarding the American states, "When some future Xenophon or Thucydides shall arise to do justice to their virtues and their actions; the glory of America will rival—it will outshine the glory of Greece."

The founders idolized Demosthenes not only as one of the greatest orators in history but also as one of the greatest models for statesmen. They studied the Athenian's speeches closely and made frequent mention of him. In 1774 John Adams contrasted the First Continental Congress' economic response to parliament's Intolerable Acts with the bolder policy of Demosthenes. Adams noted, "When Demosthenes (God forgive the Vanity of recollecting his Example) went [as] Ambassador from Athens to the other States of Greece, to excite a Confederacy against Philip [of Macedon], he did not go to propose a Non Importation or Non Consumption Agreement!" Southerners called Patrick Henry "the Demosthenes of the American Revolution." In 1777 Alexander Hamilton copied into his pay book a few lines from Demosthenes' orations, including this significant one: "As a general marches at the head of troops, so ought wise politicians, if I dare to use the expression, to march at the head of affairs; insomuch that they ought not to [a]wait the event, to know what measures to take; but the measures which they have taken ought to produce the event." If Hamilton's tenure as the first secretary of the treasury is any indication, he certainly lived by this maxim. Thomas Jefferson considered Demosthenes' speeches the finest model for "senatorial eloquence," which required logic.

Indeed, the founders made certain that their own children were as thoroughly steeped in the works of the ancient historians as they themselves had been. John Adams lectured his son John Quincy:

> I wish to hear of your beginning Sallust, who is one of the most polished and perfect of the Roman Historians, every Period of whom, and I had almost said every Syllable and every Letter, is worth Studying. In company with Sallust, Cicero, Tacitus, and Livy, you will learn Wisdom and Virtue. You will see them represented with all the Charms which Language and Imagination

can exhibit, and Vice and Folly painted in all their Deformity and Horror. You will ever remember that all the End of study is to make you a good Man and a useful Citizen.

In 1781 John Adams criticized his son for not reading Demosthenes and Cicero at the University of Leyden. The elder Adams launched into this tirade:

> I want to have you upon Demosthenes. The plainer Authors you may learn yourself at any time. I absolutely insist upon it, that you begin upon Demosthenes and Cicero. I will not be put by. You may learn Greek from Demosthenes and Homer as well as from Isocrates and Lucian—and Latin from Virgil and Cicero as well as from Phaedrus and Nepos. What should be the Cause of the Aversion to Demosthenes in the World I know not, unless it is because his sentiments are wise and grand, and he teaches no frivolities. If there is no other Way, I will take you home and teach you Demosthenes and Homer myself.

Adams's parental heckling must have worked, for when John Quincy Adams entered Harvard in 1785, his father could boast that John Quincy had translated all of Tacitus's works, as well as the writings of Suetonius, Plutarch, and numerous other classical authors. Thomas Jefferson even rebuked his daughter Martha for not keeping up with her Livy, though her gender entitled her to read the Roman historian in Italian translation. Henry Lee, the Revolutionary War cavalry officer, urged his son Carter, away at Harvard, to "dwell on the virtues & imitate, so far as lies in your power, the great & good men whom history presents to your view—Lycurgus, Solon, Numa, [and] Hannibal."

Conclusion

Fixtures in the classical canon that had dominated the Western world since the Middle Ages, the historians of Greece and Rome were virtually the sole source of knowledge concerning ancient history available in the eighteenth century. Since modern archaeology was still in its infancy, there was no source of information regarding the ancient world other than these classics, a few modern histories that uniformly idolized and parroted them, and the scattered remains of Greek and Roman buildings and works of art. Furthermore, the classical historians' eloquence, their narrative skill, and the nearly universal reverence their writings had come to enjoy all worked to inhibit the founders' critical instincts. They accepted the accuracy of these select sources as an article of faith and remained largely oblivious to the ancient historians' aristocratic and other biases. In the following chapters we shall review the lessons the Founding Fathers learned from their favorite storytellers.

CHAPTER TWO

~

Sparta and Individual Rights

From Plutarch the founders of the United States learned the story of Sparta, perhaps the first totalitarian state in history. From this tale the founders learned both the strengths and weaknesses of republics that emphasize the collective good over individual rights. In the end the founders, like Aristotle and others before them, could admire the virtues of Sparta while rejecting the harsh social practices that produced them. Like other modern republicans, the founders preferred to rest their republic on the natural rights of individuals, even while urging sacrifice for the common good.

The Legend of Sparta

At some point in Sparta's early history, legend has it that the Spartans conquered a neighboring polis called Helos and enslaved its population. Though the Spartans did allow some of the conquered people, whom they called *perioikoi* ("those dwelling around"), local self-government and freedom from forced labor, they reduced the majority, called "helots," to serfdom. The perioikoi produced war materials and other items for the Spartans and sometimes even served as reserves in the Spartan army. The Spartans paid for the supplies and allowed the perioikoi to sell surplus goods to other poleis. In a sense, the perioikoi lived more comfortably than Spartan citizens, who were not allowed to trade with other city-states. By contrast, the helots, though allowed to keep half of their crops, were owned by the state; some worked directly for the state, but most were assigned to the land of an individual Spartan and could not depart from it. Even those allotted to individual Spartans could be conscripted by the state at any time and could be freed only by the state.

In the late eighth century BC, when the Spartans faced overpopulation like the rest of Greece, they decided to solve the problem by conquering fertile Messenia to the west, rather than by colonizing distant shores of the Mediterranean and Black Seas, as many other city-states were doing. (The Spartans established only one colony, at Taras, on the southern tip of Italy.) The Spartans invaded Messenia, annexed its territory, and added its citizens to the helot population. The annexation of all of one polis's territory by another was rare in Greece, not only because the Greeks valued the smallness of their poleis but also because such a policy would require a standing army. Indeed, the significance of Sparta's expansionism is that it left the Spartans a small minority in their own country, rulers over a vast population of oppressed helots. Thus, Sparta could not hope to develop along the same lines as the other Greek city-states. The constant need to suppress the helot population necessitated the development of rigid social discipline and a military state.

The implications of the Spartan policy of conquest became apparent only after the Messenian revolt of the mid-seventh century BC. In this bloody rebellion the Messenians, with the aid of Arcadia, almost gained their independence and nearly annihilated the Spartans in the process. It was during this period that the Spartan poet Tyrtaeus wrote these stirring lines:

> For a good man to die falling beside the front-line fighters, in defense of his country, is a noble thing. . . . Since a wanderer receives no recognition, neither honor nor respect nor mercy, let us fight with all our might for this land, and die for our children. . . . Flee not, leaving behind, fallen on the ground, the elders whose knees are no longer nimble. For it is a disgrace when an older man, his hair already white and gray of beard, falls in the front line and lies before a younger man. . . . So let every man bite his lip and, with both feet firmly on the ground, take his place for battle.

Having finally suppressed the bloody rebellion of the Messenians, the Spartans, acutely aware that they now comprised but a small minority in their own country, decided that they must transform their society into a disciplined military machine or be enslaved by their own helots. At the height of Spartan power a mere nine thousand Spartan citizens ruled nearly one hundred thousand helots.

Spartan legend claimed that a lawgiver named Lycurgus had introduced the unique Spartan political and social systems around 750 BC, based on the institutions that then prevailed in Crete. Lycurgus had then made the Spartans take a solemn oath not to make any change in his constitution until he returned from a voyage to Delphi, and then he purposely starved himself to death there and even had his ashes scattered in the sea so that he could never return to Sparta in any form. The truth is that the Spartans established their distinctive institutions in the late seventh century BC in the wake of the Messenian revolt, and Lycurgus is almost certainly a mythical figure.

Though complex, the Spartan political system was largely a gerontocracy, an oligarchy ruled by a council of elders. The Gerousia, an assembly of Sparta's two kings and twenty-eight elders, the latter elected from aristocratic families by the popular assembly, possessed much of the city's legislative and some of its judicial and executive power. Members of the Gerousia held lifetime terms.

Sparta's dual kingship, controlled by two families reputedly descended from the demigod Heracles, was designed to prevent dictatorial rule and to allow one king to stay at home and preside over religious rituals while the other waged war. Rivalry between the two kings generally prevented them from effectively checking the Gerousia.

The Spartans also possessed a popular assembly, the Apella, which consisted of all citizens aged thirty and over. But the Apella was the laughingstock of Greece. It decided only the few matters presented to it by the Gerousia and could not even debate those issues. Voting in the assembly was accomplished by banging on one's shield, with the louder side winning. A group of officials shut up in a nearby shed had to decide which clamor was louder.

Each year five *ephors* (overseers) were chosen by a procedure akin to the lot. The ephors' job was to spy on the kings, each of whom was required to have an ephor at his side at all times, to initiate legislation in the Gerousia, to execute some of the laws passed by the Gerousia and Apella, to negotiate with foreign governments, to call up the army and decide who would march, to disburse government funds, to serve as moral censors, and to judge civil suits and (with the Gerousia) criminal trials. They could fine or arrest kings, pending trial. Each year the ephors issued an official declaration of war against the helots, which served as the legal basis for the execution of any troublemaker among them. Each month the kings took an oath not to exceed their authority, and the ephors took an oath not to overturn the monarchy. But the provision that ephors could not serve again after their single year in office greatly undermined their power.

Sparta was famed more for its unique social system than for its system of government. When a Spartan child was born, the ephors inspected him for signs of illness. If the child was weak or deformed in any way, he was hurled from the top of Mount Taygetus, a crude form of genetic engineering.

At seven, Spartan girls began athletic training, scandalizing most Greeks by running about in revealing skirts. The girls' training, which included running, wrestling, and hurling the discus and javelin, was considered unusually rigorous. The Spartans hoped to make their women physically fit so that they might better endure childbirth and produce healthier babies. First and foremost, girls were trained to be the mothers of warriors. On special occasions, standing nude before dignitaries, they sang songs in praise or ridicule of specific boys (also nude), as a powerful incentive to their good conduct.

So successful was the girls' indoctrination that Spartan mothers became notorious for their patriotism and martial fervor. When a Spartan woman inquired about a battle and was informed that all five of her sons had been killed, she replied testily, "That isn't what I asked you, vile slave, but rather how our country was doing." Spartan mothers told their sons departing for battle, "Come back with your shield—or on it!"

At the age of seven, boys were taken from their mothers and trained at a boot camp. The "herds" of boys were taught to read (but "no more than was necessary"), count, sing patriotic songs, and recite Homer. They were not taught lyric poetry or philosophy because such subjects "softened men." The carefully selected superintendent of the camp maintained a strict discipline with the aid of brutal older boys. The young boys were taught to steal most of their food from gardens and mess halls as training in endurance and stealth; they were beaten if caught. They walked barefooted, received only one cloak per year, bathed only a few days per year, and slept on beds of reed. They were trained in running, swimming, and dancing (for dexterity). Spartan athletic training was so rigorous the Spartans generally won the most prizes at the Olympic Games. The boys marched silently in a mass, keeping their hands in their cloaks and their eyes fixed on the ground before them. They were encouraged to play a savage game of "king of the mountain," a game in which the "king," a boy at the top of a hill, must maintain his position by fighting off all challengers and preserve his "reign" at all costs.

At twenty, Spartan males went into concealment—the *krypteia*, from the same root as "crypt," "cryptic," and "cryptography"—with nothing but a dagger. Only at night could they leave their hiding places to secure provisions and to kill any helots who were out after curfew.

At twenty-one, Spartan males joined a *synousia*, an "association" or brotherhood of fifteen men in the army. Each male had to be accepted unanimously by the brotherhood. Since a rejection meant social death, this rule served as a powerful incentive for Spartan boys to display courage, reverence, and obedience daily. Few ever had to be rejected. The soldiers of the brotherhood spent all of their time together, eating in a common mess hall and sleeping in a common barracks. Because Spartan men were professional soldiers, they were forbidden to perform manual labor of any kind. Helots furnished by the polis farmed their land, part of which was provided by the state, part by inheritance. Soldiers contributed grain from their farms to their own mess hall. To fail to do so, or to reject training, meant the loss of citizenship. Soldiers were not allowed to carry torches after dark, so that they might learn to travel fearlessly at night. Each year the three hundred best warriors were chosen to fight beside the king. Anyone who was not selected could challenge one of the three hundred to a fight for his position. Those who behaved cowardly in battle were deprived of citizenship and were made to wear cloaks with colored patches and to shave only one cheek as badges of their dishonor. When one Spartan soldier ran from battle, his grandmother killed him. Even the Spartans' statues of the gods depicted them armed.

At thirty, Spartan males became full citizens and joined the popular assembly. Between this time and age forty-five, they were expected to marry. They generally married women approximately eighteen years of age, in contrast to most other Greek men, who married girls soon after they reached puberty. Those males who failed to marry by forty-five were fined and ordered to walk naked through the marketplace on a certain winter day every year, singing a song about how their shame was justified, since they had disobeyed the law. For their failure to provide little warriors for the state, these men were also deprived of the respect normally accorded to elders. Even Dercyllidas, one of the best Spartan generals, was denied his rightful seat at a social gathering by a young man. The young man explained, "You have not fathered a son who will offer his seat to me." Marriage was affected by forcibly carrying off the bride (more training in warrior skills). Once married, Spartan males continued to live in the barracks with their brethren and were technically forbidden to visit their wives, though, in actuality, they were expected to do so. It was understood that the husband would periodically sneak away to his wife, in the dead of night, all the while trying not to get caught (more stealth training). Some men allegedly fathered children before ever seeing their wives in the daylight. Some Spartan males shared their wives with other "virtuous" men, with the blessing of the state. A Spartan husband would not think of denying his wife to another male, nor would the wife consider refusing such a request, if the suitor were an honorable man. The point was to produce more children but without the passionate feuds that resulted from surreptitious sex. By institutionalizing adultery, the Spartans hoped to rob it of its power to destabilize society.

At forty-five, Spartan males could return to their wives and homes. There they lived for the rest of their lives.

At sixty, Spartan males could retire from military service if they wished. The elders of noble families became eligible for election to the Gerousia. Newly elected members of the Gerousia received the dubious privilege of a double mess of porridge when dining in public mess halls. They generally gave the extra serving to a friend or family member as a token of honor.

Sparta lost no opportunity to teach each age group its vital role in the survival of the polis. At festivals, a choir of old men sang, "We were once valiant young men"; a group of young men sang, "But we are the valiant now; put us to the test, if you wish"; and a collection of boys sang, "But we shall be far mightier."

Like all other social systems, the Spartan system possessed distinct advantages and disadvantages. The deleterious effects of the system are obvious to the modern individualist. First, the Spartan fear of foreign ideas, a fear stemming from the need to preserve their unique system, hurt the Spartans both intellectually and economically. Spartans were forbidden to trade and travel, lest foreigners corrupt them. Soldiers patrolled the polis's borders to discourage visitors. When a foreigner asked a Spartan how many Spartan citizens there were, he replied, "Enough, my friend, to keep out undesirables." The few invited guests were escorted around by a guard and sometimes expelled without explanation. As a result of its intellectual isolation, Sparta left posterity no art, even in the broadest sense of the term, in sharp contrast to Athens. Even Spartan history has come down to us from the Athenians, since the Spartans did not write history. When an Athenian politician criticized Sparta for its lack of education, a Spartan king replied proudly, "Your point is correct, since we are the only Greeks who have learned nothing wicked from you Athenians." While Athens possessed an intelligently controlled currency, accepted even by the primitive tribes of northern Europe, the Spartans purposely used unwieldy iron bars for that purpose because they feared the seduction of wealth.

Second, the need to maintain discipline caused the Spartans to feed and clothe themselves miserably. The very word "spartan" has come to mean "bare" or "unadorned." After tasting the infamous black porridge of Sparta, a Sybarite who had the misfortune to be a guest at a public mess hall there declared, "Now I understand why you Spartans do not fear death!" Spartan law decreed that the ceiling in every house be constructed using only an ax and the doors with only a saw, the object being to encourage frugality in furniture and cutlery (who would adorn a shack with golden goblets and velvet chairs?). As a result of this practice, an astonished Spartan king who visited a lavish dining hall in Corinth asked his host if the timber there grew square. The Spartans were proud of their ability to survive on horrendous food and shabby clothing. One of their kings, Agesilaus II, claimed that the greatest benefit of the Spartan system was the "contempt for luxury" it inspired. When Agesilaus met outdoors with a Persian *satrap* (provincial governor) to negotiate peace, the satrap arrived with embroidered rugs and soft cushions to keep from soiling his splendid robes, while the Spartan king plopped himself down on the grass. The Spartans' pride in their frugality could sometimes be obnoxious. Once, when the Athenian philosopher Diogenes the Cynic saw Rhodians parading about in fine clothes at the Olympics, he scoffed, "Affectation!" But when he saw the Spartans parading about in their rags soon after, he declared, "More affectation!" Aristotle noted that, while the Spartans' single-minded pursuit of courage had provided them with essential security, it had also deprived them of "the ability to live in a way that has real value." By sacrificing personal freedom so completely to the considerations of security, they had defeated the whole purpose of security, which was to defend that degree of freedom necessary to self-fulfillment. By the very means with which they had sought to avoid enslavement at the hands of foreigners, the Spartans had enslaved themselves.

Finally, the collectivized Spartan system left individual Spartans with personality deficiencies. Plutarch, who admired the Spartans, compared them with bees because they were incapable of leading private lives, being "organic parts of their community, clinging together around their leader, forgetting themselves in their enthusiasm, and belonging wholly to their country." Spartans became notorious for their lack of humor. When a man asked a Spartan if he wished to hear him imitate a nightingale, the Spartan declined, saying, "I have heard the nightingale herself." The very word "laconic," derived from Laconia, the Spartan home in the southern Peloponnesus, became a synonym for "terse."

But the Spartan system possessed advantages as well. First, it encouraged a selflessness lacking in most individualistic societies. When an old man looking for a seat at the Olympics was jeered away by other Greeks, the Spartans rose up en masse, even the elders, to offer him a seat. The old man sighed, "All Greeks know what is right, but only the Spartans do it."

Second, the Spartans' lifelong discipline produced skilled, rugged, courageous, and patriotic soldiers. By 550 BC, the Spartan army was the best in Greece. Combined with the Athenian navy, the Spartans later saved Greece from enslavement by the Persians. So strenuous was Spartan training that their soldiers considered war a vacation from its rigors. The Spartans were the only people who actually relaxed their discipline in wartime. When asked why Sparta was not surrounded by a wall, King Agesilaus II pointed to Spartan soldiers and said, "These are the Spartans' walls." King Agis remarked that Spartans did not ask how many the enemy were, only where they were located. A Spartan with a crippled leg refused to leave the army, saying, "What's needed to fight our foes is a man who stands his ground, not one who runs away." The Spartans became famous for their patriotism. When a foreigner tried to curry favor with King Theopompus by claiming that in his own polis he was called a "friend of Sparta," Theopompus replied sternly, "Stranger, it would be more honorable for you to be called a friend of your own city."

Finally, the Spartan system produced strong, independent women. As the mothers of warriors, Spartan women possessed a much higher status in society than Athenian women. In Sparta only women who died in childbirth and soldiers who died in battle were permitted headstones above their tombs. Since Spartan males lived in the barracks and spent all of their time preparing for war, the women had to oversee the helots. As the managers of Spartan farms, living without male supervision, Spartan women developed practical skills and an independent caste of mind.

The Spartans did not lack admirers, even in the rival city of Athens. Socrates and his students, Plato and Xenophon, greatly respected their frugality, discipline, stability, courage, and patriotism. Above all, they admired the Spartans for having rationally devised their own unique lifestyle, rather than meekly continuing a traditional way of life. Whatever one thought of the Spartan system, it was certainly not a mindless copy of any other. Yet one contemporary made the telling observation, "Despite the universal praise for such a code of behavior, not a single city is willing to copy it."

By 500 BC the Spartans had established the Peloponnesian League, an alliance of Peloponnesian (and a few other) poleis sworn to mutual defense and determined to suppress democracy in the region. The Spartans feared the instability they associated with democracy above every other danger. Legend has it that when a man urged Lycurgus to create a democracy in Sparta, the lawgiver had replied, "Make your own household a democracy first." The man withdrew his request.

Problems with Plutarch's Account

The Founding Fathers derived this account of Sparta largely from Plutarch's life of Lycurgus, whom most modern historians consider to have been a mythological figure, as well as from Plutarch's *Sayings of the Spartans*. Since Plutarch lived over half a millennium after Sparta's heyday, it is not surprising that modern historians question some of the details in Plutarch's account. While Sparta was far less individualistic than Athens and most other Greek poleis, as attested by other writings that were much closer to the era chronologically (though even these accounts were written by outsiders), it is likely that Plutarch's account of the polis is at least somewhat exaggerated.

The Lesson

Nevertheless, the founders derived valuable lessons concerning the strengths and weaknesses of collectivistic republics from the story of Sparta. When Samuel Adams, the "Father of the American Revolution," prayed that Boston would become a "Christian Sparta," he was referring to Spartan frugality, selflessness, valor, and patriotism. Similarly, in his *Letters from a Pennsylvania Farmer*, John Dickinson reserved his praise for Spartan calm and courage, writing,

> To such a wonderful degree were the ancient Spartans, as brave and free a people as ever existed, inspired by this happy temperature of soul that rejecting even in their battles the use of trumpets and other instruments for exciting heat and rage, they marched to the scenes of havoc and horror, with the sound of flutes, to the tunes of which their steps kept pace—"exhibiting," as Plutarch says, "at once a terrible and delightful sight, and proceeding with a deliberate valor, full of hope and good assurance, as if some divinity had sensibly assisted them."

Americans ought to imitate this calm firmness in resisting unconstitutional taxation, Dickinson claimed. The Boston town meeting publicly thanked Dickinson for his "Spartan, Roman, British Virtue, and Christian spirit joined." In 1790 James Wilson applauded the Spartan emphasis on the training of youth: "In Sparta, one of the most respectable members of the state was placed at the head of all the children. Would not some similar institution be eligible with regard to such of them as are deprived of their parents?" Benjamin Rush admired Spartan frugality. In 1798 he wrote, "The black broth of Sparta and the barley broth of Scotland have been alike celebrated for their beneficial effects upon the minds of young people." In 1814 John Taylor, the American laissez-faire economist, contrasted the virtues of the landed aristocracy of Sparta with the vices of the British commercial elite.

But while the founders admired many of the traits the Spartans' intense military training had instilled in them, few were prepared to advocate so complete a suppression of individuality. Thomas Jefferson referred to the Spartans as "military monks." In *Federalist* No. 6 Alexander Hamilton noted, "Sparta was little better than a well-regulated camp." John Adams agreed. He called Sparta's communal ownership of goods "stark mad." To the Abbe de Mably's statement, "How right Lycurgus was in forbidding Spartans to communicate with other Greeks!" Adams retorted, "Is it such a felicity to be confined in a cage, den, or cave? Is this a liberty?" The founders sought the Spartans' numerous admirable qualities without the brutal system of socialization that produced them.

Although the Founding Fathers were less individualistic than most modern Americans, they were less collectivistic than the ancients, who lived in small, vulnerable city-states that were almost constantly at war with one another. Most of the ancient republics considered a high degree of individual liberty a luxury they could not afford, conflicting with the requisites of stability and security. The founders experienced enough warfare, and possessed enough appreciation for stability and security, to see the value in Spartan cultural traits. But they also enjoyed enough peace and desired enough individual freedom to prevent them from ever adopting Sparta as a precise model for the new republic they sought to create.

⌒

CHAPTER THREE

The Persian Wars
and the Superiority
of Republican Government

From Herodotus and Plutarch the Founding Fathers learned the story of the Persian Wars, the near miraculous victory of the tiny Greek republics over the seemingly invincible Persian Empire. From this tale the founders learned that it was possible for a collection of small republics to defeat a centralized, monarchical empire in a war for survival. This was a crucial lesson because the founders faced such a power in the Revolutionary War. Just as few contemporary observers had expected the Greek republics to defeat the Persian Empire, the greatest power on earth in the early fifth century BC, few observers of the founders' day expected the weak and undisciplined collection of American republics to defeat Great Britain, the greatest power on earth in the eighteenth century.

The Persian Wars

The Persian Empire
In 539 BC, Cyrus the Great, the king of Persia (central Iran), overthrew the Babylonian Empire. Soon after, he added the Lydian Empire (central Turkey) to his possessions. Croesus, the king of Lydia, had made the fatal blunder of attacking Persia. When Croesus had asked the oracle of Delphi, "What will happen if I attack the Persians?" she had replied, "A great empire will fall." On the assumption that the oracle meant the Persian Empire, Croesus had attacked Persia. But the oracle had really meant Croesus's own empire—or so it was assumed later, after his kingdom had been conquered.

In any case, having conquered the Lydian Empire, Cyrus hardly paused before swallowing the undisciplined Greek poleis of Ionia (western Turkey), which had already come under the informal control of Lydia, and the rest of western Asia Minor. Cyrus imposed puppet dictators on the Ionians. The Persian conquest of Lydia and Ionia placed the empire's massive forces on the doorstep of Greece. The same Cyrus who had freed the Hebrew prophets from their Babylonian captivity now threatened Greek liberty.

In 529 BC Cyrus died fighting the Scythians, the savage nomads of southern Russia, who decapitated him. Using camel caravans to maintain his water supply, Cyrus's son, Cambyses II, extended Persian rule south to Egypt and to the Greek colony of Cyrene in what is now eastern Libya in 525 BC. In emulation of the Egyptian pharaohs, Cambyses then married his own sister and began acting like a god. Going completely mad after failing to conquer Nubia due to water supply problems, Cambyses committed suicide in 522 BC.

The following year Cambyses' distant cousin Darius I succeeded him. Darius quickly extended the Persian Empire eastward to the doorstep of India. In 513 BC he conquered eastern Thrace but failed to push north beyond the Danube. Darius constructed the famous "royal road" from Sardis to Susa, thereby converting a three-month, 1,500-mile journey into a three-day trip when using swift horses. He also increased government efficiency by reorganizing the empire and by dispatching investigators to each of the provinces. The Persians established their chief administrative centers at Susa, Ecbatana, Persepolis, and Sardis. The first three cities were located in what is now western Iran, Sardis on the western frontier in Asia Minor. At its height, the Persian Empire consisted of one million square miles containing nearly seventy million people.

The Persians were relatively capable and mild rulers, as long as subject peoples paid their tribute. The growth of a new ethical religion, built upon the teachings of the Persian philosopher Zoroaster, moderated Persian rule. Since honesty was the most important requirement of the religion, Zoroastrians like Cyrus were shocked at the immorality of the Greek marketplace (the *agora*), claiming that the Greeks maintained "a special place, marked out, where they meet to cheat one another."

The Rise of Athenian Democracy
In 510 BC a popular uprising forced the Athenian dictator Hippias to flee to Persia. The Spartans, who had helped the Athenians drive Hippias and his friends out of Athens, attempted to impose an oligarchy of three hundred Athenian aristocrats on the city. Two years of civil war ensued.

In 508 BC Cleisthenes and the democratic party of Athens expelled the Spartan king Cleomenes and a small contingent of Spartan soldiers. The Athenians then defeated the armies of Sparta's allies, Chalcis and the Boeotian League, in two separate battles. Sparta was not sufficiently intent on imposing an oligarchy on Athens, which was not a Peloponnesian polis, to press the matter.

It was at this time, following the overthrow of Hippias, that the Greek word *tyranos* became a pejorative term in Athens, rather than simply a word for "dictator." This antidictatorial strain would later culminate in the writings of Aristotle, who portrayed tyrants as enemies of free speech and assembly, employers of spies, builders of distrust, impoverishers of the people, and initiators of wars.

Cleisthenes was made the sole *archon* (magistrate) for one year in order to revise the laws of Athens. He reduced the power of the Areopagus, the council of nobles, and made the Ecclesia, the assembly of all citizens (adult males twenty and older, except for slaves and resident foreigners), the supreme legislative body of Athens. The Ecclesia passed all laws, and its decisions could not be appealed. The Ecclesia assembled to vote on legislation every ten days; the average attendance was about five thousand. The new Council of Five Hundred prepared the assembly's agenda, executed its laws, handled public finances, and received foreign envoys. The Council of Five Hundred was completely responsible to the Ecclesia. Since council members were chosen by lot and citizens could not serve more than twice in a lifetime, each citizen was likely to sit on the Council at least once during his lifetime. Cleisthenes abolished the four-tribe organization, based on bloodlines, through which Athenians had elected their local leaders, since it gave the aristocrats too much power and divided the polis by clan and by region. He replaced the system with ten new tribes. Each tribe consisted of *demes*, subdivisions containing citizens from each part of Athens and from different clans. The new system forced Athenians of all persuasions to cooperate, thereby increasing unity. All Athenians came to see the city of Athens as their own, since the city was the logical meeting place of the new multiregional tribes. Each tribe also elected a *strategos* (general). The only elected leaders in Athens, the strategoi soon became the most influential leaders of the polis, gradually taking over the responsibilities of the archons. Cleisthenes also instituted the practice of ostracism, though it was not successfully applied until 487 BC. Every spring, Athenian citizens voted for the banishment of the Athenian they considered most dangerous to the polis. Provided that at least six thousand votes were cast, the man who received the largest number of votes would be exiled for ten years to a place more than three days' journey from the polis. Each citizen wrote his choice on an *ostrakon*, a shard of pottery. (A few citizens added expletives and caricatures.) Although ostracism was often abused by influential popular leaders called *demagogues* ("leaders of the people"), who had their rivals banished, it was intended as a way of neutralizing overly ambitious aristocrats, who might otherwise subvert the democracy.

The reforms of Cleisthenes completed the transformation of Athens from a backwater polis, torn by economic and political strife, into a flourishing city-state with a new sense of purpose, a new self-confidence, and the first major democracy in world history. The transformation proved vital to the defense of Greece against a massive Persian invasion.

The Ionian Rebellion

In 499 BC, disgruntled with Persian taxes and puppet dictators, the Ionians rebelled against Persia. The Ionians succeeded in expelling most of the dictators and the small Persian garrisons that kept them in power. Most of the Ionian poleis then replaced the dictatorships with democratic governments. Sympathetic to the Ionian cause for cultural and ideological reasons and concerned that Persian control of the Hellespont might disrupt vital grain shipments from the north, Athens dispatched twenty warships to the aid of the Ionians. The polis of Eretria, located north of Athens on the island of Euboea, contributed an additional five ships. By contrast, the Spartans refused to send an army to Ionia, fearing that, while their army was so far from home, their traditional rival Argos would attack Sparta and incite a helot revolt. In the following year, the Ionians, with Athenian and Eretrian help, burned Sardis. In 494 BC Darius put down the Ionian revolt and burned Miletus in revenge. The surviving men of Miletus were deported to Mesopotamia, and the city's women and children were enslaved. Nevertheless, in an attempt to mollify the other Ionians, Darius allowed them to maintain their democratic systems, though they still had to follow the orders of the satraps in matters important to the empire.

In 492 BC Darius, who had already shown signs of interest in adding Greece to his empire, dispatched a Persian fleet to attack Athens and Eretria in retribution for their aid to the Ionians. The fleet was destroyed by Aegean storms, which drove the Persian ships onto the sharp rocks of Mount Athos. Nevertheless, Mardonius, the fleet's commander, completed the conquest of Thrace and persuaded Macedon to form an alliance with Persia, thereby extending Persian influence into northern Greece.

Still determined to gain revenge against the Greeks as well as to add Greece to the Persian Empire, Darius sent a second fleet across the Aegean Sea to attack Eretria and Athens in 490 BC. The Persians captured and burned Eretria and enslaved its citizens through the treachery of some of its dissident factions, who opened one of the city gates to the enemy. The Eretrians were deported to Persia, where they were held in the village of Ardericca. Their despair was captured on a tombstone: "We who once left behind the loud-roaring swells of the Aegean lie here in the midst of Ecbatana's plain. Farewell, famous Eretria, our lost fatherland; farewell, Athens, bordering on Euboea; farewell, beloved sea. We are Eretrians from Euboea by birth, but we lie here, near Susa—alas!—so far from our country."

The Battle of Marathon (490 BC)

After sacking Eretria, the Persians executed a flawless landing at Marathon, twenty-five miles northeast of Athens. Persian commanders Datis and Artaphernes selected Marathon as the landing site on the advice of Athens' former dictator Hippias because it possessed a protected beach and level ground for the Persian cavalry. Hippias also hoped that the Persians might gather aid from his former supporters as they marched toward Athens. (Darius had agreed to make Hippias satrap of Athens once it was conquered.) But the Athenians had no intention of allowing the Persians to march on Athens. They quickly dispatched a force under the command of Miltiades. The Persians were astonished when the outnumbered but more heavily armored Athenians charged their illustrious army. By keeping his center weak, Miltiades fooled the Persians into attacking it, breaking through it, and surging forward. These Persians then found themselves surrounded, after the right and left wings of the Athenians defeated the Persians' weak wings, composed of Ionian subjects, and closed in around them. The Persians fled in a panic, leaving behind 6,400 dead out of a total force of 30,000, while the Athenians lost only 192 out of 10,000 soldiers. The Spartans arrived late from an important religious festival, grunted their approval at the Athenian victory, and returned home.

After the battle, Miltiades ordered Phidipides, who had trained as a long-distance runner, to run from Marathon to Athens and to proclaim the victory. According to legend, Phidipides ran the twenty-five miles to Athens, cried, "We have been victorious!" collapsed, and died. In honor of this exploit the modern Olympic Games instituted the "marathon race."

The Athenians' stunning victory at Marathon punctured the Persian aura of invincibility and gave the Athenians a tremendous sense of self-confidence. The victory convinced the Athenians that their radical experiment in democracy might actually succeed.

The revolt of Egypt against Persia (487–485 BC) and the death of Darius (486 BC) combined to delay the next, and by far the largest, Persian invasion of Greece. Darius had become so single-minded in his quest for vengeance that he instructed a slave to whisper in his ear three times every night while serving dinner, "Master, remember the Athenians!" Xerxes I, his successor, initially cared little about gaining revenge, until his brother-in-law Mardonius, who wished to be satrap of all of Greece, began provoking him to rage over the humiliating defeat at Marathon.

Themistocles (ca. 524–459 BC)

Meanwhile, Themistocles, strategos and leader of Athens, made two vital contributions to the Greek victory in the Persian Wars. First, he persuaded the Athenians to allocate new funds for the expansion of the Athenian fleet from seventy to two hundred ships. After the mines at Laurium, south of Athens, yielded an unusually large quantity of silver in 483–482 BC, some Athenian leaders proposed dividing the money among the citizens, since few expected the Persians to return. Themistocles was able to convince the Athenian people to support his alternative proposal to expand the fleet by playing upon popular fears of Athens' traditional enemy, Aegina, and by persuading them to accept his interpretation of an important prophecy. When an Athenian delegation had asked the oracle of Delphi for advice on the Persian threat, she had shrieked that they should "flee to the ends of the earth"—by which she had meant that they should leave Greece to the Persians and establish a colony in the western Mediterranean, the ends of the known world. But the stubborn Athenians had refused to leave until she gave them "some better oracle about our country." The oracle had then replied that Athens would be destroyed. But she had added, "Safe shall the wooden wall continue for you and your children. . . . Holy Salamis, you shall destroy the offspring of men." While some Athenians interpreted this prophecy as advising them to huddle behind the "wooden wall" of the Acropolis, Themistocles persuaded most Athenians that the "wooden wall" represented the fleet, an interpretation strengthened by the mention of Salamis, one of Athens' island possessions. Since the priestess had used the term "Holy Salamis," instead of "Cruel Salamis," Themistocles argued that the Athenians were destined to win a major victory there. Themistocles had probably known for a long time that the narrow strait between Salamis and Attica, Athens' territory on the mainland, was the ideal location for a battle with the Persian navy. He might even have included a reference to Salamis in his question in order to coax the priestess into answering as he desired. At any rate, the construction of so large a fleet meant that the new Athenian ships had to be manned, in large part, by rowers paid by the state. The lower classes had never before played so large a role in Greek warfare. It was the Athenian fleet, expanded between 483 and 480 BC, that proved the most crucial factor in the Greek victory over the Persians.

Second, Themistocles played a leading role in reconciling many of the quarrelsome cities of Greece and forging them into a confederacy against Persia. In 481–480 BC representatives from thirty-one Greek poleis met at Corinth to formulate defensive plans. The Athenians agreed to grant Sparta command of the combined army and navy, though Athens was contributing more than half of the Greek fleet. Themistocles understood that this concession was necessary to avoid dangerous squabbling. But Athens and many other poleis strongly objected to the Spartan proposal to station the entire Greek army at the Peloponnesian isthmus, a plan that would have surrendered all of northern and central Greece to the Persians. The Spartans argued that the Persian army so outnumbered the Greek infantry that the Greeks' only hope of victory was to make their stand at a narrow point like the isthmus. But since the other Greeks were unwilling to surrender their homes to the Persians, the Spartans were forced to agree to a compromise plan, which involved keeping most of the army at the isthmus but stationing a Greek detachment at a mountain pass in northern Greece called Thermopylae.

The Beginning of the Persian Invasion (480 BC)

The Persian invasion force was the largest ever fielded in Greece, consisting of two hundred thousand men and one thousand ships. The empire's motley army consisted of Persians and numerous subject peoples and mercenaries, including Ethiopians, who carried stone weapons and painted themselves red and white before battle, an Arab camel corps, and Iranian horsemen with lassoes. Though Xerxes knew that these subject peoples were less loyal to him than were his own Persians, he considered them useful because they were more expendable and because their outlandish dress and behavior might frighten the enemy. The Greek army was much smaller than the Persian army, and the Greek fleet consisted of only about 450 ships.

Starting from Sardis in May 480 BC, the Persian army marched to the Hellespont. The Persians crossed the turbulent Turkish Straits by lashing ships together to form a bridge. The army had to raise walls on either side of the bridge so that the expedition's animals would not be alarmed at the sight of the sea surrounding them as they crossed. In June the Persians marched through Thrace, clearing forests to fashion a road for their huge army. In July and August they crossed Macedon and Thessaly. Meanwhile, Persian emissaries were collecting enough bowls of earth and water from terrified Greeks to hold a mud wrestling contest. Persian custom required a surrendering nation to present a bowl of earth and a bowl of water to the imperial messenger, to symbolize Persian control of the surrendering nation's land and water. Every polis except Athens and Sparta obliged the Persians in this manner. The Athenians threw their messenger into a pit and told him to collect his own earth; the Spartans threw theirs into a well and told him to collect his own water.

The Battle of Thermopylae

At its narrowest, the mountain pass at Thermopylae is only fifty-feet wide, making it a perfect defensive position for a small number of men. The Persians would not be able to use their overwhelming numerical superiority to advantage by surrounding the Greeks, since they could only fit a certain number of soldiers onto the battlefield at a given time—nor would so small an area allow the Persians to take advantage of their superiority in cavalry and archery. (According to Herodotus, Persians were taught only "to ride, to shoot, and to tell the truth.") A mere seven thousand Greeks, led by King Leonidas I and his three hundred Spartans, awaited the massive Persian army in the August heat. Leonidas had ascended one of the two Spartan thrones after his half brother King Cleomenes had lost his mind and begun beating respected aristocrats with his walking stick. (While imprisoned for his insanity, Cleomenes died a mysterious death, which the Spartans called suicide.) Leonidas's army at Thermopylae was supposed to have been larger than it was, but most of his troops were delayed by the Olympics.

When Xerxes' scouts reported that the Spartan soldiers were lounging around, combing their hair, the Persian king laughed at their effeminacy. But Demaratus, a former Spartan king who had been deposed through the conspiracy of his colleague Cleomenes and had taken refuge in Persia, told Xerxes that he should not laugh. The Spartans always took care to groom themselves before a battle because they were prepared to die and wished to look good when they did so. Xerxes was hardly impressed. He could not believe that anyone would dare to oppose his massive army, particularly the Greeks, who lacked kings to instill a proper fear and obedience in their soldiers. But Demaratus shrewdly identified the source of Greek power and discipline: "They are free, but not completely free; for law is their master, and they fear it more than your men fear you. They do whatever it commands, and it always commands the same thing: they must never flee from battle, no matter how many are their enemies; they are to hold their ground, and there they are required either to conquer or die." When a Spartan soldier reported the rumor that the Persians were so numerous their arrows blocked out the sun, Leonidas remarked, "How pleasant then, if we're going to fight them in the shade."

Amazed that so small a force would dare to resist his huge army, Xerxes ordered his men to *capture* the Greek army. But the Spartans, fighting at the front of the Greek line, repelled three charges, sending the Persian lines crashing backward each time. Jumping up and down in frustration, Xerxes then called on his elite corps, "the Immortals," to attack the Greek line. Handicapped by the shorter length of their spears, most of the Immortals died. On the third day of the battle, however, a Greek named Ephialtes showed the Persians a secret pass that led behind the Greek army. Once a Persian detachment had gotten behind him, Leonidas realized that his army would be encircled and slaughtered. He ordered all but his three hundred Spartans to retreat. Seven hundred Thespians remained with the Spartans, refusing to leave. Leonidas instructed the remaining one thousand Greeks to eat breakfast in expectation of dinner in Hades.

Although the Spartans and Thespians fought well, driving some of the Persians into the sea and killing two of Xerxes' younger brothers, all but two of the Spartans and most of the Thespians were slain. The two surviving Spartans were so disgraced they later committed suicide. One of them, who was blind, was called a coward for requesting and receiving permission to retreat because of his disability. The Spartans claimed that a soldier did not require sight where the fighting was close and the enemy provided so many targets. At any rate, the infuriated Persians decapitated Leonidas's corpse and placed his head on a stake.

Why did Leonidas choose to die at Thermopylae? First, someone had to cover the retreat of the rest of the army. Second, the oracle of Delphi had prophesied that the Persians would either destroy Sparta or kill a Spartan king. Knowing this, Leonidas was prepared to sacrifice his life for his city. Fully conscious of the perilous nature of the situation, he had brought with him to Thermopylae only those Spartans who possessed living sons, so that their family lines would continue if they died. After the war a monument honoring the Spartan dead was erected at Thermopylae. On that monument was inscribed the famous epitaph, "O stranger, go and tell the Spartans that we lie here, obedient to their commands."

The Persians lost twenty thousand men to the Greeks' four thousand in the Battle of Thermopylae. Xerxes' clumsy attempt to hide this fact from his own men—by having nineteen thousand of the Persian casualties secretly buried in a poorly camouflaged pit—fooled no one. Persian morale was badly damaged, and Xerxes grew suspicious of his contingent of Ionians. Hoping to encourage such suspicion, Themistocles had scrawled Greek messages to them on the rocks. The Battle of Thermopylae inspired the Greeks and became an enduring symbol of courage in a seemingly hopeless cause. To cite just one example, Texans at the Alamo remembered Thermopylae. The battle also provided the Greeks with the time required to inflict a serious naval defeat on the Persians at Artemisium, which, in turn, made possible the crucial victory at Salamis.

The Battle of Artemisium

At roughly the same time as the Battle of Thermopylae, the Greek fleet, under the Spartan Eurybiades, waged a fierce battle against the Persian fleet nearby at Artemisium. The Persians had already lost two hundred of their one thousand ships merely advancing across the notoriously stormy Aegean Sea. According to Herodotus, a Greek named Ameinocles made a fortune from the Persian goblets that washed up on his beachfront property.

Many Greeks wanted to leave Artemisium, so as not to risk the 271 ships stationed there against the remaining eight hundred Persian ships. But Themistocles bribed Eurybiades and another leading general to insist that the fleet stand and fight. The Persians then made a fatal error. They were so certain of victory that they detached one hundred ships from the fleet for the sole purpose of capturing any Greek ships that attempted to escape. Learning of this tactic, the Greeks decided on a surprise attack on the main Persian fleet. The battle itself, fought intermittently for three days, was indecisive: both the Greeks and the Persians lost one hundred ships. But the Persian detachment of one hundred ships whose task was to prevent a Greek escape was utterly destroyed by a storm. Nevertheless, the defeat of the army at Thermopylae forced the Greek fleet to retreat southward to Salamis.

The Destruction of Athens

The Persian army then marched into southern Greece. Xerxes' soldiers found few people in Athens, which had been largely evacuated. The women and children had fled to Troezen in the Peloponnesus, and nearly all of the men had joined the fleet at Salamis. The rest of the men refused to leave the city, insisting that the oracle of Delphi's "wooden wall" was the wall that encircled the Acropolis. Unfortunately, that wooden wall became a blazing wall after the Persians pounded it with flaming arrows. Still, the feisty Athenians refused to surrender. They extinguished the fires and rolled boulders down on the Persians. But when the Persians found a temple outside of the Acropolis close enough to allow a steep climb over the wall, the situation became hopeless for the Athenians. Some committed suicide, while others were killed. Reveling in their revenge, the Persians burned Athens to the ground. Xerxes dispatched a messenger to Persia to announce the long-sought victory. The Athenians later buried the remnants of these temples, now considered defiled, and rebuilt from scratch. Happily for historians, the burial preserved a great deal of early Athenian architecture and sculpture.

The Battle of Salamis (480 BC)

The Greek naval commanders at Salamis voted to sail for the isthmus to support the Greek army there, which was building a wall across it in preparation for the Persians. But Themistocles realized that, if the commanders were allowed to sail away, each would make a panic-stricken dash for his own polis, and Greece would be enslaved. Even if the commanders sailed for the isthmus, they would find themselves fighting the Persians in the open sea, where the Persians could exploit their greater numbers and maneuverability. Therefore, Themistocles persuaded Eurybiades, this time without a bribe, to call a second council meeting. There Themistocles noted the wisdom of facing the Persians in the narrow strait of Salamis. When Adeimantus of Corinth rebuked Themistocles for speaking, since he no longer had a polis to represent because Athens lay in ruins, Themistocles retorted that Athens had a greater polis than Corinth, since, with its ships and soldiers, it could take any polis it desired. Finally, Themistocles warned that, if the Greek fleet did not remain and fight at Salamis, the Athenians would immigrate to Siris in Italy. Without the Athenian fleet, Greece would surely fall to the Persians. Themistocles' threat persuaded the other commanders to remain at Salamis for a while.

But soon the Peloponnesian commanders, fearful of being cut off from their homes, began to agitate for a third council meeting. In fact, it appeared that these commanders might even sail away without permission. To prevent their flight, Themistocles dispatched a trusted slave to tell Xerxes that he wished to defect to the Persian side and that the Persians should encircle Salamis to keep the Greek fleet from escaping. His message also exaggerated the degree of disunity within the Greek camp, implying an easy Persian victory.

Xerxes swallowed the bait. When the news that Xerxes had surrounded Salamis reached the Greek captains, they were left with no other choice but to stand and fight.

Although outnumbered by 600 to 370 ships, the Greeks possessed two significant advantages that help explain their victory in the Battle of Salamis. First, the narrowness of the strait, only one mile in width, prevented the Persians from using their greater numbers and maneuverability to surround the Greeks and allowed the Greeks to use their battering rams to great effect. Second, the Greeks were more highly motivated than the Persians. While the Greeks were fighting for their families, their poleis, and their liberty, the conscripted Phoenician, Egyptian, and Ionian sailors who formed the bulk of the Persian navy would benefit little from the conquest of Greece. This is what Herodotus meant when he wrote, "Free men fight better than slaves."

The battle proceeded disastrously for the Persians. On the frequent occasions when the Persian captains were forced to retreat, they found it impossible, since the waters behind them were crowded with other Persian ships. Trapped, the Persian ships were rammed by the Greek triremes. The Persian ships sank, and their crews, floundering in long robes, generally drowned. In one instance, the brilliant Queen Artemisia of Caria (south of Ionia), in a desperate attempt to escape an Athenian battering ram, bore down on a Persian ship blocking her retreat and sank it. This act of "friendly fire" by the queen, who commanded five ships in the battle, actually redounded to her benefit, since none of the crew of the ill-fated ship survived. Assuming that Artemisia had defected from the Persians, the captain of the Athenian ship who had been chasing her broke off his pursuit, and Xerxes, who assumed that the ship she had sunk was Athenian, heaped praise on her. In fact, overwhelmed by frustration and anger at the looming disaster, Xerxes, who was watching the battle from a throne erected on a nearby hill, declared, "My men have behaved like women, my women like men!" Later, the Athenians, who were perhaps the most chauvinistic of Greeks, offered a ten thousand drachma reward for Artemisia's capture, since, as Herodotus put it, "there was great indignation felt that a woman should appear in arms against Athens."

Because the Battle of Salamis determined the outcome of the Persian Wars, which determined the fate of Western civilization, it must rank as one of the most significant battles in history. The Greeks sank more than two hundred Persian ships, killing as many as forty thousand Persians, while losing only forty ships. Essential to furnishing the massive Persian army with food and other vital supplies and to maintaining communications with the Persian Empire, the Persian fleet had been routed. Xerxes issued a frantic order for his remaining ships to retreat to Persia.

Mardonius's Final Offensive

Fearful of what might happen to him, since he had been the one who had urged Xerxes to invade Greece, Mardonius begged the king to allow him to remain in Greece with a large detachment. Xerxes agreed. After wintering in Thessaly, Mardonius prepared to resume hostilities in the spring of 479 BC.

Mardonius dispatched the king of Macedon, an old friend of Athens, to persuade the Athenians to form an alliance with the Persians. Alarmed, the Spartans sent their own envoys to Athens to convince the Athenians to reject the Persian offer. The Macedonian king reported that Xerxes would give the Athenians whatever land in Greece they desired and would rebuild their city if the Athenians joined with him. On the other hand, if the Athenians did not form an alliance with the Persians, they could expect Mardonius to single them out for further reprisals. The Spartans then appealed to the Athenians' reputation as a freedom-loving people and to the common bonds of Greek culture. Finally, the Spartans offered to help feed Athens, since Xerxes had destroyed the harvest, and even promised to give the Athenians a new home in the Peloponnesus, which could be better defended against future Persian attacks.

According to Herodotus, the Athenians replied to the Macedonian king as follows:

We know as well as you that the power of the Mede [Persian] is many times greater than our own. We did not need to have *that* cast in our teeth. Nevertheless, we cling so to freedom that we shall offer what resistance we may. Tell Mardonius this: "So long as the sun keeps his present course, we will never join alliance with Xerxes." Nay, we shall oppose him unceasingly, trusting in the aid of those gods and heroes whom he has lightly esteemed, whose houses and whose images he has burnt with fire. And come not again to us with words like these; nor, thinking to do us a service, persuade us to unholy actions. You are the guest and friend of our nation; we would not have you receive hurt at our hands.

To the Spartans, the Athenians replied as follows:

It was natural no doubt that the Lacedaemonians [Spartans] should be afraid that we might make terms with the barbarians. But, nonetheless, it was a base fear in men who knew so well of what temper and spirit we are. Not all the gold that the whole earth contains, not the fairest and most fertile lands, would bribe us to take part with the Medes and help them to enslave Greece. Even could we have brought ourselves to do such a thing, there are many very powerful motives that would now make it impossible. The first and chief of these is the burning and destruction of our temples and the images of our gods. . . . Again, there is our common brotherhood with the Greeks, our common ancestry and language, the altars and sacrifices of which we all partake, the common character we bear. . . . Know then . . . that while one Athenian remains alive we will never join alliance with Xerxes. We thank you, however, for your forethought on our behalf and for your wish to give our families sustenance, now that ruin has befallen us . . . but, for ourselves, we will endure as we may, and not be burdensome to you.

In the spring of 479 BC Mardonius again occupied and destroyed Athens. Still, the Athenians refused an offer of alliance, even killing one of their own councilors who dared propose its consideration.

The Battles of Plataea and Mycale (479 BC)

The Athenian rejection of Xerxes' offer of alliance made another battle inevitable. This final battle was fought at Plataea, on the spurs of Mount Cithaeron, where the ground was impassable for the Persian cavalry. Under the leadership of the Spartan Pausanias, Leonidas's nephew, a large Greek army faced off against an even larger Persian army. Each Greek soldier swore an oath before the battle: "I shall fight to the death, and I shall not count my life more valuable than freedom." After withstanding a fierce assault by Persian archers, the Spartans charged the Persian center. Mardonius was killed, along with fifty thousand of his troops. The Persians fled in panic, nearly all of them slaughtered in their retreat from Greece. Pausanias then ordered that the lavish dinner the Persians had prepared beforehand be served to his own staff, exclaiming, "By the gods, with food like this what greedy characters the Persians were to chase after our barley-bread!" The same day a Greek fleet of 110 ships, under Latychidas of Sparta and Xanthippus of Athens, attacked remnants of the Persian fleet beached at Mycale off the coast of Asia Minor. Fighting off the Persian marines, the Greeks torched the fleet.

The poet Simonides composed two of the greatest epitaphs in history for those who died in defense of Greek liberty at Plataea. For the Athenian dead he wrote, "Hastening to ensure the freedom of Greece, we lie here, enjoying ageless glory." And for the Spartan dead he wrote, "And though they have died, they have not died, for their courage raises them in glory from the rooms of Hades."

Problems with Herodotus's Account

While archaeology has tended to support much of Herodotus's account—even the lopsided casualty figures for the Battle of Marathon—there are problems with it. For instance, he claimed that the Persian army that invaded Greece included millions of men, so many that they drank several rivers dry along their approach. No doubt Herodotus's Persian sources were much fewer in number and much less reliable than his Greek sources. Even his Greek sources were probably heavily weighted in Athens' favor, since it was while living in that city that he first decided to write a history of the Persian Wars. It is likely that the stories of the Persian Wars he heard in Athens tended to maximize the city's role in the victory and to glorify the city in other respects. In particular, the story of Athens' rejection of an alliance with Persia, while essentially true, is presented in a suspiciously dramatic form. Rather than identify an individual speaker, Herodotus presents "the Athenians" speaking collectively. Their stirring speech bears a striking resemblance to the monologues of the chorus in the plays of Sophocles, Herodotus's friend.

The Lesson

Nevertheless, the Founding Fathers read with admiration Herodotus's *Histories* and Plutarch's life of Themistocles. They accepted without reservation Herodotus's conclusion as to the source of the Greek victory over the Persians: "Free men fight better than slaves."

This insight inspired the founders to believe that they could defeat the British army and secure American independence, at a time when few objective observers accepted the possibility of such an outcome. After the Coercive Acts (which the colonists called the Intolerable Acts) were passed in 1774, John Adams expressed a common view: "The Grecian Commonwealths were the most heroic Confederacy that ever existed. . . . The Period of their glory was from the Defeat of Xerxes to the Rise of Alexander. Let Us not be enslaved, my dear Friend, Either by Xerxes or Alexander."

The founders idolized the heroes of the Persian Wars, especially Themistocles and Leonidas. When Jefferson wished to compliment John Adams, a staunch supporter of a strong American navy, he compared Adams with Themistocles, whose success in building the Athenian fleet had secured victory for Greece in the Persian Wars. Similarly, Jefferson celebrated the courage and patriotism of Leonidas's Spartans, comparing the asinine question of which American had contributed the most to the success of the American Revolution with the question, "Who first of the three hundred Spartans offered his name to Leonidas?"

In the years after the Revolutionary War the founders did not forget the chief lesson they had learned from the story of the Persian Wars, the superiority of republican government to centralized monarchy. Indeed, the Antifederalists went further, opposing any centralization of power within the new republican government on the grounds that the Persian and Revolutionary Wars had proved centralization unnecessary. They argued that the clause of the proposed U.S. Constitution that would allow the existence of a federal army in peacetime was not only dangerous to freedom but also unnecessary, since both the Greeks and the Americans had proven that militias composed of common citizens, motivated by love of liberty, were superior to professional armies. George Mason praised "the little cluster of Greek republics which resisted and almost constantly defeated the Persian monarchy." Of course, the Antifederalists were defeated by the Federalists, who, as we shall see, had derived their own lessons from the study of Greek and Roman history.

CHAPTER FOUR

~

Athens and the Perils of Democracy

From Plutarch the Founding Fathers learned the story of the growth of democracy in Athens, from both Thucydides and Plutarch the tale of Sparta's victory over Athens in the Peloponnesian War. Since neither Plutarch nor Thucydides were sympathetic to the democratic system of government in Athens, it is not surprising that the founders connected the two developments, blaming Athenian democracy for the disastrous defeat. In addition, they learned from Plato the story of Socrates' execution by the Athenian masses on false grounds. The negative view of democracy the founders derived from ancient historians and philosophers played no small part in their decision to create a "republic," a system of mixed government in which the masses would have a share of government power but would be counterbalanced by a powerful executive and by a strong senate, rather than a simple democracy.

The Delian League

Once the Persians had been driven from Greece, Sparta, a land power, had neither the motivation nor the ability to free Ionia and to end the Persian naval threat. In order to accomplish these goals, in 478 BC, a large number of poleis bordering on the Aegean Sea formed the Delian League, headquartered on the sacred island of Delos. The league agreed to maintain a two-hundred-ship fleet. The confederation was funded by the contributions of member poleis and by money seized from those city-states that had collaborated with the Persians during the war. Each member polis was required to contribute either a specific number of manned ships or their equivalent in money, based on its degree of wealth. Since nearly all of the other city-states chose to contribute money, Athens provided almost all of the league's ships.

It was the duty of the Athenian leader "Aristides the Just," one of the founders of the Delian League, to assess the wealth of each polis and to determine its contribution. No assessment of his was ever challenged. Many poleis were assessed at only one ship.

Plutarch told many stories about Aristides' integrity. One such story claimed that, during a vote for ostracism, an illiterate man whom Aristides did not know asked the statesman to write the name "Aristides" on his potsherd for him. Startled, Aristides asked the man, "Has this Aristides injured you in some way?" The man replied that he did not even know Aristides but was just sick and tired of hearing all of this praise of "Aristides the Just." Shaking his head sadly, honest Aristides wrote his own name on the man's potsherd. (Indeed, Aristides was banished that year, 483 BC, at the instigation of his rival Themistocles, though he was later recalled when the Persians invaded Greece, and he distinguished himself leading the Athenians at Plataea. Athens was fortunate that Aristides had been banished in 483 BC, since he had been one of the leading opponents of Themistocles' naval construction program. Virtue and wisdom do not always go together.) On another occasion, when Aristides was prosecuting an opponent and the jury refused to listen to the defendant's case, Aristides jumped to his feet and demanded they do so. At another time, when Aristides acted as an arbitrator in a dispute, one party reminded him that the other party had once injured Aristides. Aristides replied, "Do not tell me about that. Tell me what he has done to you. I am here to judge your case, not mine." Before the Battle of Marathon, Aristides relinquished his turn at command to Miltiades and persuaded the other generals to do so as well, since Miltiades was the best of the generals. After the battle, when Aristides was placed in charge of guarding the enemy's spoils, he did not help himself to any. Despite the numerous opportunities for the acceptance of bribes that his tenure as the league's assessor afforded him, Aristides left the post poorer than when he assumed it. Indeed, since he did not even leave behind enough money to pay for his own funeral, the state paid for it and for his daughters' dowries.

The turning point in the history of the Delian League came in 465 BC, when Thasos, a polis rich in precious metals, decided to leave the confederacy. Although Ionia had been liberated and the Persian threat had been considerably reduced, Athens treated the secession of Thasos as a revolt and crushed it. The Athenians not only reimposed the polis's assessment but also demolished the city's walls and seized a gold mine from it. Athens then forced some Aegean poleis that had not joined the league to do so, a policy that raised the number of member states to approximately 140. The Athenians explained that, if they were forced to reduce the fleet through lack of funds, Persia would again threaten Greece. Why shouldn't all of the Aegean poleis that benefited from Athenian naval protection pay what all agreed was a fair price for it? The poleis that refused were taking advantage of their neighbors.

Athens established and maintained democratic governments in those member poleis that revolted. The Athenians explained that the imposition of democracy on league members was merely designed to ensure their future loyalty to democratic Athens and to protect their citizens from greedy and powerful aristocrats. (Indeed, many poleis that did not belong to the Delian League, such as Argos and Syracuse, voluntarily established democratic systems without the slightest pressure from Athens.) The Athenians considered it a dangerous policy to allow foreign aristocrats who had proved themselves disloyal to Athens to continue to rule their poleis. They noted that Sparta had long since installed oligarchies in the poleis of the Peloponnesian League.

In 454 BC, after losing a whole army and two fleets helping Egypt launch an ill-fated rebellion against Persia, the Athenians moved the headquarters of the Delian League from Delos to Athens in order to better protect it from a resurgent Persian navy. In 445 BC the Athenians required that disputes between league members—even those between Athens and its allies—be settled in Athenian courts. The Athenians explained that settling disputes in the relatively fair Athenian courts was better than settling them through internal warfare, which would destroy the league. Most imperial powers of the day did not use courts at all. As the Athenians told the Spartans, the attitude of most powerful cities was that, "where force can be used, courts of law are unnecessary." Indeed, most of the league members' complaints did not concern the fairness of Athenian courts but rather regarded the expense of staying in Athens while awaiting a hearing, a need exploited by the city's greedy innkeepers. Finally, the Athenians offered the right of appeal to Athenian courts for any allied citizen facing the death penalty or the deprival of citizenship in his own polis. To some citizens of member poleis, especially to aristocrats already angry with Athens for robbing them of their power, these actions constituted clear evidence that Athens had become a tyrannical power and that the Delian League had become the Athenian Empire.

Indeed, the Athenians did effect an air of imperialism. Aristides' successors increased league members' assessments. The Athenians expropriated land from their "allies" to build their own settlements, which were often little more than garrisons to watch over the allies. The Athenians also used the league fleet to establish colonies elsewhere. They used their control of the Hellespont to levy a 10 percent tax on grain exported through the Turkish Straits anywhere but to Athens. They mandated the use of Athenian coinage within the league, though this policy was partly due to the desire to substitute a standardized, silver currency for the heterogeneous coinage of the allies, which varied considerably in substance and weight. Finally, they demanded that each ally send a cow and a panoply of arms as an offering at the city's Panathenaic Festival. Athens had become the political, military, economic, and cultural center of the Aegean.

The Banishment of Themistocles and Cimon

The Ostracism of Themistocles

In 471 BC Themistocles' rivals succeeded in having him ostracized. Themistocles complained that the Athenians treated him like a plane tree: when it was stormy, they ran under his branches for shelter, but as soon as the storm cleared, they plucked his leaves and lopped off his branches. On another occasion he used a more pungent analogy to convey the fickleness of the Athenian people toward him, saying, "I do not admire the sort of men who use the same vessel as a wine pitcher and a chamber pot."

Themistocles lived in Argos for several years, until called back to Athens to stand trial on the ridiculous charge of plotting treason against Athens with Persia. The accusation was the work not only of Themistocles' rivals in Athens but also of the Spartans, who might have feared his presence in Argos, Sparta's traditional enemy. The Spartans pressed Athens to force Themistocles to stand trial before a general Greek congress, which the Spartans dominated, rather than before an Athenian jury.

Realizing that he could not prevail in such a trial, Themistocles made his way to Persia, ironically the only secure place of refuge from his Greek enemies. The shrewd Athenian learned the Persian language within a year and acquired influence at the court of Artaxerxes, Xerxes' son, who had assumed the throne following his father's assassination in 465 BC. Thrilled to have in his custody the Athenian who had inflicted so great a defeat on Persia, Artaxerxes gave Themistocles three cities in Asia Minor, including Magnesia, where Themistocles died around 459 BC.

The Ostracism of Cimon

Cimon, a son of Miltiades who had distinguished himself at Salamis, succeeded Themistocles as the leader of Athens. Though not particularly eloquent, Cimon was brave and just, refusing all bribes. It was Cimon who greatly reduced the Persian threat to Greece by defeating them and capturing two hundred Persian ships in a naval battle near the Eurymedon River on the western coast of Asia Minor in 466 BC. On the same day he defeated Persian land forces, thereby freeing parts of Asia Minor. Cimon also led the Delian League in clearing the Aegean Sea of pirates. He ordered the construction of sturdy walls from the city to Piraeus, Athens' best harbor. These walls would allow Athens to resist sieges by continuing to import food via the sea. Although Cimon's aristocratic sympathies inclined him to maintain friendly relations with the Spartans, even naming his own sons after them, the Spartans remained deeply suspicious of the new Delian League. (As early as 479 BC an anxious Sparta had suggested that all poleis outside the Peloponnesus destroy their own walls, since they might prove useful to the Persians in the event of another invasion, and rely on the Spartan army for protection instead. Most poleis had simply ignored the suggestion. Themistocles, on the other hand, had quietly accelerated work on the reconstruction of Athens' walls, had presented Sparta with the fait accompli, and had warned that thenceforth Sparta must consider Athens capable of defending itself.)

Although Cimon won popularity for a while by giving his own money, food, and clothes to the poor, his aristocratic leanings and pro-Spartan policies finally led to his ostracism in 461 BC. After the helots, with help from some of the perioikoi, had taken the opportunity to revolt afforded by a devastating earthquake, an embarrassed Sparta had requested Athens' assistance in crushing the revolt. Cimon had persuaded the reluctant Athenians to dispatch four thousand soldiers to Sparta, asking, "Will you look on Greece lamed and Athens without her yoke-fellow?" But alarmed by the democratic spirit of the Athenian soldiers and worried that these soldiers might go over to the helots' side, the Spartans had changed their minds about Athenian aid. The Spartans had told the Athenians that their services were no longer needed and that they should go home. The Athenians blamed Cimon for this humiliation, since they had not wanted to aid the Spartans in the first place.

Following his decade of exile, Cimon returned to Athens and died fighting against the Persians on Cyprus. Plutarch later offered Cimon the backhanded compliment that his accomplishments were especially impressive considering that he was exceptionally lazy and drunk most of the time.

The Further Democratization of Athens

The victories of the Persian Wars had given the Athenians a strong sense of pride and confidence. Interpreting the outcome of the Persian Wars as the victory of democracy over monarchy, Athenians began to perceive their system of government as the source of their strength and became determined to expand the power of the majority even further.

Ephialtes

Ephialtes, Cimon's successor, led Athens less than one year before a Boeotian assassin hired by Athenian aristocrats killed him. While in office, Ephialtes persuaded the Ecclesia to transfer all judicial power from the aristocratic Areopagus, except for its ancient authority to hear homicide cases, to the democratic heliaea. First created by the Athenian statesman Solon (594 BC) but given little power, the heliaea was a body of six thousand jurors chosen by lot annually from among citizens thirty years and older. Between 101 and 2,501 jurors (usually 501) were selected by lot out of the six thousand to serve on each particular jury. Due to the large size of the juries, a majority vote, cast by secret ballot, was sufficient for a decision. A chairman presided over the trial. There were no lawyers. The defendant had to plead his own case, though he might hire a speechwriter to assist him. Whoever brought forth the charge acted as the prosecutor. Each side argued its case in six minutes, or in some multiple of six minutes, as measured by water dripping from a special jar. Whenever a jury found a defendant guilty of a crime for which there was no specific penalty, the jurors then decided between the penalties proposed by the defendant and the prosecutor. Whenever a plaintiff brought forth a case so frivolous he was unable to win at least one-sixth of the jury vote, he was punished. (Like modern Britain's "English rule," which states that if a plaintiff loses a civil suit he must pay the defendant's court costs, this policy was designed to discourage frivolous litigation.) Significantly, Ephialtes also pushed through the Ecclesia a measure authorizing the payment of jurors, thereby making it possible for the poor to serve on juries.

Pericles

Pericles, son of Xanthippus (the hero of Mycale) and protégé of Ephialtes, led Athens from 454, when he was about thirty-six, until his death in 429 BC. Pericles forced all outgoing members of the Council of Five Hundred to submit to the assembly an audit, an account of their official acts. Until a council member did so, he could not leave Athens or sell property. Under Pericles, the polis used "surplus funds" from the Delian League to pay members of the Council of Five Hundred one drachma per day, thereby allowing the poor to participate in the council. He also used league funds to rebuild the temples of the Acropolis and to fill them with some of the greatest art ever produced. These public works programs provided employment, especially for rowers put out of work by peace, and increased Athens' beauty and fame. One critic, who was later ostracized by the people, questioned the propriety of using league funds in such a manner and added that Pericles was dressing Athens "like a vain woman with precious stones and statues and thousand-talent temples." Pericles retorted that since Athens had lost her temples fighting the same Persians the league had been created to oppose, it was only just that the league reimburse Athens for its losses. He also deflected criticism by offering to spend his own money on some of the works, if the people considered his public spending excessive. The people refused his offer. Pericles created prestigious offices (the *litourgoi*), held by the wealthy, that required the officeholder to pay for ships, plays, statues, and other public services, which would be dedicated to himself. In this way Pericles made the wealthy vie with one another for the honor of strengthening, educating, and beautifying Athens.

Pericles was the kind of man who was equally comfortable discussing the finer points of poetry and charging into battle. A man of immovable dignity, Pericles once ignored the taunts of a heckler for an entire day while conducting business in the agora. The heckler even followed Pericles home at the end of the day, still spouting insults. By then it was dark, so Pericles dispatched a servant with a torch to lead the man home. Pericles never attended parties, saving all of his energy for state affairs. He was very frugal, to the distress of his daughters-in-law. He was a man of great eloquence. Comics depicted him wielding a thunderbolt in his tongue, and a political rival who was fond of wrestling used this analogy concerning Pericles' rhetorical ability: "Whenever I throw him in wrestling, he beats me by arguing that he was never down, and he can even make the spectators believe it." Yet Pericles spoke only about important subjects, leaving his friends to speak on minor matters, so that the people would not tire of him.

Unfortunately, Pericles used his eloquence to promote a harsh stance toward Sparta that ultimately proved fatal to Athens. Athenian and Spartan forces, joined by some of their allies, fought a series of battles in Boeotia between 460 and 446 BC, leading some historians to call the conflict the "First Peloponnesian War."

Pericles was willing to use bribery to prevail in this conflict. In 446 BC a huge Spartan army poised to attack Athens retreated for no apparent reason. When Pericles submitted his audit to the assembly that year, there was one item in his account concerning which he refused to speak: ten talents "for necessary purposes." Since everyone knew what had happened earlier in the year, and since everyone knew that Pericles would not steal money (he cared so little about wealth he allowed his own estate to decay), no one questioned the expenditure. The furious Spartans executed the royal advisor whom Pericles had bribed into persuading King Pleistoanax to retreat, and they imposed so large a fine on the king himself that he was forced to flee Sparta. The words "for necessary purposes" remained good for a laugh on Athens' comic stage for another generation.

The Peloponnesian War

Causes

The Peloponnesian War was a Greek civil war. It was not only a struggle between the Peloponnesian and Delian Leagues, both of which grew larger and larger as more and more neutral poleis were drawn into the conflict, but also a class war between the commoners and aristocrats of nearly every polis. The commoners of most city-states favored an Athenian alliance, the aristocrats a Spartan alliance, and the two groups battled each other with ever increasing ferocity. In reality, all of Greece lost the Peloponnesian War, at that time the bloodiest conflict in the history of Greece. At least half of the Athenian population died during the war, along with large numbers of Spartans and other Greeks. At the war's end Greece lay in ruins.

The three underlying causes of the Peloponnesian War were fear, pride, and fatalism. The Spartans had been suspicious and fearful of the Delian League from the time of its establishment and now felt threatened by Athens' newfound power and by its democratic system.

Relations between the two poleis were worsened by a long-standing commercial rivalry between Athens and Corinth, Sparta's principal ally in the Peloponnesian League. In 434–433 BC Corinth waged war against Corcyra (Corfu), a neutral Greek island in the Adriatic Sea, due to a dispute over Epidamnus in what is now Albania, a colony that the two poleis had founded jointly. In 433 BC, alarmed by a Corinthian naval construction program, Corcyra abandoned its traditional policy of neutrality and asked Athens for aid.

Athens decided to aid Corcyra in its conflict with Corinth for three reasons. First, the Athenians feared the results of a Corcyraean defeat. At the time, the three greatest naval powers in Greece were Athens (300 ships), Corcyra (120 ships), and Corinth (100 ships). If the Corcyraean navy fell into Corinthian hands, the Peloponnesian League, already superior to the Delian League in land power, would approach it in naval power. Second, the Athenians were dazzled by the Corcyraeans' offer to join the Delian League if the Athenians aided them in their war against Corinth. Such an alliance between Athens and Corcyra would give the Delian League complete naval supremacy. Third, fatalism contributed to Athens' decision. Many Athenians considered war with Sparta inevitable and sought to increase Athenian power in preparation for that conflict. According to Thucydides, the Corcyraeans encouraged Athenian fatalism, saying, "If any of you imagine that war is far off, he is grievously mistaken, and is blind to the fact that Lacedaemon [Sparta] regards you with jealousy and desires war." Pericles shared this perspective, since he doubted that Greece could remain half democratic and half oligarchic. Territorial disputes might be settled by negotiation, but ideological differences could not be compromised.

Although Athens dispatched only thirty ships to defend Corcyra, Corinth was forced to retreat in humiliation, rather than risk war with Athens. Nevertheless, fearful of Corinthian machinations in Potidaea, which was both a Corinthian colony and a member of the Delian League, Athens ordered the Potidaeans to expel their Corinthian ambassadors and to raze their walls on the seaward side. The Athenians also increased Potidaea's assessment to the league from six to fifteen talents. When Potidaea revolted, the Athenians surrounded the city, trapping Corinthian envoys inside.

Corinth, now infuriated enough to desire war, called a meeting of the Peloponnesian League at Sparta (432 BC). There, again according to Thucydides, the Corinthians played on Spartan pride and fear:

> The world used to say that you were to be depended upon. . . . If our present enemy, Athens, has not again and again annihilated us, we owe more to her blunders than to your protection. Indeed, expectations from you have before now been the ruin of some whose faith induced them to omit preparation. . . . Do not sacrifice friends and kindred to the bitterest enemies, and drive the rest of us in despair to some other alliance.

The Corinthians' threat to secede from the Peloponnesian League was unmistakable.

Megara, another Spartan ally, complained about Pericles' harsh decree prohibiting Athenian allies from trading with the Megarians. The Athenians were still angry with the Megarians for breaking away from Athens, and massacring an Athenian garrison in the process, in 446 BC. More recently, the Athenians believed the Megarians had killed an Athenian herald.

The able Spartan King Archidamos warned against the devastation that war would bring to Greece, noting that young men often romanticized war because they had no experience of it. But Archidamos's rivals portrayed his wisdom as cowardice, and Sparta declared war on Athens.

The Spartan Invasion of Attica

Nine months later, the Spartan army invaded Athenian territory (431 BC), forcing the country people to retreat behind the walls of the city. But though the Spartans destroyed the Athenians' crops, the Athenians could still furnish themselves with food and other essential supplies as long as they controlled the seas. Athens and its allies possessed 600 ships to the 150 ships of Sparta and its allies. Better yet, while the Athenians possessed six thousand talents, the Spartan treasury was virtually empty.

The Speech

It was the Athenian custom to honor all of the city's fallen soldiers with a public funeral each year. Each of the polis's ten tribes carried a giant cypress coffin containing the remains of its casualties, in a procession leading to the public cemetery outside the city. The coffins were carried on biers, an empty eleventh bier representing those missing in action. The public funeral featured an oration, delivered by the most distinguished and respected citizen of Athens. In 430 BC that man was Pericles, and he delivered one of the most famous speeches in Western history.

Pericles began his speech (as recounted by Thucydides) by denying his ability to honor Athens' fallen heroes. Rather, through their supreme sacrifice, the soldiers had bestowed honor on him and on all other Athenians. Pericles then glorified the individualistic, democratic way of life the heroes had died defending, contrasting it with the totalitarian, oligarchic system of Sparta:

> Our constitution does not copy the laws of neighboring states; we are a pattern to others rather than imitators ourselves. Its administration favors the many rather than the few; this is why it is called a democracy. If we look to the laws, they afford equal justice to all in their private differences . . . class conditions not being allowed to interfere with merit; nor again does poverty bar the way— if a man is able to serve the state, he is not hindered by the obscurity of his condition. . . . We do not feel called upon to be angry with our neighbor for doing what he likes. . . . But all this ease in our private relations does not make us lawless as citizens. Against this, fear is our chief safeguard, teaching us to obey the magistrates and the laws, particularly such as regard the protection of the injured. . . . We throw open our city to the world and never exclude foreigners from any opportunity of learning or observing. Although the eyes of an enemy may occasionally profit by our openness, we trust less in system and policy than in the native spirit of our citizens; while in education, where our rivals from their very cradles by a painful discipline seek after manliness, we live exactly as we please, and yet are just as ready to encounter every legitimate

danger. . . . We cultivate refinement without stinting and knowledge without effeminacy; wealth we employ more for use than for show, and place the real disgrace of poverty not in owning to the fact, but in declining to struggle against it. . . . Again, in our enterprises we present the singular spectacle of daring and deliberation, each carried to its highest point. . . . In short, I say that as a city we are the school of Hellas; and I doubt if the world can produce a man who . . . is equal to so many emergencies, and graced by so happy a versatility, as the Athenian.

In this speech Pericles transformed the traditional heroic ethic, the quest for immortality through fame and glory, by applying it to a city rather than to an individual hero. The new heroes of his day, he proclaimed, fought not for their own individual glory, like Homer's Achilles, but rather for the immortal fame of their city. Pericles' funeral oration is similar in argument, if not in style, to Abraham Lincoln's Gettysburg Address. But, in stark contrast to Lincoln, Pericles never mentioned the gods, though the occasion was perfectly suited to such a reference. It is unclear whether this glaring omission was due to Pericles' irreligiousness or to Thucydides'.

The Plague
Unfortunately, the overcrowding caused by the migration of the country people into Athens created the perfect breeding ground for a plague that devastated Athens in 430–429 BC and again in 427–426 BC. The plague (perhaps bubonic), carried from Egypt to Athens by a trading vessel, ravaged parts of the Persian Empire as well. Thucydides, who contracted and survived the plague and nursed many sick friends, described the plague's symptoms:

> It [The internal body] burned so that the patient could not bear to have on him clothing or linen even of the very lightest description. . . . What they would have liked best would have been to throw themselves into cold water; as indeed was done by some of the neglected sick, who plunged into the rain tanks in their agonies of unquenchable thirst . . . though it made no difference whether they drank little or much. Besides this, the miserable feeling of not being able to rest or sleep never ceased to torment them.

Physicians were among the first to die, since they contracted the disease from its earliest victims. Some men managed to escape death by severing infected extremities. Even predatory birds avoided the unburied bodies, or died after eating them. Thucydides continued, "No remedy was found that could be used as a specific; for what did good in one case did harm in another. Strong and weak constitutions proved equally incapable of resistance, all alike being swept away, although nursed with utmost precaution." Those who became ill were filled with despair. Athenians avoided one another but perished anyway. Thucydides concluded,

> The bodies of dying men lay one upon another, and half-dead creatures reeled about the streets and gathered round all the fountains in their longing for water. The sacred places also in which they [the country people] had quartered themselves were full of corpses . . . for as the disaster passed all bounds, men, not knowing what was to become of them, became utterly careless of everything. . . . All burial rites before in use were entirely upset, and they buried the bodies as best they could. . . . [Wood, used for pyres, became scarce.] Sometimes getting the start of those who raised a pile, they threw their own dead body upon the stranger's pyre and ignited it. . . . Present enjoyment, and all that contributed to it, was considered both honorable and useful. Fear of gods or law there was none to restrain them. . . . No one expected to be brought to trial for his offenses, but each felt that a far severer sentence had been already passed upon them all.

One-quarter of the Athenian population died at this time, including Pericles himself. Pericles had been elected strategos almost thirty times; holding the office thirteen straight years before the people had ousted him and fined him in 430 BC. In their rage the people had blamed the plague on Pericles' strategy of retreating within the city. But, of course, Pericles had possessed no alternative to that strategy, since it would have been suicidal to engage the larger and better-trained Spartan infantry. Overcome with remorse, the people had reinstated Pericles in 429 BC. By then, two of Pericles' sons, his sisters, some of his other relatives, some of his friends, and his assistants had all died of the plague, and he had contracted it himself. Although Pericles survived the disease itself, he died of a resultant exhaustion, at the age of about sixty, later that year. Pericles' successors, lesser men who lacked the courage to oppose the people when they were wrong, would lead Athens to ruin.

The Mitylene Debate

In 428 BC the oligarchy at Mitylene, the largest polis on the island of Lesbos, revolted against the Delian League. By the following year Athens had crushed the revolt, with the considerable help of the common people of Mitylene, who turned against the oligarchs when the latter armed them for a suicide attack against the Athenians. Nevertheless, the Athenians were filled with such rage that they voted to execute the whole adult male population of Mitylene and to sell its women and children into slavery. But some Athenians, who had not attended the first assembly meeting and were astonished by the decision, called for a second meeting. The second meeting produced a dramatic exchange of arguments concerning the relationship between democracy and empire.

Cleon, Pericles' demagogic successor (429–422 BC) and a tanner by trade (the playwrights often made fun of his smell, his crude manner, and his lowly origins), defended the harsh decision. He began, "I have often before now been convinced that a democracy is incapable of empire. . . . Fears or plots being unknown to you in your daily relations with each other, you feel the same with regard to your allies . . . entirely forgetting that your empire is a tyranny and your subjects disaffected conspirators." Nevertheless, having asserted that majority-controlled governments were less capable of preserving empires, Cleon proceeded to flatter his audience by adding, with complete inconsistency, that "ordinary men" (who formed the majority) were better judges of foreign affairs than aristocrats:

> Ordinary men manage public affairs better than their more gifted fellows. The latter are always wanting to appear wiser than the laws, and to overrule every proposition brought forward, thinking that they cannot show their wit in more important matters, and by such behavior too often ruin their country. . . . [Common citizens], being fair judges, rather than rival athletes, generally conduct affairs successfully . . . [while aristocrats are] slaves to every new paradox, despisers of the commonplace . . . more like the audience of a rhetorician than the council of a city.

Cleon then noted the danger in allowing rebellions within the Delian League to go unpunished:

> We meanwhile shall have to risk our money and lives against one state after another . . . and shall spend the time that might be employed in combating our existing foes in warring with our own allies. . . . The three failings most fatal to empire [are] pity, sentiment, and indulgence. . . . If they were right in rebelling, you must be wrong in ruling. . . . Reflect on what they would have done if victorious over you.

An opponent named Diodotus began his response by assaulting Cleon's rhetorical tactics. He declared,

> The two things most opposed to good counsel are haste and passion. . . . [He who opposes discussion, like Cleon] must be either senseless or self-interested: senseless if he believes it possible to treat of the uncertain future through any other medium; self-interested if, wishing to carry a disgraceful measure and

doubting his ability to speak well in a bad cause, he thinks to frighten opponents and hearers by well-aimed calumny.

Diodotus then complained of Cleon's attempt to preempt dissent by portraying all dissenters as traitors or fools:

> The charge of dishonesty makes him [the dissenting speaker] suspected, if successful, and thought, if defeated, not only a fool but a rogue. The city is no gainer by such a policy, which deprives it of its advisers; although, in truth, if our speakers are to make such assertions [as Cleon's], it would be better for the country if they did not speak at all. The good citizen ought to triumph not by frightening his opponents, but by beating them fairly in argument; and a wise city . . . far from punishing an unlucky counselor, will not even regard him as disgraced. . . . We are the only city, which, owing to these refinements, can never be served openly and without disgrace, he who does serve it openly being always suspected of serving himself in some secret way. . . . We, your advisers, are accountable, while you, our audience, are not. For if those who gave the advice and those who took it suffered equally, you would judge more calmly.

This last remark was a well-aimed shot at the assembly, which often banished leaders whose advice proved unfortunate, though the assembly itself had passed their recommendations. Diodotus then criticized the decision against Mitylene. He argued that the executions would not deter future rebellions but rather worsen them, since those who rebelled would be desperate, knowing the fate that awaited them if they failed. Furthermore, the Athenian decision to kill the whole adult male population, making no attempt to distinguish the leaders of the rebellion from its numerous opponents, would encourage "innocent people" to join future rebellions, since all could expect execution.

Diodotus won a close vote to overturn the previous decision. Only the ringleaders of the Mitylene rebellion, though reckoned broadly at over one thousand, would be executed; none would be enslaved. A trireme arrived in Mitylene in the nick of time to save most of the city's population from execution.

The Destruction of Plataea

The Plataeans were not so fortunate. In 427 BC the Spartans executed two hundred Plataeans, sold the rest into slavery, and razed Plataea. Plataea had committed the unpardonable sin of taking the side of Athens, its traditional ally. Ironically, the city where the Greeks had won their freedom was now destroyed by the very polis that had led the Greeks in that battle against the Persians.

Moral Degeneration

The war between the poleis soon degenerated into a class war within each polis. The first instance of full-fledged class warfare occurred at Corcyra (426 BC), where the common people massacred many aristocrats, with the tacit consent of Athens. Thucydides vividly recounted the moral condition of Greece:

> In peace and prosperity, both states and individuals are more generous, because they are not under pressure; but war, which cuts down the margin of comfort in daily life, is a teacher of violence and assimilates ordinary people's characters to their conditions. . . . [During the class wars,] the meaning of words changed. Reckless daring was counted the courage of a good party man; prudent hesitation, cowardice in disguise; moderation, a cover for weakness; and the ability to see all sides, inability to do anything. . . . The violent speaker was always trusted, and his opponent held suspect. . . . In short, credit went to the man who struck first, or who stirred up those who had no such intentions. The tie of party took precedence over that of the family . . . and even the solidarity of parties depended not on solemn oaths but on being jointly compromised. . . . And the cruder intellects generally survived better; for, conscious of their deficiencies and their opponents' cleverness, and fearing that they might get the worst of it in debate and be victims of some cunning plot if they delayed, they struck boldly and at once.

Though somewhat more socially stable than Corcyra, Athens revealed its own moral decline in 422 BC, when, after crushing the revolt of Skione in Chalcidice, the Athenians executed all of the city's adult males and sold the women and children into slavery. This time there was little opposition to the decision and no reprieve for the rebels.

The Peace of Nicias

By surviving the Spartan siege of their city, by harassing the Spartan coastline, and by inspiring Spartan fears of helot revolt, the Athenians secured a favorable peace treaty with Sparta in 421 BC. Cleon and Brasidas, the leaders of the two poleis, had both fallen in battle the previous year, and both cities were exhausted after a decade of war. The country people of Athens were particularly anxious to return to their farms without harassment from the Spartans.

Nevertheless, although the peace, negotiated by the Athenian leader Nicias, was supposed to last fifty years, it proved no more than a half-time break in the Peloponnesian War. Since Sparta had essentially sacrificed its allies' interests in the treaty in order to obtain the release of 120 Spartan prisoners of war whom the Athenians had captured at Sphacteria, Sparta's principal allies, Corinth, Megara, and the poleis of Boeotia, refused to sign the treaty. Indeed, they even spoke of breaking away from the Peloponnesian League and forming "a third force." Although sporadic fighting continued, including a Spartan victory over an Athenian and allied force at Mantinea in 418 BC, Athens had clearly won the first half of the war.

The Massacre at Melos

But Athenian morality continued to decline. In 416 BC the Athenians invaded the neutral island of Melos in order to force the polis into the Delian League. When the Melians resisted, Athenian demagogues secured the Ecclesia's approval for the execution of the city's adult males and the sale of its women and children into slavery. Again, there were no second thoughts and no reprieve. When the Melians protested to the Athenians that it would be wrong to kill them, the Athenians replied brutally, "The strong do what they may, and the weak do what they must." The Melians responded that it was foolish for the Athenians to disregard justice, since it was "a principle which affects you as much as anybody, since your own fall would be visited by the most terrible vengeance and would be an example to the world." The Athenians retorted, "You must allow us to take the risk of that."

The Origins of the Sicilian Campaign

Athens' military campaign in Sicily proved its downfall. Segesta, an Athenian ally in Sicily, became involved in a war against Selinus. When Selinus secured the support of Syracuse, the largest and most powerful polis in Sicily, the Segestans knew they would be conquered if Athens did not aid them. Segesta asked Athens to attack Syracuse with sixty ships.

The Athenians debated the issue. Nicias, the leader of the aristocratic party, a man renowned for his piety, opposed the invasion. Alcibiades, the handsome, charming, ambitious, and unprincipled leader of the democratic party, was the chief advocate of the expedition.

Alcibiades had been raised by his uncle, Pericles, after Alcibiades' father had died when he was only three. As a youth, Alcibiades had studied under Socrates, to whom he was always a sore disappointment. (Nevertheless, Socrates once saved Alcibiades' life in battle.) Once, when Pericles had told his young nephew that he had no time to talk, since he had to prepare the annual account of his administration for the assembly, the boy had retorted that his time would be better employed finding a way to avoid the audit. The story is indicative of Alcibiades' propensity to cut corners. Although Alcibiades had become extremely wealthy through marriage, no amount of money seemed capable of supporting his lavish lifestyle. Highly competitive and ambitious even as a child, he had once bitten an opponent to avoid losing a wrestling match. He was also exceedingly vain. As a boy, he had refused to play the flute because it contorted his facial features; as a man, he walked through the agora trailing long purple robes. Nevertheless, many citizens admired his looks, his wealth, and his prowess at chariot racing (he placed three times at the Olympics), relished his flamboyant antics, and even found his lisp charming. Although Alcibiades possessed Spartan connections (both his great-great-grandfather and his nanny were Spartans), he quickly decided that war was more profitable to a general than peace. Hence, Alcibiades used his charm to secure an Athenian alliance with Argos (420 BC), a long-standing enemy of Sparta, whose thirty-year peace treaty with that polis had just lapsed.

In opposition to the Sicilian expedition Nicias first noted that Sparta would like nothing better than to see Athens dispatch its ships and soldiers far away across the Mediterranean Sea. Second, he argued that, even if Athens succeeded in conquering Syracuse and controlling grain-rich Sicily, it was too far away to be ruled without great difficulty. Finally, he noted that if Athens did not attack Syracuse, the Sicilian city would probably stay out of the Peloponnesian War, but if Athens attacked and failed to conquer the polis, Sparta would have a powerful new ally. Nicias declared, "You leave many enemies behind you here to go yonder and bring back more with you."

In support of the Sicilian expedition Alcibiades first argued that since Syracuse had been established by Corinth, and since Syracuse was already supplying Sparta with grain, it was likely that Syracuse would join the war on the Spartan side regardless of Athens' actions. He declared, "Men do not rest content with parrying the attacks of a superior, but often strike the first blow to prevent the attack being made." Second, Alcibiades claimed that the people of Syracuse were so divided that they would not be able to resist Athens. Third, Alcibiades contended that the Carthaginians of Sicily would side with Athens. Fourth, he noted that the first part of the Peloponnesian War had proved that Sparta could not harm Athens as long as Athens controlled the sea. Fifth, appealing to the Athenian love of action for its own sake, Alcibiades argued that Athens must avoid complacency. He declared, "If we cease to rule others, we are in danger of being ruled ourselves. . . . By sinking into inaction, the city, like everything else, will wear itself out, and its skill in everything will decay." Finally, he noted that Segesta had agreed to pay sixty talents for the sixty ships it requested from Athens. Athenian diplomats sent to Segesta had verified the existence of the gold.

Seeing that most Athenians supported Alcibiades' position, Nicias then tried a different tack. He attempted to frighten the Athenians by listing in meticulous detail the enormous resources and exertions a Sicilian expedition would require. Far more than sixty combat ships would be needed to land the requisite number of Athenian and allied heavy infantry, mercenaries, and archers and to keep the sea lanes open for the enormous number of supply ships that would be required. The supply ships would have to be filled with grain, bakers, carpenters (to make rams that could breach Syracuse's walls), and stonemasons (to build forts).

Nicias's tactic backfired. His arguments made the supremely confident Athenians even more eager to undertake the expedition, since they loved nothing better than an impossible task. Many young men looked forward to adventure and military pay. The Athenians selected three commanders to lead the expedition: Nicias, Alcibiades, and Lamachus (a renowned soldier).

Immediate Setbacks

The expedition was plagued by misfortune from the outset. Before the armada even sailed, Alcibiades' enemies in the city accused him of attempting to undermine Athenian democracy by creating chaos. More specifically, his opponents accused him of sending henchmen out one evening to disfigure the faces of *hermae*, the square, stone figures of the god Hermes kept in doorways and sanctuaries. Alcibiades' alleged motive was to create chaos and alarm, which he allegedly intended to use to gain power. Alcibiades' enemies also accused him of hosting elaborate satires of religious rites at his home. Though Alcibiades was an irreligious man, it is highly unlikely that he would have been so foolish as to risk antagonizing the people in such a manner. But the people were in a panic, lest such sacrilege bring down the wrath of the gods on them. Alcibiades requested a trial before the expeditionary force departed, but his enemies persuaded the assembly that the expedition was too important to delay. They advanced this argument because they wished to use the absence of Alcibiades and his loyal soldiers to turn the people in the city against him and because they did not want the soldiers from Argos whom he had recruited to go home.

The expeditionary force, which consisted of 134 combat ships, numerous supply transports, 5,100 heavy infantry, 480 Cretan archers, and 700 Rhodian slingers, departed in 415 BC. Each soldier was paid one drachma per day, the captains more. Captains lavished money on their own ships. Each soldier brought money with him in case of emergency. In short, Athens' military and financial investment in the expedition was enormous.

When the Athenians reached the southern tip of Italy, they learned that the Segestans had deceived them. Segesta possessed only thirty talents in its entire treasury. Before the Athenian ambassadors had arrived, the Segestans had gathered all of the city's private wealth and placed it in the treasury and had borrowed numerous gold items from neighboring cities and distributed them to a select group of their own aristocrats, who had hosted the ambassadors lavishly.

More ominously, the three Athenian commanders discovered that they disagreed on basic strategy. Nicias argued that, if the Segestans did not raise the money they had promised, the Athenians should display their might a few times to avoid embarrassment and return home. By contrast, Lamachus proposed an immediate attack on Syracuse while some Syracusans were still in a panic and others still doubted the approach of the force. The Athenians would catch the Syracusans unprepared and take many of their supplies before they could be stored in the city. But Alcibiades proposed a delay in order to collect allies and to prepare for the impending assault on Syracuse. Alcibiades was certain he could employ his famous charm to win numerous allies. Unfortunately, Alcibiades' proposal, the worst of the three, prevailed, after he converted Lamachus to his position. Only one Sicilian polis, Catana, allied itself with Athens, and the opportunity to surprise and overwhelm the Syracusans was lost.

Meanwhile, in Athens, rumors that some traitors were prepared to turn the city over to the Spartans swept the populace. When a terrified suspect was bullied into handing over a fictitious list of coconspirators, innocent men were arrested and executed. People began falsely accusing one another in order to receive pardons—a classic "witch hunt." Since Alcibiades' name was on the original list of coconspirators, probably at the instigation of his enemies, he was called home to stand trial for satirizing religious rites.

Fearing the paranoid state of the Athenian citizenry, Alcibiades decided to flee, defecting to Sparta. Along the way he warned Messana (Messina), strategically located at the northeastern tip of Sicily, that some of its citizens were about to betray the city to Athens. The same demagogue who had once curried favor with the Athenian masses by praising democracy now curried favor with the Spartans by remarking that democracy was "a system which is generally recognized as absurd." Athens sentenced Alcibiades to death in absentia and seized his property.

The First Battle of Syracuse

Meanwhile, the Athenians used a double agent to deceive the Syracusans concerning their location outside Syracuse. When the Syracusans left the city to attack the wrong site, the Athenians occupied a strong position before Syracuse. As a result of this ruse, the Syracusans were forced to fight in a position that nullified their cavalry advantage. On one side stood cliffs, on the other walls, houses, trees, and a marsh. Though the Athenians won the battle, losing only 50 men to Syracuse's 260, the Syracusan cavalry protected the retreat of their infantry, thereby preventing the Athenians from routing them and taking the city. It became obvious that the Athenians could take Syracuse—a necessity, if they were to survive in hostile territory—only by attacking the city directly, where the Syracusan cavalry would not be as effective as in open country. But attacking a walled city was no easy task. Meanwhile, Alcibiades persuaded Sparta to dispatch one force to aid Syracuse and another to invade Attica once again.

The First Battle of Naupactus

The Syracusan navy surprised the Athenian fleet at Naupactus, south of the city. Knowing that the Athenians possessed lighter prows because they liked to maneuver around the enemy's flanks, the Syracusans had shortened the area of their prows and had made them more solid, placing nine-foot stays in the sides of their ships. Thus prepared, the Syracusans rammed the Athenians in the narrow bay of Naupactus (ironically, much as the Athenians had rammed the Persians in the narrow strait of Salamis), sinking some of their ships. Syracusan infantry occupied the coast, so that those Athenians who made it ashore were captured, along with their ships. The rest of the Athenian fleet barely escaped to sea.

The implications of the First Battle of Naupactus should have deeply disturbed the Athenian commanders, causing them to alter their location or their tactics or to withdraw altogether. But the lessons of the First Battle of Naupactus were completely lost on the strategoi.

The Second Battle of Syracuse

An Athenian general named Demosthenes (not to be confused with the famous orator who lived a century later) then arrived with seventy-three more ships, five thousand more heavy infantry, and numerous slingers and archers. Athens was sinking deeper and deeper into the Sicilian morass.

After many daytime attacks on the Syracusan walls had been repulsed, Demosthenes attempted an exceedingly risky night assault. His thinking was that the Syracusans would not be able to see at night. Unfortunately, it did not occur to him that his own soldiers would have the same problem.

The assault was utterly disastrous. The weak link in the city wall that Demosthenes chose to attack stood atop a hill. Although the Athenians did surprise and rout the Syracusans guarding the wall there, they were so eager to exploit their success that they advanced in great disorder. As a result, when Syracuse's Boeotian allies rushed upon the Athenians in tight formation, the Athenians were routed in turn. The first Athenian line then retreated back down the hill in panic, running directly into the second line of Athenians, who were rushing up to fight. Unable to see in the dark and assuming that the men sprinting toward them were Syracusans, many soldiers in the second line killed their own comrades. The scattered Athenians were so terrified that they constantly asked each other the password, thereby allowing the Syracusans to learn it.

Retreating soldiers had only three ways out: back down the hill, where their own comrades were likely to kill them; across hostile plains, where Syracusan cavalrymen were likely to cut them off and slaughter them; and over a cliff, off of which many Athenians accidentally charged, unable to see in the darkness. Many who escaped did so by abandoning their shields and climbing down the side of the cliff. The Syracusans had thoroughly routed the Athenians.

The Second Battle of Naupactus

Disgusted at the outcome of this battle and hearing the disease-ridden men complain of the unhealthy environment at their camp, Demosthenes wanted to return home. But Nicias, who had been the severest critic of the expedition, now insisted on staying, for three reasons. First, spies told him that Syracuse was about to go bankrupt and lose its mercenaries and that some of the city's citizens were going to betray it. Second, yet another Athenian fleet was on its way. Third, Nicias predicted that the same soldiers who were demanding to go home would claim, once they reached Athens, that they had never wished to leave and that their commanders had been bribed into departing. (He was probably correct.) Nicias remarked that he would rather die at the hands of the enemy than at the hands of his own people.

Though Demosthenes persuaded Nicias to move the force to Catana, so that the Athenians could regain their health and open sea in which to fight, a sudden lunar eclipse foiled this reasonable plan. Greek religious tradition warned against making important moves during an eclipse. Nicias consulted a soothsayer, who told him not to leave the area for another twenty-seven days.

Meanwhile, the Syracusans, who had been reinforced by Spartans under Gylippus, since Nicias had failed to set up a watch to intercept him, attacked the Athenians at Naupactus again. Using the same tactics they had used in the First Battle of Naupactus, the Syracusans inflicted an even greater defeat on the Athenian navy. The Syracusans now controlled the seas. They no longer thought of mere victory but also of capturing the whole Athenian army in Sicily. The Syracusans sealed the harbor with old ships lashed together. Now the Athenians fought only for survival.

The Third Battle of Naupactus (413 BC)

As the fleets prepared for yet another clash, Nicias reminded each captain of the importance of the upcoming battle, both for himself and for Athens, recalled to him the memory of any heroic ancestor he might have had, and implored him not to fail his family and his polis. The Athenians attached grapples to their ships and filled them with heavy infantry. If the Syracusans rammed them again, the Athenians planned to grapple their ships, board them, and capture them.

Learning of this plan, the Syracusans tied hides to the sides of their ships, so that the Athenians could not grapple them. Loaded down with armored men, the rammed Athenian ships went down even faster than in the two previous battles. Syracuse scored a decisive victory, sinking or capturing nearly every remaining Athenian ship. The battle sealed the fate of the Athenian soldiers in Sicily and, to a large degree, of Athens itself.

The End of the Sicilian Fiasco

The Athenian soldiers' only remaining hope, now that no fleet remained to support them, was to reach Catana by land and hold out there. The supreme confidence and ambition that had launched the Sicilian expedition was now a faint memory. In the need for haste the Athenians were forced to take the unusual step of leaving behind the wounded. Some of these soldiers stumbled behind the army as far as their weak legs could carry them, all the while crying out to their friends, begging not to be left behind. Thucydides recorded, "So that the whole army, being filled with tears and distracted after this fashion, found it not easy to go, even from an enemy's land, where they had suffered evils too great for tears, and in the unknown future before them feared to suffer more."

They did suffer more. Since the Syracusans occupied all of the passes, the Athenians were forced to follow an indirect route to Catana. The Syracusan cavalry harassed them day and night and prevented them from obtaining any food or water. When Nicias's troops got five miles ahead of Demosthenes' force, Syracusan cavalry and archers ambushed and decimated the latter detachment. Demosthenes surrendered.

Nicias's force pushed on to the Assinarius river, south of Syracuse. When his parched men saw the river, they trampled one another to death to get to the water. Syracusans hiding on the opposite bank let loose with their javelins, impaling the Athenians, who continued to drink even as the water filled with the blood of their comrades. Some, entangled in their own equipment, were swept downstream and drowned. A Spartan force attacked the Athenians from the rear. The mangled bodies piled up in the river. Nicias surrendered.

Although Gylippus ordered the Syracusan soldiers to relinquish all captured Athenians as prisoners of war, they ignored him, killing some Athenians, hiding others away as private slaves, and employing others in state quarries. This last group of Athenians was treated worse than animals. Denied any shelter or sanitation, they received only a pint of grain and a half-pint of water per day, half the usual slave's ration. Most died within eight months. Syracusan masters later freed a few of the slaves in gratitude for the slaves' teaching them lines from the Athenian playwright Euripides. When these former slaves returned home to Athens, they thanked the old playwright for their freedom.

Against Gylippus's protests, Syracuse also executed Nicias and Demosthenes and threw their bodies outside the city gates as a public spectacle. Thucydides summarized the Athenians' experience in Sicily: "Having done what men could, they suffered what men must."

As chance would have it, the story of the decimation and surrender of the Athenian forces in Sicily reached Athens from a foreigner who plopped himself down in a barber's chair and started talking about it as though it were common knowledge in the city. Since the Athenians did not believe the stranger's story, they tortured him on the wheel as a rumormonger and public agitator. When the Athenian people learned that the story was all too true, their agitation was exceeded only by their fury. As Thucydides put it, "They turned against the public speakers who had been in favor of the expedition, as though they themselves had not voted for it."

The End of the War

The Athenians had lost 4,500 of their own men, 40,000 allies, and 200 ships—one-third of their army and most of their navy—in Sicily. To say that the Sicilian Campaign was the Athenian Vietnam would be a vast understatement. The United States did not lose the Cold War as a result of its defeat in Vietnam, but the Athenians did lose the Peloponnesian War as a result of the Sicilian Campaign.

The Sicilian disaster produced revolts among Athens' allies and even inspired a coup that produced a brief period of oligarchic rule in Athens itself (411 BC). More importantly, sensing a golden opportunity to gain the vengeance against Athens that had so long eluded them, the Persians began financing the construction of a large Spartan fleet and the payment of its crews. The destruction of the Athenian fleet in the Sicilian campaign, when combined with the construction of a new Spartan fleet, proved the turning point in the war, threatening Athenian control of the seas.

Nevertheless, the Athenian leader Cleophon refused to accept a generous Spartan peace offer that would have preserved the status quo. Although the Athenians won a naval victory at Arginusae in 406 BC, victory soon turned to defeat, when the short-tempered Athenian assembly executed the six victorious generals for failing to rescue drowning rowers in stormy seas. Five thousand men had drowned in the great confusion of that stormy evening. The Greeks believed that the souls of such men, denied a proper burial, could not enter Hades but must wander the earth as shades. The generals, one of whom was Pericles' son, were denied a proper trial. The generals insisted that they had instructed a captain to rescue men clinging to the wreckage; for obvious reasons, the captain denied the order had been issued.

Ever optimistic (or stubborn), the Athenians again rejected a Spartan peace overture that would have left them part of their former empire. In 405 BC, largely through the incompetence of Athenian generals (their best commanders had just been executed), the brilliant Spartan general Lysander caught the remaining Athenian navy by surprise on the beach at Aegospotami at the Hellespont. Not only had the Athenian generals chosen a poor location on an exposed beach, but they had also allowed the rowers to roam about at will, and had even failed to post a watch. Alcibiades, who had worn out his welcome at Sparta by impregnating the wife of a king and had been readmitted to Athens only to leave again after one of his subordinates had suffered an embarrassing defeat, left his nearby retirement villa to warn the Athenian generals against these mistakes. In response one of them snapped, "It is we who are in command here, not you!" The Spartans destroyed or captured all but 9 of the 170 remaining ships in the Athenian fleet. They also captured three thousand rowers, all of whom they put to death. By then, neither side had the slightest claim to the moral high ground. The Spartans had massacred the prodemocratic leaders of Miletus, and Athens had decreed that the right thumbs of all prisoners must be severed so that they could not hold a spear again.

The Spartans controlled both land and sea for the first time. They used it to prevent Athens from importing food and collecting money from allies. Meanwhile, the Spartan troops stationed on Athenian soil prevented them from cultivating a crop of their own and from using the silver mines at Laurium. As a result, the Athenians had to melt down sacred statues for gold and replace their famous silver coins with silver-coated copper coins. Athenian slaves used the opportunity to flee (only to be enslaved by others). To worsen the city's food shortages, Lysander returned all prisoners to Athens and decreed that any Athenian caught outside the city would be killed.

By 404 BC Athens had been starved into submission. Legend has it that, in Lysander's excitement at the end of this twenty-seven-year war, he wrote home to the ephors, "Athens is taken," to which the ephors, irritated by Lysander's un-Spartan verbosity, replied, "'Taken' would have been enough."

One of Sparta's allies (by one account Thebes, by another Corinth) proposed that Athens be razed and that the entire Athenian population be sold into slavery—just as the sleepless Athenians expected. But after a man from Phocis sang a few lines from Euripides' *Electra*, the allies decided that it would be an outrage to destroy a city that had produced such a poet. Instead, the Spartans dismantled Athens' walls, as well as the "long walls" connecting the city with Piraeus, and demolished all but a few of Athens' ships. They also replaced Athenian democracy with the rule of the "Thirty Tyrants," a group of ruthless Athenian aristocrats led by Critias, and maintained a garrison on the Acropolis. Ironically, through Greek disunity the Persians had managed to secure the revenge against Athens that they had failed to gain by their own efforts in the Persian Wars.

The Execution of Socrates

A mere five years after the Peloponnesian War, Athens executed Socrates. A pronouncement of the oracle of Delphi had first led Socrates, the son of a sculptor and a midwife, on a search for philosophical truth. When asked by one of Socrates' friends if Socrates was the wisest man in the world, the oracle had replied, "Wise is Sophocles, wiser is Euripides, but wisest of all is Socrates." This statement had astonished Socrates. He could not believe that he was the wisest man in the world, since he did not think he knew anything at all. But surely Apollo would not lie. Socrates began to question all Athenians reputed to be wise—politicians, playwrights, and craftsmen—to discover if any were wiser than he. Employing the "Socratic method," an intense line of questioning aimed at defining objects and ideas and refining propositions by examining their logical consequences, Socrates revealed numerous inconsistencies in the arguments of these "wise men." Socrates finally concluded that the oracle's statement was "a kind of joke": Socrates was the wisest man because he alone recognized his own ignorance.

By making public fools of the leading men of Athens, to the delight of the city's youth, who began to idolize and emulate Socrates (they also admired his fearlessness in combat and his ability to drink enormous amounts of wine without any visible effect), Socrates helped bring about his own death. The philosopher created other enemies in the city by finding fault with democracy, by speaking well of the dreaded enemy, Sparta, and by criticizing the traditional portrayal of the gods. He believed, contrary to the stories recited by the poets, that the gods were completely virtuous and that they did not honor the sacrifices of the wicked. Still other critics of Socrates noted that both the traitor Alcibiades and the bloodthirsty Critias had been his students. Some Athenians recalled that Critias had written a poem claiming that the gods were the invention of an ingenious ruler, who had hoped to make evildoers fearful of an all-seeing eye. Although nothing could have been further from Socrates' beliefs, and though Socrates had once risked his own life by defying Critias's order that he arrest one of Critias's political opponents, many Athenians assumed that Socrates was to blame for Critias's cynicism. Finally, Anytus, one of the most powerful men in Athens (one of the two men who had led a successful revolution against Critias and the Thirty Tyrants), was angry with Socrates for turning his son against him by filling his head with philosophy. When Anytus ordered his son to devote his time to the family tannery rather than pursuing Socratic philosophy, the young man became a bitter drunkard.

In 399 BC Socrates was arrested for impiety and for corrupting the youth. Socrates was convicted by a jury vote of 281 to 220. Even then Socrates could have avoided death by offering exile as his punishment. Instead, he proposed a fine of three thousand drachmas, to be paid by wealthy friends, since he himself possessed only one hundred drachmas. Even this penalty he offered only belatedly and with great reluctance. His first suggestion had been that the city should pay him for his essential service as a "gadfly" who stung the citizens out of their lethargy. Indeed, he had declared, "Being convinced that I have wronged no man, I certainly will not wrong myself; I will not give a sentence against myself and say that I am worthy of something bad." Outraged by his insolence, the jury chose the death penalty (the prosecutors' alternative) by a larger margin than that which had convicted him.

Socrates' final address to the jury, as recorded in Plato's *Apology of Socrates* ("apology" meant an explanation or defense; Socrates never apologized for anything), remains one of the most powerful speeches in Western history. Socrates declared, "It is not death which is difficult to escape, gentlemen; no, it is far more difficult to escape wickedness, which pursues us more swiftly." He warned those who had convicted him not to rejoice too quickly:

> You have done this thing to me in the hope that you might thus avoid having to give an account of your lives, but I tell you that the result will be just the opposite of what you expected. For now there will be many who will call you to account, men whom I have held back, though you were not aware of it. They are young men, and so they will be more severe with you, and you will be even angrier and more upset than you are now. You are mistaken if you think that by putting men to death you will prevent anyone from chastising you for not living as you should.

To those who had voted for his acquittal Socrates concluded warmly,

> And you also, judges, must regard death hopefully and must remember this one truth: that no evil can come to a good man, either in life or after death, and the gods do not neglect him. . . . When my sons are grown, I would ask you, my friends, to punish them, and I would have you trouble them, as I have troubled you, if they seem to care about money, or anything else, more than virtue; or if they pretend to be something when they are really nothing, then reprove them, as I have reproved you, for not caring about that which they ought to care, and for thinking that they are something when they are really nothing. And if you do this, both I and my sons will have received justice at your hands. And now is the hour to depart, I to die, and you to live. Whichever of these fates is the better one is by no means clear to anyone, except to the gods.

Socrates then rejected an informal arrangement that would have allowed him to escape. He told his friend Crito, who urged him to flee, that he did not wish to live in another polis, to dislocate his sons, and to put his friends' lives and property in peril. More importantly, he noted, in a quintessentially Greek fashion, that the Law, which had given him life (his mother and father had been married through it) and nourishment, was even more worthy of respect than one's parents, since it was the lifeblood of the entire polis. By remaining in Athens when he had come of age, he had consented to be governed by its laws. Should he now break this solemn covenant in order to gain a few more years of life? (He was seventy years old.) And what kind of life would it be? One without self-respect or the respect of others. For it was not the Law itself but rather a mere jury of men that had injured him. If he were to raise his hand against the Law, he would place himself in the wrong, destroy his whole life's work, and make a mockery of his own teachings concerning virtue. How could he be trusted in any other decent polis if he showed contempt for the laws of his own? Would he not validate the unjust decision against him; would it not appear likely that a corrupter of laws might also have been a corrupter of youth? Socrates asked, "Shall I not obey the laws, which have protected me until now? I stood my ground in the army, where my generals posted me; shall I not stay at my post now, where the gods have placed me?"

Socrates was executed by ingesting a cup of hemlock. He went to his death serenely, saying that he was looking forward to meeting *and questioning* all of the great figures of history. He assumed that they would not evict him from Hades for asking questions. He assured his weeping friends that only his body, which was but a meaningless shell, would die. The real "Socrates" was the soul, not the body, and the soul was immortal. Complete truth could be acquired by the soul only after death, since "so long as we have the body with us in our inquiry, and our soul is mixed up with so great an evil, we shall never attain sufficiently what we desire, and that, we say, is truth." Hence, of all people, philosophers should most welcome death: "If you see a man fretting because he is to die, he is not really a philosopher but a philosoma—not a wisdom-lover but a body-lover." Socrates hinted that only philosophers enjoyed a blessed state of complete wisdom, as companions of the gods, in the afterlife. Like the Pythagoreans, but far less dogmatically, Socrates intimated the possibility of reincarnation for other souls: souls virtuous by "habit and custom without philosophy" entered into new human bodies, while impure souls entered into animal bodies or became shadowy apparitions wandering the earth. When one of Socrates' students offered him a beautiful garment in which to die, Socrates said, "What, is my own good enough to live in but not to die in?" Socrates' last words were as follows: "Crito, we owe a cock to Asclepius. Pay it, and don't forget now." Most historians believe that Socrates was referring to a severe illness from which Plato had just recovered: those who recovered from an illness were expected to donate a chicken to the priests of Asclepius, the god of healing. But there is another, more intriguing possibility—that the cock was for himself, that Socrates was equating the passage from this miserable world into a better existence with the healing of an illness. At any rate, Socrates' execution transformed him into a martyr for philosophy, virtue, and free speech, an enduring inspiration to countless people for 2,400 years.

Traumatized by the death of his mentor, Plato, who already had grave misgivings about the democratic government of Athens, went on to propose for his ideal republic an oligarchy of "guardians" led by a philosopher-king. Perhaps perceiving the flaws in such a system, Plato then penned a series of more practical treatises on politics, in the process introducing the influential theory of mixed government. In the *Laws*, a work in which Plato suggested a legal code for a small city to be established in Crete, Plato stated that there were three simple forms of government: monarchy (rule by the one), aristocracy (rule by the few), and democracy (rule by the many). But each of these forms degenerated over time. Monarchy degenerated into tyranny, aristocracy into oligarchy, and democracy into ochlocracy ("mob rule"). Plato then suggested that perhaps the best government would be a mixed government, one that balanced the power of the one, the few, and the many. Plato's mixed government theory became one of the most significant theories in Western history. Aristotle, Plato's pupil, made mixed government theory the centerpiece of his *Politics*, in which he cited numerous examples of mixed government in the ancient world. Polybius then applied the theory to Roman history, influencing Cicero, the classical author whom the Founding Fathers most revered.

Problems with the Accounts of Plutarch, Thucydides, and Plato

The Founding Fathers learned the story of the growth of Athenian democracy from Plutarch's lives of Aristides, Cimon, and Pericles; encountered the tale of the Peloponnesian War in Thucydides' history and in Plutarch's lives of Nicias, Alcibiades, and Lysander; and learned the story of Socrates' execution from Plato's dialogues, especially the *Apology*, the *Crito*, and the *Phaedo*. From these sources the founders learned to see Athens as the epitome of the democratic state, a chronically unstable, often hellish, society controlled by violent and erratic mobs that frequently executed their nation's best citizens on the flimsiest of grounds.

In sharp contrast to the founders, modern historians emphasize both the limited nature of democracy in Athens and the polis's staggering intellectual achievements. They note that the Athenians granted citizenship to 50,000 adult males at most, out of a total population of about 250,000. The Athenians excluded women, metics (resident foreigners—from *metoikoi*, "those who dwell with" us), and slaves from the franchise. After Pericles' nativist legislation of 451 and 450 BC, which made Athenian descent on both sides a requirement for citizenship, it became virtually impossible for metics to become citizens. A metic could not own land, speak in court, or marry a citizen, though they were otherwise well treated.

The status of women in Athenian society, like that of women in most other Greek societies, was unenviable. Few women were educated, since their sole functions were to bear children and manage the household. Custom forced women to stay in their own quarters in the back of the house when their husbands entertained guests. By necessity, lower-class Athenian women worked as spinners, weavers, and vendors, but upper-class women were not allowed to work outside the home. Women were allowed to attend plays but sat apart in the back rows. Athenian women possessed few legal rights. They could own only clothes, jewelry, and slaves. They could not enter into any business transaction involving more than a small amount of money. Wealthier men generally kept an educated, foreign-born mistress called a *hetaira* (companion). The hetairai sometimes owned businesses and often moved about the city more freely than the sequestered wives, sisters, and daughters of many citizens, who could only leave the house during festivals or on other special occasions. In Sophocles' *Tereus*, Procne, while preparing to kill her own son in revenge for her husband's seduction of her sister, declares, "We [women] are nothing. When we reach puberty and understanding, we are thrust out. . . . Some go to strangers' homes, others to foreigners', some to joyless houses, some to hostile. And all this, once the first night has yoked us to our husbands, we are forced to praise and to say that all is well."

Yet it would be wrong to assume that all Athenian women were docile. Socrates' wife, Xanthippe, was notoriously harsh toward her husband—justifiably so, since his philosophical dialogues did not bring in any money with which to feed the family. Xanthippe once even assaulted Socrates in the agora, tearing the cloak off his back. When Socrates' friends advised him to hit back, he refused to take the bait, replying, "Yes, by Zeus, in order that, while we are sparring, each of you may join in with, 'Well done, Socrates!', 'Good punch, Xanthippe!'" When Xanthippe scolded Socrates and drenched him with water, he said, "Did I not say that Xanthippe's thunder would end in rain?" When one of their three sons complained bitterly to his father about his mother's nagging, Socrates urged the young man to be patient with her, reminding him of the aggravations and troubles Xanthippe had endured on his behalf when he was a baby. Socrates said of his wife's scolding, "I have gotten used to it, as to the continued rattle of a windlass." When asked why in the world he had married her, he replied that one of his chief goals in life was to get along well with people, and he figured that if he could get along with her he could get along with anyone. Despite these good-natured jests, theirs was hardly a loveless marriage. Xanthippe wept profusely at his execution.

Legend has it that Pericles' mistress, Aspasia, played a large role in his public decisions. Pericles had divorced his wife, by mutual consent, years before he took Aspasia as his mistress in 445 BC. At the time he was about forty-five, and Aspasia about twenty-five. Plutarch later claimed that Aspasia was responsible for an Athenian decision to aid her home polis of Miletus against its traditional enemy, Samos. Politically adept, Aspasia had once been a diplomat of sorts for the king of Persia. Socrates and other Athenian philosophers visited her frequently, and she tutored numerous would-be politicians in the art of public speaking. Socrates called Aspasia "the admirable mistress I have in the art of speaking—she who has made so many good speakers, one of whom was the best among all the Greeks—Pericles." When Pericles' enemies tried her for impiety in the 430s BC (the real purpose of the trial was political), Pericles had to weep and plead for her until the jurors, always gratified to see their leaders cut down to size, voted for acquittal.

Of course, women were not guaranteed the right to vote by the U.S. Constitution until 1920 and did not begin to approach social equality until the 1960s. Indeed, modern criticism of Athens as "undemocratic" highlights the ambiguity of the word "democracy." If democracy means the political participation, however indirect, of all adults, then democracy is a twentieth-century invention. If, on the other hand, it means the direct political participation of all citizens, however narrowly the citizenry is defined, then democracy was a purely ancient phenomenon, since every modern democracy is representative, not participatory.

At any rate, modern historians are much more apt to attribute Athens' stunning intellectual achievements to its democracy than were the founders or their antidemocratic Athenian sources. Whatever its faults as perceived through the subjective lens of modern values, the participatory nature of Athenian democracy prevented the rise of an inefficient and haughty bureaucracy and produced citizens who were excellent soldiers, sailors, legislators, administrators, and judges. Athens demanded so much talent from its citizens and gave them so much freedom to express their talent that the city produced an incredible array of geniuses who laid the foundations of Western art, architecture, drama, historical writing, and philosophy. The classicist C. E. Robinson was correct when he wrote, "Athens' heyday lasted less than eighty years, and the number of her adult male citizens scarcely exceeded fifty thousand. Yet his handful of men attempted more and achieved more in a wider variety of fields than any nation great or small has ever attempted or achieved in a similar space of time."

The Lesson

But the Founding Fathers, following in the tradition of Plutarch, Thucydides, Plato, and the other ancient historians and philosophers, considered the story of Athens a cautionary tale against an excess of democracy in a republic. John Adams typified the common opinion of Athenian democracy when, in his *Defence of the Constitutions of Government of the United States of America* (1787), he attributed Athens' downfall to it. According to Adams, the Athenians had condemned their own society to destruction by consolidating all power in the hands of the masses and failing to balance that power with a strong executive and a powerful senate. Adams wrote that simple democracies like Athens were "but a transient glare of glory, which passes away like a flash of lightning, or like a momentary appearance of a goddess to an ancient hero, which by revealing but a glimpse of celestial beauties, only excited regret that he had never seen them." He added, "The republic of Athens, the school mistress of the whole civilized world, for more than a thousand years in arts, eloquence, and philosophy, as well as in politeness and wit, was, for a short period of her duration, the most democratical commonwealth in Greece." But through the establishment of a mixed government and through such modern innovations as representation and the separation of legislative, executive, and judicial powers, the United States could escape "the tumultuous commotions, like the raging waves of the sea, which always agitated the ecclesia at Athens." Adams concluded regarding the American experiment, "This will be a fair trial, whether a government so popular can preserve itself. If it can, there is reason to hope for all the equality, all the liberty, and every other good fruit of Athenian democracy, without any of its ingratitude, convulsions, or factions."

The Founding Fathers not only cited and praised Thucydides and Plutarch but also idolized the individual Athenians these historians had touted, most of whom had been critics of democracy. "Aristides" was a popular pseudonym throughout the eighteenth and early nineteenth centuries. Benjamin Rush considered Aristides a model of integrity. David Ramsay wrote of George Washington, "Enemies he had, but they were few, and chiefly of the same family with the man who could not bear to hear Aristides always called the just."

Thomas Jefferson and Benjamin Franklin were so enamored of Socrates, the great philosopher and critic of Athenian democracy, they occasionally distorted the historical record concerning him. In his autobiography Benjamin Franklin audaciously paired Socrates with Jesus as the two greatest models of humility. Whatever Socrates' virtues, humility had never been one of them. In spite of the philosopher's claim that he knew nothing, the gleeful arrogance with which he had enticed his opponents into admissions of inconsistency persuaded few Athenians to consider him a humble truth-seeker. Jefferson so revered Socrates that he refused to acknowledge that the Athenian philosopher had ever believed in the intervention of the gods in human affairs, a belief at odds with Jefferson's own convictions. Jefferson speculated that the *daemon* (divine entity) that Socrates claimed spoke to him was reason. Jefferson wrote regarding Socrates, "He was too wise to believe, and too honest to pretend, that he had real and familiar converse with a superior and invisible being. He probably considered the suggestions of his conscience, or reason, as revelations, or inspirations from the Supreme Mind, bestowed, on important occasions, by a special superintending providence." Such a view ignored Socrates' faith in the oracle of Delphi, as depicted not only in Plato's *Apology* but also in Xenophon's *Memorabilia*.

While the founders followed the ancient historians in praising the Athenian opponents of democracy, they also joined them in criticizing its supporters. In 1766 George Mason compared British prime minister George Grenville, the leading advocate of the Stamp Act, with Pericles, recalling Plutarch's accusation that Pericles had drawn Athens into the fatal Peloponnesian War in order to deflect attention from his own misuse of funds. Mason wrote regarding the repeal of the Stamp Act, "No thanks to Mr. Grenville and his party, who without his genius or abilities, has dared to act the part that Pericles did, when he engaged his country in the Peloponnesian War, which, after a long and dreadful scene of blood, ended in the ruin of all Greece, and fitted it for the Macedonian yoke." Alexander Hamilton used the same story to argue, in *Federalist* No. 6, that a strong central government was necessary to prevent warfare between the states. Surely, Hamilton contended, the American states could not remain forever free of such leaders as Pericles, who had started the Peloponnesian War, a war that "terminated in the ruin of the Athenian commonwealth," to cover up his own misdeeds.

The founders were even more fervent in their denunciation of Pericles' successors, Cleon and Alcibiades, whose vices Thucydides had recounted so vividly. In his *Letters from a Pennsylvania Farmer* John Dickinson warned that passions against Britain should not overwhelm reason to the point at which "the sway of the Cleons . . . the designing and detestable flatterers of the prevailing passion, becomes confirmed." In 1767 Benjamin Franklin compared English Tories who supported violent action against America with Athenian demagogues like Alcibiades, who had urged the ill-fated invasion of Sicily during the Peloponnesian War. Franklin argued ominously,

> Athens had her orators. They did her sometimes a great deal of good, at other times a great deal of harm; the latter particularly when they prevailed in advising the Sicilian war, under the burthen and losses of which war that flourishing state sunk, and never again recovered itself. To the haranguers of the ancients succeed among the moderns your writers of political pamphlets and newspapers and your coffee-house talkers.

Thus, it is not surprising that the Founding Fathers favored mixed government over democracy when drafting state and federal constitutions. The framers of the new state constitutions that emerged from the Revolution never doubted that their governments should be mixed. Rather, their dilemma was how to mix them in a society that no longer possessed a monarch and that had never possessed a titled aristocracy. The framers decided that these essential roles should be played by an elected governor and a senate consisting of an aristocracy of wealth. Ten of the thirteen states created a senate, nearly all of them establishing property qualifications for senate candidates that exceeded those for members of the lower house.

Even Thomas Jefferson, the future champion of representative democracy, fervently embraced mixed government during the Revolution. In 1776 Jefferson argued that "the wisest men" should be elected to the Virginia Senate and should be, "when chosen, perfectly independent of their electors." Experience taught Jefferson "that a choice by the people themselves is not generally distinguished for its wisdom." He proposed a nine-year, nonrenewable term for Virginia senators, so that they would not always "be casting their eyes forward to the period of election (however distant) and be currying favor with the electors, and consequently dependent on them." Jefferson could even accept Edmund Pendleton's suggestion "to an appointment for life, or to any thing rather than a mere creation by and dependence on the people." Jefferson even proposed the indirect election of state senators and the elimination of all previous restrictions on the Senate's power to originate or amend any bill. He added that the governor should appoint the state's judges, in order to make the jurists "wholly independent of the Assembly—of the Council—nay, more, of the people."

Similarly, at the Constitutional Convention, James Madison ("the Father of the Constitution") argued for a nine-year term for U.S. senators, declaring,

> Landholders ought to have a share in the government to support these invaluable interests and to balance and check the other [the many]. They ought to be so constituted as to protect the minority of the opulent against the majority. The senate, therefore, ought to be this body; and to answer these purposes, they ought to have permanency and stability. Various have been the propositions; but my opinion is, the longer they continue in office, the better will these views be answered.

It was useless to deny the existence of an American aristocracy, though there were no "hereditary distinctions," and though inequalities of wealth were minor by comparison with Europe. Madison added, "There will be debtors and creditors, and an unequal possession of property, and hence arises different views and different objects of government. This, indeed, is the ground work of aristocracy; and we find it blended in every government, both ancient and modern." In Madison's notes for *Federalist* No. 63, in which he again championed an aristocratic Senate, Madison cited Aristotle, Polybius, and Cicero, all supporters of mixed government and opponents of democracy. Madison warned Jefferson,

> Wherever the real power in Government lies, there is the danger of oppression. In our Governments the real power lies in the majority of the Community, and the invasion of private rights is chiefly to be apprehended not from acts of Government contrary to the sense of its constituents, but from acts in which the Government is the mere instrument of the major number of constituents.

For that reason, Madison endorsed a federal veto on state laws, claiming that, without it, states would continue to be controlled by "interested majorities" who would trample "on the rights of minorities and individuals." Alexander Hamilton, John Adams, John Dickinson, and numerous other founders endorsed the Constitution as having established a mixed government that balanced the power of the one (the president), the few (represented by the aristocratic Senate), and the many (represented by the House of Representatives). Both the president and the Senate were indirectly elected, the president by the Electoral College and the Senate by the state legislatures. There is truth to John Adams's claim that the writings of Polybius "were in the contemplation of those who framed the American constitution."

It is true that by the 1790s the Democratic-Republican Party, led by Jefferson and Madison, began to endorse reforms that would create a more democratic government. These reforms included an end to property qualifications for voting and the linkage of the Electoral College to the popular vote. But even then the Democratic-Republicans tended to use the term "republic" rather than "democracy" concerning their favored system and tended to emphasize the crucial role of representation. No one endorsed the direct democracy of Athens, so brilliantly vilified by the ancient historians.

Yet even the limited reforms of the Democratic-Republicans were enough to send John Adams into despair. In 1806 Adams complained, "I once thought our Constitution was quasi or mixed government, but they have now made it, to all intents and purposes, in virtue, in spirit, and effect, a democracy. We are left without resources but in our prayers and tears, and having nothing that we can do or say, but the Lord have mercy upon us." The specter of a new Athens hung ominously over Adams's head.

Not until the next generation, the "Age of the Common Man," when democracy ceased to be a dirty word, was Athens thoroughly rehabilitated. Only then did Athens replace Rome as the preferred ancient model for the United States. Colleges began to promote the study of the Greek language, which had always occupied a secondary position to Latin, with greater fervency and began to assign the works of the Athenian dramatists, among other Greek works.

CHAPTER FIVE

The Fall of Greece and the Need for a Strong Central Government

In the works of Plutarch, Polybius, and Demosthenes the Founding Fathers encountered the story of the conquest of the Greek republics by Macedon and Rome. From this tale most of them learned the importance of a strong central government to bind the American states together in a powerful union. Without such a union, these founders believed, there was a real danger that the United States would suffer the same fate as the Greeks, who lost their liberty because of constant internal strife that left them vulnerable to foreign invaders.

Fourth-Century Greece

Spartan Domination

Having won the Peloponnesian War, the Spartans installed puppet oligarchies throughout the former Athenian Empire and in Thebes and interfered in the internal affairs of other Greek states. The oligarchies were so ferocious that the Spartan king Pausanias allowed the restoration of democracy in these poleis after only a year or two, rather than face a massive rebellion.

Even so, the Spartan social system was ill suited to the imperial policy the Spartans now pursued. The wealth that resulted from the control of Greece corrupted luxury-starved Spartan leaders, who began secretly violating the city's prohibition on private wealth. One war hero, Gylippus, hid gold under the tiles of his roof. After a servant turned him in, saying there were "owls" roosting under those tiles (Athena's sacred owl graced Athenian coins), Gylippus was forced to leave Sparta in disgrace.

Worse yet, constant warfare had dramatically reduced the number of Spartan citizens, and Greece remained restive. Indeed, even Corinth, Sparta's erstwhile ally, joined Athens, Thebes, and Argos in rebellion against Sparta, with some financial help from Persia. This so-called Corinthian War (395–386 BC), in which Lysander, Sparta's greatest general, was killed, was followed by continual skirmishes that lasted another decade. The numerous wars of the fifth and early fourth centuries BC took such a toll on the Spartan army that only 1,200 citizens remained by 371 BC.

The Battle of Leuctra

With their numbers diminished and their discipline weakened, the Spartans suffered an astonishing defeat at the hands of the Thebans at the Battle of Leuctra that year. Although the Spartan force at Leuctra outnumbered the Thebans and their allies eleven thousand to six thousand, only seven hundred of the Spartan number were citizens; the rest were allies and perioikoi. When Epaminondas, one of Thebes' elected leaders, attempted to outflank the Spartan right wing, the Spartans were forced to shift their formation. Pelopidas, another Theban leader, struck the right wing quickly and with great force at that precise moment, crushed it, and created confusion and panic throughout the Spartan army. As a result, the Thebans were able to rout the Spartans, killing four hundred of their citizens, including King Cleombrotus. Even more humiliating for Sparta, the survivors ran ignominiously from the field. In fact, so many Spartans retreated that the Spartan people had to suspend the law depriving them of citizenship for cowardice.

The Thebans and their allies then invaded the Peloponnesus with seventy thousand men, the first time in Spartan history a foreign army had entered Laconia. The army burned and plundered the territory, freed some helots, and restored Messenia to its former inhabitants, thereby undermining Spartan power and traditional Spartan culture.

But Thebes was not to lead Greece for long. Epaminondas, the leader upon whom it depended, was speared to death, on the verge of victory, while fighting the odd new alliance of Athens and Sparta at Mantinea in 362 BC. Pelopidas was killed in a different battle soon after.

Philip II of Macedon

Meanwhile, virtually unnoticed, the power of Macedon was growing. The Macedonians were a relatively primitive, tribal people who were closely related to the Greeks but who possessed a distinct culture of their own. Macedon was not divided into democratic and oligarchic poleis like the rest of Greece but rather was governed by a single, centralized monarchy. By the fourth century BC Macedon had become wealthy enough to possess cities and a Hellenized aristocracy.

In 359 BC, at the age of twenty-two, the brilliant Philip II seized the throne while serving as regent for his infant nephew after his brother had been killed in battle. Taken hostage by Thebes at the age of fifteen in 367 BC in order to guarantee the Theban-Macedonian alliance, Philip had learned the art of warfare from Epaminondas himself. Immediately after assuming power in Macedon, Philip decreed that his infantry be trained in complex tactical maneuvers and close-order drills and sent them on thirty-five-mile marches. He also hired distinguished mercenary officers from various parts of Greece. Philip improved Epaminondas's phalanx by lengthening the standard eight-foot spear to eighteen feet and by fitting this *sarissa* with a heavier iron point and a stouter bronze butt spike. Held six feet from the butt, the fifteen-pound sarissa now extended twelve feet, thus allowing the soldiers' shields to be shortened by two-thirds and their bronze breastplates and helmets to be replaced with lighter leather. The greater length of the spear also meant that the first four or five rows of soldiers could thrust instead of the usual three. (The chief problem of Philip's phalanx was to keep the spears free of the enemy's ruined equipment and mutilated corpses.) To the phalanx Philip added cavalry (great numbers of horses, largely unavailable in southern Greece, grazed in the northern pasture land), armed with lances and broad, slashing swords. Having learned from the success of Thebes' "Sacred Band" the importance of esprit de corps within elite units, Philip created an elite cavalry unit known as "the Companions." (Indeed, the very name "Philip" means "horse lover.") Philip learned to use his cavalry to drive the enemy onto the long spears of his phalanx, a hammer-and-anvil tactic that proved highly effective.

Having ended the threat posed by the primitive Illyrians of what is now Yugoslavia, Philip seized the Athenian colony of Amphipolis and other points in gold-rich Thrace to the east in 357 BC. Thracian gold and silver mines, which produced one thousand talents per year, provided Philip with the means to expand his army. The following year the Thebans called on Philip for aid in their holy war against the Athenian ally Phocis for control of sacred Delphi. Philip was only too glad to help, thereby extending his influence into central Greece. In 355 BC Philip gained control of Thessaly by allying himself with some of its partisans in a civil war.

Unfortunately, even the extraordinarily eloquent and passionate orations of Demosthenes (the *Philippics*, 351–341 BC) could not persuade the Athenians to oppose Philip. Despite the warnings of Demosthenes, the Athenians adopted a policy of appeasement toward Philip, who bribed some Athenian leaders and convinced others that he was a friend who had no further territorial ambitions. Some Athenians even welcomed Philip's leadership in a joint invasion of Persia. They considered Greek unity more important than resistance to tyranny. Others were simply tired of war and the high taxes required to pay for it.

In 349–348 BC Philip conquered many cities of the Chalcidician League in northern Greece, several of which were Athenian allies. Having taken Olynthus, the league's capital, with the help of traitors, Philip then sold its entire population into slavery. In 348 BC, with the help of traitors he had bribed, Philip used an army to set up puppet dictators in Euboea. The same year he seized the rest of Thrace. In 346 BC the Athenian Philocrates, who was also on Philip's payroll, negotiated a disastrous peace treaty with Macedon, in which Athens accepted the loss of Amphipolis, the historical equivalent of the Munich Agreement of 1938 between Neville Chamberlain and Hitler. With Athens' guard down, Philip conquered Phocis the same year. He now acquired the prestige of acting as the guardian of sacred Delphi. When Philip attacked Byzantium, thereby threatening Athens's grain supplies from the Black Sea region, Athens, Thebes, Corinth, and a few other poleis finally joined together to stop him.

The Battle of Chaeronea

It was too late, however. In 338 BC Philip destroyed the coalition's reserve force of ten thousand mercenaries in a surprise attack. He then engaged the coalition's main army at the decisive Battle of Chaeronea in Boeotia. Both sides possessed about thirty thousand troops. Philip led the right wing of his army ahead of the rest of his force. He engaged the Athenians, who had not put an army in the field in twenty years, then withdrew up a hill in an orderly fashion. The inexperienced Athenians, thinking they had a rout, advanced incautiously, opening a gap between themselves and the Thebans. Philip's cavalry, stationed on the left and commanded by his eighteen-year-old son Alexander, then struck the Thebans on their now exposed flank. Meanwhile, Philip turned and launched a counterattack against the Athenians, charging downhill. The Macedonians killed one thousand soldiers and took another two thousand captive. The rest of the coalition forces fled. The Macedonian infantry then rushed to help the cavalry slaughter the courageous Thebans, who refused to flee. Nearly all three hundred of the Sacred Band, a unit that had never before been defeated, were killed at Chaeronea. Philip wept over their slain bodies, piled up where they had died defending one another in a futile effort. He buried them there in seven soldierly rows.

Philip was magnanimous toward Athens because he did not relish expending further resources on a siege of the city and because he admired Athenian culture. He organized the Greek poleis into the "Corinthian League," which he dominated. Each polis was obligated to contribute men and supplies for a full-scale invasion of the Persian Empire.

But Philip would not live to see the invasion of Persia. In 336 BC he was stabbed to death by a Macedonian nobleman while walking in a procession at his daughter's wedding. The javelins of three pursuers killed the assassin before he could be questioned. While some contemporaries believed that the Persians, who feared Philip's planned invasion of their empire, had hired the assassin, others believed the assassin had been employed by one of Philip's wives, Queen Olympias of Epirus, who feared that the son produced by his latest marriage to young Cleopatra—not to be confused with the more famous Cleopatra who lived three centuries later—would threaten her son Alexander's ascension to the throne. Indeed, the three pursuers who killed the assassin all happened to be close friends of Alexander. More revealingly, Olympias placed a crown on the assassin's corpse, buried it, and dedicated the murder weapon (a short sword) to Apollo. Soon after, Alexander had Cleopatra's powerful uncle quietly liquidated and encouraged his mother to kill Cleopatra's infant son, his rival for the throne. Requiring little encouragement, Olympias exceeded her instructions, roasting both the infant and a daughter of Cleopatra over a charcoal brazier, then forcing Cleopatra to hang herself. A member of the cult of Dionysus, Olympias enjoyed sleeping in a bed filled with large snakes, an unintentional form of birth control that had driven Philip from her bed long before. She was also suspected of having administered drugs that caused brain damage to the child of another of Philip's wives.

Empire, Division, and Destruction

Alexander then conquered the vast Persian Empire in a remarkably brief time, thereby spreading Greek culture throughout the Near East. When Alexander died in 323 BC, his only heir was an embryo, a child later murdered at age thirteen. When asked on his deathbed to whom he bequeathed his empire, Alexander whispered, "To the strongest." After forty years of bloody struggle between his former generals for the control of his empire, it was divided into three parts, each controlled by a general. Ptolemy, who had been Alexander's personal staff officer and his governor of Egypt, ruled that province. Antigonus the One-Eyed, who had once saved Alexander's supply line in an important battle, ruled Macedon and much of Greece.

The brilliant Seleucus, who had commanded Alexander's infantry, ruled the rest of Alexander's empire.

The easternmost portion of the Seleucid Empire was captured by an Indian ruler. The rest of the eastern Seleucid Empire fragmented into independent states, which were absorbed by the Parthians (of Iran) in the second century BC. Egypt was conquered by Rome in the first century BC.

Greece revolted against the Antigonids, fragmented into a number of states, and also fell to the Romans. One of these Greek states, the Achaean League, was an early model of a federal system. Reestablished from a looser version by four Peloponnesian poleis around 280 BC, the league was governed by a representative body elected by the adult males of each member polis. This assembly met four times per year to formulate a common foreign policy and to enact economic legislation, such as laws regulating the coinage. At its height, the league successfully combined as many as sixty different poleis in rough equality and harmony under a single government and currency. Previous leagues had been empires, dominated by a single member, not federations of equal states. Another federation, the Aetolian League of central and northwestern Greece, varied representation according to population.

The Roman conquest of Greece began with the humbling of Macedon. In 197 BC the Romans responded enthusiastically to the call of Pergamum (in Asia Minor) and Rhodes for aid against Philip V of Macedon, one of Antigonus's successors. A Roman legion under Titus Flamininus defeated Philip at Cynoscephalae in Thessaly, killing twenty thousand Macedonians and capturing another eleven thousand.

As in most of the Romans' other battles against the Macedonians and Greeks, the chief cause of Roman victory was the army's ability to take advantage of the phalanx's woeful lack of maneuverability. Relying on the careful overlapping of long and heavy spears, the phalanx was highly effective in opening charges but required level ground without obstructions and a perfect coordination between soldiers that the Romans, with their more maneuverable maniples, quickly learned to disrupt. The Romans surged into the inevitable gaps in the phalanx that formed during battle and assaulted the enemy from the side and rear. When the Greeks had to turn their bulky, unwieldy spears to face such threats, they inevitably lost the close coordination on which the phalanx depended.

As a result of the victory at Cynoscephalae, the Romans were able to impose a treaty on Philip that limited him to five thousand troops, deprived him of his elephants, and fined him one thousand talents. Furthermore, they prohibited Philip from waging war outside Macedon without Roman permission.

In 190 BC the Romans halted a Seleucid invasion of Greece that King Antiochus III had undertaken on the advice of the Aetolian League, which desired territory in the Roman protectorate of Macedon. Though outnumbered seventy-four thousand to thirty thousand, Scipio Africanus and his brother Lucius defeated Antiochus at Magnesia in Asia Minor. The Romans stripped the Seleucid emperor of his navy, his elephants, and a large sum of money.

In 168 BC, the Romans, under Lucius Aemilius Paulus, defeated a coalition of Greeks, led by Perseus, Philip V's successor, at Pydna in Macedon. Under orders from the Senate to treat the rebels harshly, Paulus sold 150,000 inhabitants of Epirus into slavery. The Romans also deported one thousand leaders of the Achaean League to Rome. One of these hostages was the historian Polybius.

In 148 BC, when anti-Roman sentiment flared in Greece as a result of the Senate's policy of supporting oligarchies there, the Romans burned Corinth. They then converted all of Greece into a collection of provinces governed by a Roman proconsul.

Under the Roman Empire, Greece was converted from a collection of political and military powers into a center for study and tourism. Long after the Spartans had abandoned their own unique political and social systems, they refrained from formally repealing their most famous laws so as to attract wealthy Roman tourists. Romans traveled hundreds of miles to see the reenactment of the notorious Spartan custom of flogging their boys until they fell unconscious—an ancient practice now performed in a specially built theater, not for discipline's sake, but as a tourist attraction. The Romans looted Sicily and Greece for slaves, books, and art. The employment of well-educated Greek slaves was one of the principal means through which Roman aristocrats were Hellenized.

The Macedonian and Roman conquests of Greece undermined the central position of the polis in Greek life. Citizens of the poleis no longer made foreign policy decisions. Those were now made elsewhere, at distant imperial centers, by foreign conquerors.

The Lesson

The Founding Fathers learned the story of the fall of Greece to Macedon and Rome from Plutarch's lives of Agesilaus, Demosthenes, Philip II, and Alexander, from the orations of Demosthenes, and from Polybius's *Histories*. From this tale the Federalists among them learned that the Greeks had lost their liberty to Macedon and Rome because of their failure to unite under a strong central government.

At the Constitutional Convention, at state ratifying conventions, and in published essays, the Federalists repeatedly cited ancient Greece as a civilization destroyed by decentralization. James Wilson, Alexander Hamilton, and James Madison all made this case at the Constitutional Convention. Hamilton noted regarding the Greeks, "Philip [II of Macedon], at length taking advantage of their disunion, and insinuating himself into their Councils, made himself master of their fortunes." Americans could expect to be subjected to foreign domination as well, Hamilton insisted, if they remained a weak, disunited collection of republics similar to the Greek city-states. On the next day James Madison reiterated the point: just as Greek disunity had allowed Philip II to "practice intrigues" resulting in their enslavement, so American disunity would produce the same result. Citing Plutarch, Madison also contended that the constant warfare between the Greeks might be repeated among the American states unless they were bound together by a strong central government. At the New York ratifying convention Hamilton noted regarding the incessant wars between the Greek poleis, "Those that were attacked called in foreign aid to protect them; and the ambitious Philip, under the mask of an ally to one, invaded the liberties of each, and finally subverted the whole."

Hamilton and Madison made the same argument in the *Federalist* essays. In *Federalist* No. 6 Hamilton again cited the failure of the Greeks to rally around a strong central government as the chief reason for the fall of Greece to Philip, who became her master "through intrigues and bribes." In No. 18 Madison wrote, "Had Greece, says a judicious observer on her fate, been united by a stricter confederation, and persevered in her union, she would never have worn the chains of Macedon; and might have proved a barrier to the vast projects of Rome."

Madison had spent the three years prior to the Constitutional Convention studying ancient confederacies, especially the Achaean League, for the very purpose of learning lessons concerning federalism in anticipation of drafting a federal constitution for the United States. The founders had no choice but to turn to the ancient confederacies (and to the modern Dutch and Swiss confederacies) for such lessons, since England lacked any tradition of federalism.

John Adams's *Defence of the Constitutions of Government of the United States of America* brought attention to the Achaean League in 1787, just before the Constitutional Convention. Adams concluded, "Such is the passion for independence that this little commonwealth, or confederation of commonwealths, could not hold together." He concluded that Americans must adopt the sentiments of Aratus, one of the league's principal leaders, who, according to Plutarch, declared,

> That small cities could be preserved by nothing else but a continual and combined force, united by the bond of common interest; and as the members of the body live and breathe by their mutual communication and connection, and when once separated pine away and putrify, in the same manner are cities ruined by being dismembered from one another, as well as preserved, when linked together in one great body.

At the Constitutional Convention James Wilson also cited the Achaean League as an instance of federal government gone awry as a result of "the encroachments of the constituent members." Madison noted that the same disunity that had paved the way for Macedonian conquest of Greece in the fourth century BC led to the Roman subjection of the Achaean League two centuries later.

The Federalists appealed to the Achaean precedent at the state ratifying conventions as well. At the New York ratifying convention Hamilton declared regarding the Greek confederacies, "Weakness in the head has produced resistance in the members; this has been the immediate parent of civil war; auxiliary force has been invited; and foreign power has annihilated their liberties and name." The Romans subverted the Achaean League, just as the Macedonians had subverted the Greek republics two centuries earlier. Madison took great pains to ensure that the Virginia ratifying convention was not deprived of the same lesson.

Hamilton and Madison referred to the Achaean League in their *Federalist* essays as well. In No. 16 Hamilton praised the league for being among the most centralized of the ancient confederacies, though it had not been centralized enough. In No. 18 Madison reviewed the "valuable instruction" that the league provided. The member states of the Achaean League, all of which were democracies, were equally represented in the federal council. The federal council exerted complete control over the league's foreign policy and appointed its chief magistrate. The chief magistrate commanded the army and administered the government with the advice of ten assemblymen. Madison claimed that "there was infinitely more of moderation and justice in the administration of its government, and less of violence and sedition in the people, than were to be found in any of the cities exercising singly all the prerogatives of sovereignty." He contended, "Popular government, so tempestuous elsewhere, caused no disorders in the members of the Achaean republic, because it was there tempered by the general authority and laws of the confederacy."

Madison was not dissuaded from such assertions by the scarcity of knowledge concerning the Achaean League. True, he admitted, "It is much to be regretted that such imperfect monuments remain of this curious political fabric. Could its interior structure and regular operation be ascertained, it is probable that more light would be thrown by it on the science of federal government than by any of the like experiments with which we are acquainted." Nonetheless, Madison was confident that enough was known about the league to warrant his assertion that disunity caused by decentralization had produced its downfall. The Achaeans' Roman ally "seduced the members from the league, by representing to their pride the violation it committed on their sovereignty." Madison concluded, "By these arts, this union, the last hope of Greece, the last hope of ancient liberty, was torn to pieces; and such imbecility and distraction introduced, that the arms of Rome found little difficulty in completing the ruin which their arts had commenced. . . . It emphatically illustrates the tendency of federal bodies rather to anarchy among the members, than to tyranny in its head." He repeated the message in *Federalist* No. 45, pointing out that though the league had "a considerable likeness to the government framed by the convention," its downfall did not result from encroachments by the federal government, of the kind that Antifederalists feared, but rather from "the dissensions, and finally the disunion, of the subordinate authorities."

John Dickinson was even more vociferous in praise of the league, though equally aware of its fatal flaw. Whereas John Adams doubted Polybius's objectivity, seeing "the fond partiality of a patriot for his country" in the historian's discussion of the league, Dickinson quoted Polybius enthusiastically: "From their incorporation may be dated the birth of that greatness, that by a constant augmentation, at length arrived to a marvelous height of prosperity." He also paraphrased Polybius's exaggerated claim that the members of the league "seemed to be but one state." Nevertheless, Dickinson concluded that even this prosperous and happy confederacy was destroyed by internal dissension fomented by a foreign power. Had it been more unified and had it comprised all the Greek republics, the outcome of history would surely have been different. Dickinson wrote,

> Let any man of common sense peruse the gloomy but instructive pages of
> their mournful story, and he will be convinced that if any nation could have
> successfully resisted those conquerors of the world [Macedon and Rome], the
> illustrious deed had [could have] been achieved by Greece, that cradle of

republics, if the several states had been cemented by some league such as the Achaean, and had honestly fulfilled its obligations.

He added regarding the Achaean League and its lesson,

> The glorious operation of its principles bear the clearest testimony to this distant age and people, that the wit of man never invented such an antidote against monarchical and aristocratical projects, as a strong combination of truly democratic republics. . . . The reason is plain. [Since] the energy of the government pervaded all the parts in things relating to the whole, it counteracted for the common welfare the designs hatched by selfishness in separate councils.

Dickinson concluded with an appeal to American pride: "How degrading would be the thought to a citizen of United America that the people of these states, with institutions beyond comparison preferable to those of the Achaean league, and so vast a superiority in other respects, should not have wisdom and virtue enough to manage their affairs with as much prudence and affection for one another as these ancients did."

Even Thomas Jefferson, an advocate for state sovereignty who worried that the new constitution might give the federal government too much power, recommended that John Adams study ancient confederacies for what they might reveal about federal systems and sent copies of Polybius's *Histories* to James Madison at the Convention. Perhaps Jefferson did not anticipate the lesson that so many of his colleagues would draw from the history of these confederacies.

Indeed, some Antifederalists came to different conclusions about the demise of the Achaean League. At the Virginia ratifying convention, the future president James Monroe, who was pleased with the league because member states had "retained their individual sovereignty and enjoyed a perfect equality," in marked contrast to the system proposed by the Constitution, argued that the Achaean League had been overwhelmed by three great powers (Macedon, Sparta, and the Aetolian League), making Roman aid necessary and submission to the vast Roman power inevitable.

Problems with the Federalist Lesson

While there is truth in the contention that Greece fell to Macedon and Rome because of the inability of the Greeks to unite under a common government, it is important to note that Greek culture revolved around the polis, a city-state small enough to invite citizen participation in government.

Aristotle was well within tradition when he recommended that the polis include no more people than was necessary for self-sufficiency. While unification under a strong central government might have preserved Greek liberty, it might also have stifled the creativity that so distinguished the Greeks. Furthermore, Greek defeats at the hands of Macedon and Rome had as much to do with outdated military tactics as with a lack of centralized government. As we have seen, the military success of Philip II of Macedon rested largely on his improvement of the phalanx, and the chief cause of the Roman conquest of Greece was the Romans' ability to take advantage of the phalanx's woeful lack of maneuverability.

Conclusion

Nevertheless, the lesson the founders had learned from the Persian Wars during the Revolutionary War was partially reversed by a lesson learned from the fall of Greece thereafter. While the Persian Wars had proven that a small cluster of republics, animated by patriotism and love of liberty, could triumph over a large, centralized monarchy, a lesson vital to the United States during the Revolutionary War, the fall of these same republics to the centralized powers of Macedon and Rome also proved instructive to the Founding Fathers in their quest to build a stronger union following the war. The founders learned that a certain degree of centralized power was necessary even to a confederacy of republics.

~

CHAPTER SIX

Early Rome and Republican Virtue

The Founding Fathers considered the early Roman republic, not Athens or Sparta, the greatest ancient model for the United States. Athens was too democratic and unstable, and Sparta too collectivistic and militaristic, to serve as close models. By contrast, the Roman republic, the founders believed, had given the masses enough power to avoid a tyrannical oligarchy without giving them so much control as to establish a chaotic ochlocracy. Furthermore, the founders believed that the early Romans had personified the virtues so vital to a republic. Thus, the founders viewed the Romans not only as political models but also as models of personal behavior—that is, as heroes. It is probably no accident that the founders' preference for the Romans over the Greeks mirrored the educational system's traditional preference, reaching back to the Middle Ages, for the Latin language over the Greek.

The Reasons for Roman Success

How is it that a small people possessing relatively poor soil and harbors came to rule over the largest empire in the world, spanning several million square miles and containing seventy-five million people? The Romans' geographical advantages and cultural traits account for much of their success.

Location, Location, Location

Around 1000 BC various Latin tribes migrated from the Balkans into central Italy and intermarried with the locals. Though familiar with iron, the Latins were mostly shepherds and herdsmen. During the ninth century BC, some of these tribesmen settled on the Palatine and Esquiline hills, two of Rome's famed seven hills, overlooking a convenient crossing of the Tiber, the second largest river in Italy. Twenty miles from the sea, Rome was close enough for transportation and communication but distant enough to have warning of raiders. Located near valuable salt beds, Rome's hills were easily defensible and free from flooding. Most significantly, Rome was located at the crossroads between the Etruscans to the north and the Greeks to the south. The Romans learned much from both of these peoples.

By 700 BC the Etruscans had settled in Etruria, the land northwest of Rome. The Greeks called the Etruscans "Tyrrhenians," whence comes the name "Tyrrhenian Sea" for the gulf that separates Italy from Corsica and Sardinia. The precise origins of the Etruscans are not known for certain, but their language was not Indo-European, and in all probability they came from Asia Minor. The Etruscans were famous for their music and for their love of war. They also enjoyed dancing, hunting, wrestling, juggling, and feasting. Initially, the Etruscans cremated their dead, but in the late eighth century BC they began burying the deceased in stone coffins. In the following century they hewed massive, lavish chamber tombs out of subterranean rock, often covering them with large mounds of earth. Surrounded by painted walls, the dead were laid on benches or interred in sarcophagi, on the lids of which reclined stone images of the deceased. The Etruscans became fairly wealthy through agriculture, iron mining, and piracy. They traded fine pottery, candelabra, jewelry, mirrors, chariots, and leather for luxury goods from Greece, Phoenicia, and Egypt. Their cities were well planned and fortified. They were the first people to use a dental bridge (made of gold) to anchor a false tooth (made of wood or ivory) to the two adjacent teeth. Their women possessed a relatively high status, socializing with men to an extent impossible for a respectable Greek or Roman woman.

The Etruscans expanded southward to the Bay of Naples, intermarrying with the locals and organizing much of northern and central Italy and some of southern Italy into three different confederations of Etruscan-dominated city-states. By about 625 BC an Etruscan adventurer from Tarquinia, the wealthiest and most powerful of the Etruscan cities (forty miles north of Rome), had become king of Rome. Tarquinia's control of Mount Tolfa, which contained large deposits of iron, tin, and copper, contributed greatly to its wealth and power. This city of twenty-five thousand people also produced metalwork, pottery, and linen, and traded widely. At that time there was much freedom of movement between cities, and intermarriage between

Etruscan and Latin aristocrats was common. In fact, more than a few Roman family names were Etruscan in etymology.

The Etruscans contributed much to Roman civilization. Etruscan kings transformed Rome from a collection of huts into a real city possessing streets, public buildings, markets, and temples. The Etruscans furnished such words as "Roma," "Italia" (meaning "calf land"), "Tuscany" (from "Etruscan"), and "Adriatic" (from the Etruscan settlement of "Hatria"). The Etruscans also contributed a few gods, the custom of making statues of deities, and the practice of prophesying by examining the entrails of sacrificial animals, by monitoring the flight of birds, and by following the positions of heavenly bodies. Some historians even credit the Etruscans with the relatively high status of Roman women. The Etruscans taught the Romans the art of construction, including the use of the arch. Their temples, shrines, private homes, aqueducts, and roads greatly influenced Roman architecture and engineering. When one of their kings drained the Forum, Rome's marshy central valley, which had previously been used as a burial site, it was the first step toward the Forum's eventual fame as the world's greatest marketplace. The Etruscans also furnished the toga and introduced the *fasces*, an ax bound by a bundle of wooden rods tied together, as a symbol of executive authority. (The ax symbolized the power to put to death, the rods the power to flog.) The Etruscans were also responsible for the Roman use of the color purple, which was the Etruscan state color, as a symbol of royalty. Finally, the Etruscans introduced chariot races and gladiatorial contests.

Between 775 and 400 BC, the Greeks colonized southern Italy and Sicily, converting parts of these regions into what the Romans called Magna Graecia (Greater Greece). From these Greeks, via the Etruscans, the Romans learned the Greek alphabet, which they adapted into the Latin alphabet now used throughout the Western world. The Romans assimilated virtually the entire Greek religion (also via the Etruscans), merely changing the names of the gods. Zeus became Jupiter, Hera became Juno (whence comes the month of "June"), Hermes became Mercury, Aphrodite became Venus, Athena became Minerva, Ares became Mars, Hephaestus became Vulcan, Kronos became Saturn, Poseidon became Neptune, Artemis became Diana, Demeter became Ceres, and the demigod Heracles became Hercules. Only Apollo remained Apollo. Even more than the Greeks, the Romans tied religion to patriotism. Roman gods seemed to exist for no other reason than to strengthen and protect Rome. Appointed by the state, Roman priests were much more powerful than their Greek counterparts. The Romans also adopted Greek-style coins and pottery early in their history. Of course, the Romans would later assimilate Greek art, literature, science, and philosophy as a result of their conquest of the eastern Mediterranean.

Cultural Traits

The Romans possessed important cultural traits that also contributed to their success. The Romans were staunch pragmatists. Cicero once declared, "Whereas our ancestors respected tradition when Rome was at peace, they were invariably guided by expediency in time of war." The pragmatism of the Romans not only proved crucial to their military success but also made them the greatest engineers of the ancient world.

The Romans were also tough and frugal. They prized strength over delicacy, power over agility, and utility over grace. They preferred *gravitas* (seriousness) to *levitas* (frivolity). They acquired this toughness the hard way, through the need to scratch out a living on rocky, barren soil.

Romans subordinated themselves to the family and to Rome. In the recesses of the central hall of their houses aristocrats kept wax busts and masks that realistically depicted the faces of illustrious ancestors. When a distinguished member of the family died, each mask was worn at the funeral by the family member most resembling the ancestor whose face was depicted in the mask. The family member even dressed himself according to the rank the ancestor had held. The eulogy was delivered by the most prominent living family member, who not only listed the achievements of the newly deceased family member but also painstakingly recounted the achievements of the whole group of ancestors, who were understood to be present in the form of their masks and borrowed bodies. This ritual instilled in young men a desire to endure hardship and even death in order to win the glory of such a eulogy for themselves one day.

The doctrine of *pater familias* (the father of the family) dominated Roman family law. The patriarch of an extended family possessed absolute authority over the entire family. Theoretically, he could even kill any member of the family and could sell his children as slaves, though such acts were exceedingly rare. (Regardless, it was not a good idea for a Roman son to tell his father he had wrecked the family wagon.) As in many other cultures, the worst crime was parricide. Anyone guilty of so heinous a crime was sewn up in a sack with a dog, a cock, a snake, and a monkey and hurled into the river or sea. Rome was regarded as an extended family, and it was but a small step from the concept of the *pater familias* to the concept of the *pater patria* (the father of the country) that later legitimated the reign of the emperors.

The Romans utilized a large collection of stirring myths, many of which were recorded by Livy, to instill courage, selflessness, honesty, and patriotism in their children. According to one popular legend, around 506 BC, Horatius Cocles saved Rome from an Etruscan army by single-handedly holding off the Etruscans while his comrades destroyed a bridge spanning the Tiber. Having no bridge left behind him, Horatius then recited a quick prayer to Father Tiber and hurled himself into the river. According to another legend, around 462 BC, a delegation of Roman officials asked Cincinnatus, a Roman farmer who was busy plowing his three-acre farm, to assume dictatorial power over Rome for six months in order to expel the Aequians, a Latin tribe threatening the village. Wiping away the sweat and grime, Cincinnatus put on his toga and set about defeating the Aequians in only fifteen days. Cincinnatus immediately resigned his dictatorship and retired to the plow. According to yet another account, in 340 BC, Titus Manlius ordered the execution of his own son for leading a reckless attack on the enemy against orders. Manlius declared, "You have . . . subverted military discipline, on which the fortune of Rome has rested up to this day. . . . It is a harsh example we shall set, but a salutary one for the young men of the future." In another legend, around 250 BC, Marcus Atilius Regulus, a Roman consul captured by the Carthaginians, was allowed to return to Rome to discuss peace terms and to negotiate the exchange of Carthaginian prisoners for himself; the Carthaginians made him pledge that he would return to Carthage if he failed. After arriving in Rome, Regulus urged the Senate to continue the war and dissuaded it from making the prisoner exchange, declaring that the Carthaginian prisoners were young and capable officers while he himself was old and worn out. True to his word, Regulus then returned to Carthage, though he knew that the enraged Carthaginians would torture him to death. In fact, they killed him through sleep deprivation.

But the greatest of all the Roman patriotic myths was the myth of the founding of Rome made famous by the poet Virgil. According to Virgil's *Aeneid*, an epic poem patterned on the Homeric epics, Aeneas, son of the Trojan aristocrat Anchises and the goddess Venus, had led a few refugees out of Troy before it fell to the Greeks. The refugees experienced numerous adventures and encountered many hardships before reaching Italy, where they settled down with local Latin tribesmen. Thirteen generations later, two of Aeneas's descendants, Romulus and Remus, established Rome. Romulus and Remus were the sons of the war god Mars and of Rhea Silvia, a priestess sworn to chastity. Rhea Silvia's uncle, the king of Alba Longa, angry with her for breaking her vows, rejected her claim that the father was Mars, imprisoned her, and had her infant sons exposed on the banks of the Tiber. But a wolf found and nursed Romulus and Remus until a herdsman discovered and raised the brothers. According to the myth, in 753 BC, the brothers returned to the site where they had been exposed as infants and Romulus traced the outlines of Rome there with his plow. Romulus killed Remus in a fit of rage over an insult and became the first king of Rome. This myth gave the Romans a noble origin and lineage; they were descended from Trojan heroes and from the god of war himself.

From such myths the Romans learned courage, discipline, persistence, patience, self-restraint, hard work, endurance, honesty, piety, dignity, and manliness. The last of these qualities was *virtus*, whence comes the English word "virtue." Indeed, most of these English terms are derived from Latin words. Many of the qualities they express were those of the farmer-soldier, who had to endure boredom, harsh weather, unforeseen calamities, and hard labor. Soldiers did not just fight; they had to dig ditches and build roads as well. Such traits were essential to success in the early struggle against nature and neighbors. In fact, Mars had begun as an agricultural god; it was Roman farmer-soldiers who converted him into the god of war.

Most importantly perhaps, the Romans possessed a sense of invincibility. Livy wrote, "It is as natural for Romans to win battles as for water to go downhill." This feeling of invincibility stemmed from the Roman belief that the gods would support them completely as long as they performed the proper rituals. Each Roman house possessed its own small shrine containing statuettes of the Lares, the household gods. Like the citizens of many other empires throughout history, the Romans possessed a sense of divine mission. When a Roman general celebrated a triumph, he proceeded through the city from the gates to the temple of Jupiter (later to the temple of Mars) and offered up to the god "the achievements of Jupiter wrought through the Roman people."

Perhaps for this reason no other people has ever been so obsessed with ritual. When the Romans declared war on another people (a frequent occurrence), one of the *fetiales*, a special group of priests, performed an ancient ceremony. After the enemy had rejected Roman demands, which were sometimes exorbitant in order to ensure their rejection, the fetial went to the enemy's border and, in the presence of at least three men of military age, announced to the gods, "Whereas the X have committed acts and offenses against the Roman people, and whereas the Roman people have commanded that there be war with the X, and the Senate of the Roman people has ordained, consented, and voted that there be war with the X: I therefore and the Roman people hereby make war on the X." The fetial then hurled a spear across the border into the enemy's territory to symbolize the beginning of a state of war. When the Roman Empire became too large to accommodate such a practice, the Romans set aside an enclosed area outside the gates of Rome called the Campus Martius, which symbolized the enemy's territory in the war-making ritual. The Romans never went to war without performing this rite.

If a mistake was made during any ritual, however lengthy, the Romans began again from the beginning. They were willing to perform the same ritual as often as necessary until it was performed without error. It did not even matter that, in some cases, the meaning of the ritual had been completely forgotten.

Many of these rituals originated in elaborate family rites, handed down from father to son, for the purpose of appealing to Ceres (the goddess of agriculture), Vesta (the goddess of the hearth), and the Lares. Even the family meal was a religious ceremony during which the Romans offered prayers, incense, and libations to the gods. Other household rituals expelled evil spirits and pleased friendly ones. Legend even has it that a Roman once marched past the astonished Gauls besieging Rome and over to Quirinal hill in order to perform a traditional family sacrifice that had to be performed on that day. After the Gauls left the city in rubble (ca. 387 BC), there was a great cry to immigrate to the nearby town of Veii, but Marcus Furius Camillus convinced the Romans that it would be impious to abandon the places in Rome where rituals must be performed. According to Livy, Camillus declared, "Surely it would be nobler to live like country shepherds amongst everything we hold sacred than to go into universal exile, deserting the gods of our hearths and homes."

Military victories reinforced the Roman sense of invincibility, which, in turn, produced more victories. On the few occasions when the Romans lost battles they believed that the gods were merely teaching them a lesson in order to keep them from becoming too proud. Nearly all Roman authors cited piety as a crucial factor in the city's success.

The Roman Conquest of Italy

Between the sixth and third centuries BC the Romans conquered all of Italy and established a republic. These two momentous developments were interrelated. The growing recognition of the rights of commoners created the internal harmony necessary for the defeat of external enemies, and the constant warfare highlighted the need to keep commoners happy by recognizing their rights.

The last of the seven kings who ruled Rome during its first two and a half centuries was Tarquin the Proud, an Etruscan who had seized power and who ruled without Senate consultation. In 509 BC Tarquin was expelled from

Rome. According to Roman legend, Lucius Junius Brutus (an ancestor of Caesar's assassin) and Publius Valerius Publicola led the rebellion. Legend held that the Romans rebelled against Tarquin when Lucretia, the married daughter of a prominent Roman nobleman, stabbed herself through the heart after being raped by Tarquin's son. After the fall of Tarquin, Lars Parsenna, king of Clusium, took advantage of the turmoil to capture Rome, but a coalition of Latins and Greeks under Aristodemus decisively defeated Lars's son, Arruns, near Aricia, thus allowing Rome to resume its independence. In any case, the Romans so hated Tarquin that the very title of "king" became a curse word. Even centuries later the Roman emperors, who had more power than Tarquin ever dreamed of possessing, adopted the designation "emperor" (*imperator*) to avoid the title of "king" (*rex*).

In 496 BC the Roman infantry suppressed a rebellion of the other Latin tribes that formed the Latin League, defeating a force composed mostly of cavalry at Lake Regillus. In 396 BC the Romans, under Camillus, tunneled into the citadel of Veii, the Etruscan city with which they struggled for control of the salt beds at the mouth of the Tiber. The Romans captured and destroyed the rival city. Situated at a river crossing from which roads radiated in all directions, Veii was a trade and craft center located only nine miles from Rome. In capturing Veii the Romans doubled the extent of their territory. By 390 BC the Latin League dominated central Italy.

Three years later the invasion of Italy by thirty thousand Gauls, fierce Celtic warriors from what is now France, threatened Rome's very existence. Having crossed the Alps and marched southward into Italy, the Gauls routed the Roman army, whose soldiers escaped to Veii, leaving Rome open. Though a small Roman garrison held out on Capitoline Hill, the Gauls burned most of the city. After seven months the Roman patricians were able to bribe the Gauls into leaving Rome. (The Gauls also left because other tribes threatened their northern territory. Naturally, Roman legend declared that they left because Camillus defeated them in battle.)

Though it took the Romans half a century to recover fully, they rebuilt their city and protected it with a new wall so sturdy that part of it still stands. The wall enclosed an area of one thousand acres. By necessity, the city was rebuilt quickly and haphazardly, which was why, according to Livy four centuries later, "the general lay-out of Rome is more like a squatters' settlement than a properly planned city." But the Romans swore that never again would a foreign army enter Rome. Indeed, it was another eight centuries before one did.

The Romans' determination to resist conquest combined with population pressures to produce a policy that some historians have termed "defensive imperialism." In the quest for ever-securer borders the Romans eventually conquered all of Italy.

Four peoples, the Latins, Samnites, Etruscans, and Greeks, blocked the Roman conquest of Italy. Though plagued by disunity, the Latin tribes repeatedly rebelled and fought the Romans tooth and nail; the last tribe was not subdued until 338 BC. The Romans dissolved the Latin League and forced each tribe to sign a separate peace treaty with them. The Romans then conquered Tarquinia by 311 BC. Meanwhile, from 343 BC to 290 BC, the Romans engaged in three fierce wars against the Samnite tribes of the hills of Campania (in southwestern Italy), who were distant relatives of the Latins. Though the Samnites possessed few towns, they were highly organized and disciplined, possessed twice the population and land of Rome, could retreat to mountainous country when in distress, and received some aid from the Etruscans and Gauls. Nevertheless, the Romans overcame numerous setbacks and defeated the Samnites and their allies decisively by 290 BC.

It was during the Samnite Wars that the Romans moved from the phalanx, learned from the Greeks via the Etruscans, to the more maneuverable formations that later enabled them to conquer the entire Mediterranean basin and all of western Europe. Roman armies were now organized around small units called *centuries* led by *centurions*. A century equaled sixty to one hundred men. Two centuries equaled a *maniple*. Three maniples equaled a *cohort*. Ten cohorts (four to six thousand men) and three hundred cavalry equaled a *legion*. When a Roman legion marched into battle, its sixty centuries did so in three lines, each able to coalesce into a mass or disperse into smaller contingents. The soldiers of two lines (the *princeps* and *triari*) watched the frontline troops (the *hastati*), intently, preparing to exploit success or prevent collapse. Roman soldiers generally cast a seven-foot javelin, then ran to meet the enemy with a razor-sharp, double-edged sword (the *gladius*). They often used their rectangular shields offensively as battering rams. The second line cast their javelins over their friends' heads to impale the enemy before them.

The Roman conquest of the Samnites left only the Greeks of southern Italy to conquer. In 282 BC the Greek city of Tarentum, fearful of the growing Roman power, sank part of a Roman flotilla and called on the brilliant Greek general Pyrrhus of Epirus for aid. In 280 BC Pyrrhus brought twenty-five thousand troops and twenty Indian war elephants to add to Tarentum's fifteen thousand soldiers, mercenaries, and large navy. After seeing the Romans in action, the sharp-witted Pyrrhus declared, "These may be barbarians, but there is nothing barbarous about their discipline."

Also, it did not take long for Pyrrhus to see the superiority of the Romans' more flexible formations over the more rigid Greek phalanx. Nevertheless, in 280 BC and again the following year, Pyrrhus defeated the Romans, losing far fewer men than the Romans each time. But Pyrrhus could not afford his losses as well as the Romans. He could rely on far fewer reinforcements, and each defeat seemed only to leave the Romans angrier and more determined to prevail. When a friend congratulated Pyrrhus on his second victory, he declared, "One more victory like that over the Romans will destroy us completely." This is the origin of the term "Pyrrhic victory," a victory that is so costly as to constitute a defeat.

Pyrrhus withdrew to Sicily for three years, where he helped the Greeks rout the Carthaginians. Following his return to the mainland, his attempt to bribe the Roman general Fabricius failed, and he was forced to fight again. (Fabricius was so ethical he even informed Pyrrhus when Pyrrhus's physician offered to poison him for money.) This time the Romans defeated Pyrrhus, and he returned home with only one-third of his original force. Three years later Pyrrhus was killed in a battle at Argos, when an old woman, alarmed at the sight of Pyrrhus engaging her son in combat, hurled a heavy roof tile at Pyrrhus and struck him below the helmet, knocking him unconscious. An Argive soldier then decapitated him.

By 275 BC the Roman army had subdued all of the Greek city-states of Italy. Only the conquest and colonization of the Po River valley, shortly after 200 BC, remained to complete Roman control of the Italian peninsula.

Roman Treatment of Conquered Italians

The Romans won the loyalty of the conquered Italians through lenient treatment. Although most subject states had to adhere to Rome's foreign policy, to supply troops for the Roman army, and to surrender 20 percent of their land (twenty-seven small Roman colonies were established in these lands by 250 BC, thereby reducing Rome's population problems), the Romans demanded no tribute and allowed each state to retain its local self-government. Some cities were even allowed full Roman citizenship and given loot and land. Such leniency was extremely uncommon in the ancient world. As we have seen, the "enlightened" Greeks often slaughtered or enslaved conquered peoples. But Roman leniency in Italy proved extremely wise. During the Second Punic War (218–201 BC), when Hannibal and the Carthaginians invaded Italy, their failure to entice Italians into widespread rebellion saved Rome and proved fatal to Carthage. As Camillus had once put it, "By far the strongest government is one to which men are happy to be subject."

The Growth of Republican Government

Until 509 BC, the Romans were ruled by monarchs selected by the Senate and approved by the people. The Senate was a council of approximately three hundred former officeholders called *patricians* (fathers) who advised the king. Nearly all of the senators were landed aristocrats.

After the Romans expelled Tarquin, the senators established an oligarchy. The chief magistrates were three to six military tribunes. By the fourth century BC, the military tribunes had been replaced by two *consuls* (colleagues). The consuls were elected annually from the patrician class by the people, subject to ratification by the Senate. In times of emergency they could appoint a dictator whose term lasted no more than six months. But, in reality, since the consuls were fatally weakened by their fractured power (they could veto each other's decisions) and exceedingly short terms, the real power in the Roman republic was held by the life-tenured Senate, which decided public policy and controlled the treasury, foreign policy, and religious affairs. The Senate could veto any actions taken by the consuls. If the consuls disagreed with each other, the Senate could make executive decisions. The Senate also served as the supreme judicial body. Common Romans, the *plebeians*, possessed little power.

Republican Reforms

Within a few centuries, however, Rome moved from an oligarchy to a more republican system. In 494 BC, short of grain and tired of fighting wars for the benefit of the patricians, the plebeians withdrew to Aventine Hill. They threatened to secede and establish their own city. As a compromise the patricians then allowed the plebeians to elect two *tribunes*. Eventually, these tribunes, whose persons were sacrosanct (to strike them was considered both a political and a religious crime), were granted the authority to halt any Senate measures they considered unfair by walking into the Senate chamber and shouting "Veto!"—Latin for "I forbid!" They could block any magistrate from exercising his office, including the punishment of a citizen. They were required to maintain an open house and were prohibited from leaving Rome overnight, so that plebeians could request their aid at any hour. The number of tribunes was gradually increased to ten.

In 451 BC the plebeians demanded a written code of laws, so that magistrates could no longer interpret Rome's customary law to suit their own interests. Drafted by ten aristocrats called the *decemviri*, the legal code was inscribed on twelve tablets and set up in the Forum for all to see the following year. Roman children memorized the laws. The Law of the Twelve Tables was the first landmark in the illustrious history of Roman law. Like most of its contemporaries, the code, which was largely formalized from existing oral law, was harsh, allowing enslavement for debt. But its terse sentences represent the first indication of the Romans' uncanny talent for legal definition.

In 445 BC plebeians were granted the right to marry patricians. (In practice, only a plebeian who had acquired some wealth would be acceptable to a patrician woman.) In 421 BC the office of *quaestor* (the consuls' finance manager) was made elective and opened to plebeians, and the number of quaestors was increased to four. (Previously, the consuls had appointed them.) In 366 BC plebeians were allowed to run for consul; in 342 BC one of the consulships was reserved for them. In 326 BC confinement and enslavement for debt were abolished. Livy later referred to this measure as "a new birth of freedom," a phrase immortalized in Abraham Lincoln's Gettysburg Address.

In the mid- to late fourth century BC new offices were created and opened to the plebeians. Most of the new offices possessed powers previously held by the consuls. One office was that of *aedile* (supervisor of the marketplace, public buildings, archives, traffic, water and grain supplies, and weights and measures, and sponsor of games), while another was that of *praetor* (supervisor of courts). A third new office was that of *censor* (administrator of the census every five years, assessor of taxes, supervisor of public morals, awarder of state contracts, and confirmer of the lineage of senators). At about the same time some wealthy plebeians were admitted into the Senate and the priesthood.

In 300 BC every citizen was granted the right to appeal to the people against a death penalty. At about the same time the college of *pontiffs* and *augurs* was opened to plebeians. The pontiffs presided over rituals and maintained the lore, while augurs recorded omens and predicted the future.

Most significantly, in 287 BC, temporary dictator Quintus Hortensius transferred supreme legislative authority from the Senate to the three popular assemblies of Rome, each of which was organized differently and authorized to vote for different offices and measures. The plebeians had gained each of these reforms by taking advantage of Rome's dependence on their military support. The patricians knew that, if the plebeians refused to serve in the army, or left to form another city, they would be destroyed. The increased wealth of some plebeians also helped produce the reforms.

The Romans called the system of government that developed in their city a *res publica* (commonwealth). They believed it was a mixed government, a system in which power of the one (in this case the two, the consuls), the few, and the many were balanced against one other. Polybius noted that the consuls needed to maintain good relations with the Senate because the Senate could block the flow of grain, clothing, and money to them in military campaigns, could replace them in the middle of a campaign if their year in office had expired, and could withhold triumphs and other prestigious awards. The consuls needed to maintain good relations with the people since they could find fault with the account that the consuls were required to submit at the end of their term and could reject the treaties they negotiated. Similarly, the Senate and the people were bound to one another by the Senate's control of lucrative contracts, by its dominance of the judicial system, and by the people's ability (through the tribunes) to veto the Senate's decisions. Likewise, the people needed to maintain good relations with the consuls since they served under them in the army.

The First Punic War (264–241 BC)

The word "Punic" is derived from *Punicus*, the Latin term for Phoenician, since Carthage had been founded by settlers from the Phoenician city of Tyre in what is now Lebanon. The Phoenicians had colonized the western Mediterranean (western Sicily, Sardinia, Corsica, Spain, and North Africa) by about 800 BC. By 500 BC Carthage, located on the coast of what is now Tunisia, had become wealthy and powerful enough to dominate the other Phoenician colonies. The chief source of Carthaginian wealth was trade (especially in metals), the chief source of Carthaginian power a large navy. Thirty merchant princes played the leading role in governing Carthage. The Carthaginian senate, controlled by the aristocracy, possessed most of the power. The popularly elected magistrates (called *suffetes*) possessed only one-year terms, and the popular assembly was consulted only when the senators and suffetes could not agree. The Carthaginians possessed little art or literature. Their chief deities were Baal, a Canaanite-Phoenician god whose worship the Hebrew prophets had denounced, and Tanit, a fertility goddess who became more prominent after the fifth century BC. The smaller size of the Carthaginian population, when compared with that of Rome, forced Carthage to rely too heavily on mercenaries.

The Cause of War

Rome and Carthage began to quarrel after the Romans conquered southern Italy, thereby extending their borders to within range of Carthaginian territory in Sicily. In 264 BC the First Punic War began as the result of a struggle over the strategic city of Messana on the northeastern tip of Sicily. When the Greek king Hiero II of Syracuse threatened to expel from Messana a group of Italian mercenaries called Mamertines, they begged both Rome and Carthage for protection. Carthage quickly provided troops. The Romans feared that, if the Carthaginians controlled the Straits of Messina, the narrow strip of water that separates Sicily from the Italian mainland, they would be able to cross over into Italy without warning and to block Rome's most important sea-lane. Hence, the Romans dispatched an army, under Appius Claudius, to besiege Messana. Fearing that army, the Mamertines fooled the Carthaginian garrison into leaving the citadel and turned the city over to the Romans. After suffering a serious defeat at the hands of Appius Claudius, Hiero also defected to the Roman side, becoming the first of Rome's many client-kings.

The War

The First Punic War was a bloody struggle that lasted twenty-three years. Some contemporaries believed that the Carthaginians' economic and naval superiority ensured their victory. In fact, the Romans possessed so few ships at the beginning of the war they had to borrow vessels from the Greeks in southern Italy just to transport their army to Messana. Yet, the Romans managed to construct a fleet and train its crews in just a few months. The Roman ships were modeled on Carthaginian vessels but were heavier and slower, since the Romans liked to keep soldiers aboard for grappling and boarding enemy vessels.

After defeating the Carthaginians in a naval battle at Mylae (260 BC) through these tactics, the Romans suffered a serious defeat in North Africa (255 BC), from which they were forced to withdraw. The Romans then lost two complete fleets and two hundred thousand men (mostly allied soldiers) in a series of other naval battles and storms.

But, unable to admit defeat, the stubborn Romans rebuilt their fleet each time. Rome was a pit bull that would not release its grip on the enemy's leg, no matter how many times it was beaten on the head or offered the milk bone of peace. In 242 BC the Romans' third fleet, under Gaius Lutatius Catulus, defeated the Carthaginian navy off the Aegates, a group of islands near the western coast of Sicily. Based on the false assumption that the Romans could not recover from the destruction of their previous fleets, the Carthaginians had allowed their own naval training to diminish. Meanwhile, the Romans had learned how to fight at sea. They had removed all nonessential equipment from their ships and had worked hard at rowing in unison. As a result, the Romans were able to sink fifty Carthaginian ships and capture seventy vessels containing ten thousand men at the Aegates. Although the Carthaginians had lost only five hundred ships to the Romans' seven hundred during the war, they now faced the threat of another invasion. Carthage sued for peace on Roman terms.

The Peace

Under Lutatius's treaty, Carthage was forced to surrender Sicily and 3,200 talents over a ten-year period. A few years later, taking advantage of a rebellion against Carthage launched by mercenaries and Libyan slaves, Rome seized Sardinia and Corsica and demanded another 1,200 talents. The Carthaginians were furious but were in no position to resist the Romans.

The islands of Sicily, Sardinia, and Corsica were the first of Rome's overseas provinces, which it ruled less leniently than its Italian possessions. The provinces were taxed and disarmed. Sicily and Sardinia were placed under the rule of Roman praetors. Local leaders, operating under Roman direction, were allowed to continue governing the other provinces until 146 BC, at which point they were replaced by Roman military governors, called *proconsuls* because they acted "for the consuls." The proconsuls ruled according to the Senate's stipulations, but the vagueness of the regulations created a tremendous opportunity for abuse.

The Second Punic War (218–201 BC)

The Roman republic reached its peak in the Second Punic War. In this war, waged against Rome's most formidable adversary, wealthy and powerful Carthage, the Romans demonstrated their most impressive quality: the ability to maintain their courage and determination in the darkest hours. The defeat of Carthage was crucial to Roman survival and, hence, to the transmission of the Greco-Roman civilization throughout western Europe. Victory in that war also made possible Roman conquest of the rest of the Mediterranean world.

The Causes

Although the First Punic War had weakened Carthage, the Carthaginians quickly regained their strength. Between 237 and 229 BC, Hamilcar Barca, Carthage's greatest general, expanded Carthaginian territory in Spain. (When the Romans asked Hamilcar what he was doing in Spain, he remarked snidely that he was fighting to obtain the money Carthage needed to pay its indemnity to Rome.) In 229 BC Hamilcar died covering a retreat that saved the lives of Hannibal, his brilliant son, and Hamilcar's staff. By 219 BC Hannibal (Grace of Baal) had further extended Carthaginian rule northward to the Iberus (now the Ebro) River. When news reached Rome that Hannibal had besieged Saguntum, an important Roman ally in Spain, the Romans were furious. When Carthage refused to repudiate Hannibal's act and turn him over to the Romans, Rome declared war (218 BC).

It is difficult to say which side was most responsible for the war. The Romans argued that, in besieging Saguntum, the Carthaginians had violated Lutatius's treaty, in which each side had agreed not to assault the other's allies. But Saguntum was not yet an ally of Rome when that treaty had been negotiated, and, in a different treaty, the Romans had agreed that the area south of the Iberus River was a Carthaginian sphere of influence. Saguntum, which lay within that area, had been inciting other towns to resist Carthage—out of fear of the growing Carthaginian power and out of confidence that Rome would come to its aid. But while an examination of the treaties leads one to the conclusion that Rome was technically in the wrong, it is also true that the Carthaginians were exceptionally bitter toward Rome because of past humiliations and that both sides eagerly embraced the conflict.

Hannibal's Expedition

It was thought that the Second Punic War, like the first, would consist largely of naval battles, with some ground combat in Spain. No one expected that the Carthaginians would attack Italy from the north. But the Romans had not reckoned with the fierce determination of Hannibal. According to Polybius, when Hannibal was only nine years old, his father had made him take a solemn oath, on an altar to Baal, to oppose Rome his whole life.

Hannibal now collected an army of ninety thousand infantry, twelve thousand cavalry, and fifty war elephants. He then subdued the tribes of northern Spain with remarkable speed. Leaving some troops behind in Spain under the command of his brother Hasdrubal, Hannibal then crossed the Pyrenees Mountains into what is now southern France with fifty thousand infantry, nine thousand cavalry, and all fifty elephants.

One of Hannibal's greatest challenges lay in crossing the Rhone River, where the Volcae, a Gallic tribe, blocked his path. Hannibal secretly dispatched a party of his best men upstream to build a bridge and ford the river. They accomplished the task swiftly. The detachment then moved back downriver toward the Volcae, who remained unaware of their presence. When the detachment was in position, they informed Hannibal through smoke signals. Hannibal then began crossing the river. In their eagerness to slaughter the Carthaginians while engaged in a difficult river crossing, the Volcae rushed to the waterfront. The Carthaginian detachment that had forded the river then emerged from hiding and attacked the Volcae in the rear, throwing the whole army into utter panic.

Hannibal then faced the difficult task of leading his thirty-seven remaining elephants across the river. The elephants followed all of their Indian drivers' orders but one: they refused to go into the water. So Hannibal had rafts constructed and fastened to the docks in such a way as to appear to be mere extensions of the docks. The elephants confidently followed their drivers onto the rafts up to the edge of the water. Imagine their surprise when the rafts were cut loose from the bank, and they began to float across the river. Some panicked and overturned the rafts. Nevertheless, none of the elephants drowned, since they could hold their trunks above water to breathe and to discharge water. Many of the drivers were not so fortunate, however.

Hannibal and the Alps

Hannibal then proceeded to the Italian Alps. Contrary to popular belief, the reason the Romans were surprised that Hannibal crossed the Alps to attack them was not because the Alps were impassable, though they were certainly difficult to cross. (The Gauls crossed the Alps constantly.) Rather, the Romans were surprised that Hannibal would risk so large an army by leading them through a mountainous area inhabited by Gauls, whom the Romans considered fierce and treacherous. But many Gallic tribes whom the Romans had treated harshly favored the Carthaginians. They supplied Hannibal and showed him safe passes through the mountains. (It is true that one tribe, the Allobroges, ambushed Hannibal, inflicting heavy casualties. On that occasion, wounded horses, laden with baggage, fell off the precipices or collided with those before and behind and with horrified soldiers, who plunged to their deaths. But the canny Hannibal defeated the tribe and took their city, thereby intimidating neighboring tribes into cooperating with him.)

Having ascended the Alps, the Carthaginians then encountered the problem of descending its steep, icy slopes. The elephants proved a mixed blessing; they terrified the Gauls, who had never seen such monstrous animals, but they were difficult to lead across mountain passes.

Hannibal managed to reach the Po River in northern Italy with twenty thousand infantry, six thousand cavalry, and a bunch of skinny elephants. (There had not been enough grass in the snow-capped mountains.) It had taken him only five months to march from New Carthage (now Cartagena) in Spain to the Alps and only fifteen days to cross the mountains.

The Battle of Trebbia

After Hannibal defeated a Roman cavalry force, Gauls serving in the Roman army rebelled and massacred Roman soldiers. Reinforcing his army with Gallic allies, Hannibal then routed forty thousand Romans, under Tiberius Sempronius Longus, at the Trebbia River (218 BC). In this battle Hannibal employed what was to become his favorite tactic: he enticed Sempronius into an ambush. Hannibal ordered a small force to attack Sempronius and withdraw, thereby drawing him into a ravine. Hannibal's main force then attacked the Romans on all sides from its positions on the overhanging riverbanks. Hannibal then armed his force with the larger shields and sturdier swords captured from the Romans in the battle.

The Battle of Lake Trasimene

Fearful of assassination attempts by treacherous Gallic chieftains (he even wore a collection of different wigs and other disguises to elude them), Hannibal then marched his men into Etruria via an obscure road that led through the marshes. The men traveled four days and three nights with little sleep, periodically collapsing on top of dead pack animals in order to keep above the water. Hannibal himself lost vision in one eye from an infection exacerbated by sleeplessness.

By laying waste to the countryside Hannibal managed to entice another Roman army, under the rash Gaius Flaminius, into pursuing and attacking him at a preselected position. Hills lay to Hannibal's left and Lake Trasimene to his right. Flaminius believed the hills provided sufficient cover for his flank. He was wrong. Aided by a thick mist, Hannibal had hidden detachments in the hills, soldiers who now fell on the Romans from the side and rear. Fifteen thousand Romans were killed, including Flaminius himself, and fifteen thousand captured. Hannibal lost only 1,500 men, and those mostly Gallic allies.

Hannibal's victories stunned and terrorized the Roman people. They had been so confident of victory that large numbers of them had followed Flaminius's army carrying chains and fetters in the hope of capturing Carthaginian slaves. Fortunately for Rome, Hannibal lacked the engines and supplies for a siege, so he turned away from the city, crossed the Apennines, and ravaged Italy's Adriatic coast.

The Strategy of Fabius

The Romans used the respite to declare a state of emergency and to appoint the fifty-eight-year-old Quintus Fabius Maximus dictator. A religious man, Fabius improved public morale by attributing the Roman defeats to a lack of piety, rather than to cowardice or ineptitude. Fabius wisely decided that Hannibal was too brilliant, and his Carthaginian veterans were too experienced (having fought with Hannibal in Spain for many years), for the Romans to oppose him in open battle. Fabius's strategy was to follow Hannibal but to avoid major engagements with him. Fabius knew that the Romans possessed two important advantages. First, while the Romans, as the native power in Italy, would always be well supplied, the Carthaginians would have to scavenge for supplies ceaselessly. Second, unlike the Romans, the Carthaginians could not easily receive reinforcements in Italy. Hence, Fabius kept his army intact and pounced on every small detachment Hannibal dispatched to forage for supplies. Through this war of attrition, Fabius gradually depleted Hannibal's force. Fabius kept to the mountains overlooking Hannibal's army—out of the reach of Hannibal's superior cavalry but close enough to pounce on Carthaginian stragglers and foragers. Everywhere the victorious Hannibal marched Fabius followed.

Fabius's strategy frustrated Hannibal. Hannibal could not defeat a force he could not fight. The losses Fabius inflicted on Hannibal's army were imperceptible to most observers but not to Hannibal, who shared Fabius's farsightedness.

Fabius under Attack

But Fabius's strategy was unpopular in Rome. Many Romans considered him a coward. They called him "Hannibal's *pedagogus*" (a pedagogus was a male slave who walked his master's children back and forth from school). When Fabius's friends begged him to risk a battle in order to save his reputation, he replied, "In that case I should be an even greater coward than they say I am."

Hannibal was one of the very few who realized that Fabius's strategy was the wisest and the most dangerous to his army. Hence, in order to discredit Fabius's strategy among the Romans, he adopted the cunning tactic of sparing Fabius's country villa while laying waste to the whole countryside around it. As Hannibal expected, some Romans then charged Fabius with colluding with the enemy. Fabius shrewdly dispelled the charge by selling the estate and contributing the proceeds to the repayment of Rome's public debt.

But the Roman people remained frustrated. When Fabius moved to punish his rash subordinate, the cavalry commander Municius Rufus, for attacking the enemy against orders, the Romans appointed Municius codictator with Fabius. The appointment of codictators was an unprecedented act.

Fabius Vindicated

Now freed from Fabius's wise restraint, Municius allowed Hannibal to lure him into an ambush at Gerunium. Hannibal hid some of his men in the small ditches and hollows of a plain. When Municius attacked his decoy force, situated on a hill, the other detachment came out of hiding and attacked the Roman force in the rear and on the flanks. If Fabius had not moved quickly to reinforce Municius, he would have lost his entire force. After seeing the vigor of Fabius's successful counterattack, Hannibal told his aides, "Haven't

I kept telling you that the cloud we have seen hovering over the mountain tops would burst one day like a tornado?"

To the credit of both men, Fabius did not gloat or criticize, and Municius placed himself and the remnants of his army under Fabius's command. The strategy of Fabius, whom the Romans nicknamed "the Delayer," had been vindicated.

The Battle of Cannae (216 BC)

Hannibal's greatest victory occurred at Cannae, on the southeastern Adriatic coast, when he had only ten days' food left and his Spanish allies were considering desertion. The Romans had ended the dictatorships of Fabius and Municius and had transferred control of the armies to the duly elected consuls, Lucius Aemilius Paulus and Gaius Terentius Varro. Although Fabius was able to persuade Paulus of the wisdom of his defensive strategy, Varro was too ambitious to heed such warnings.

On one of Varro's days to command (the consuls alternated the command), he attacked Hannibal at Cannae with eighty thousand infantry and six thousand cavalry. Hannibal possessed only forty thousand infantry and ten thousand cavalry. Hannibal placed his army with its back to a strong, choking wind. The fighting was close and desperate, but Hannibal routed the Romans in the same fashion that Miltiades had routed the Persians at Marathon. He kept his center weak, filling it with Spaniards and Gauls, and kept his wings strong, filling them with his Carthaginian infantry and cavalry. Hannibal personally led the weak center, so that it held long enough to ensure that its feigned retreat did not occur too soon. When the Carthaginian center executed its cautious retreat, the Romans foolishly pursued too far too fast, thereby allowing the victorious Carthaginian wings, led by well-trained Numidian cavalry, to close in and slaughter them. Though well armored in front and behind, Roman soldiers were vulnerable on their flanks, which the Carthaginians struck with javelins.

Rather than taking advantage of his great numerical superiority to outflank the Carthaginians or to hold a force in reserve that might be sent wherever it was needed, Varro had massed the bulk of his army in the center along a one-mile front, thereby fatally reducing his soldiers' ability to get at the enemy and to escape Hannibal's trap. Varro compounded this error by filling his wings with his least experienced troops. (Because of the previous disasters at Trebbia and Lake Trasimene, the Romans were short of experienced soldiers.)

At Cannae, the Carthaginians slaughtered fifty thousand Roman soldiers (including a bleeding and dejected Paulus, who refused a Roman soldier's

offer of a horse for his escape), and captured another ten thousand. Aston-
ishingly, the Carthaginians lost only 4,000 Gauls, 1,500 Spaniards and
Carthaginians, and 200 cavalry.

The Romans perceived the defeat at Cannae as the greatest calamity in
their history. Looking for the cause of divine disfavor, they discovered that
two of their priestesses called Vestal Virgins were no longer such; against
one they carried out the prescribed punishment, burying her alive, while
the other was allowed to commit suicide. Indeed, the Romans became so
desperate for the favor of the gods they even briefly adopted the ancient
Carthaginian practice of human sacrifice, burying alive a pair of Gauls and
a pair of Greeks in the Forum. (Ironically, by that time the Carthaginians
themselves had abandoned the practice of their Phoenician forebears of
sacrificing small boys to Baal.)

Only the commanding presence of Fabius (and the guards he placed at
the city gates) kept many citizens from fleeing Rome. In order to prevent
the people's confidence from declining even further, Fabius even prohibited public lamentation for the dead. He also cut the property qualification
for infantry service in half, and even offered eight thousand slaves their
freedom in exchange for such service, in an effort to replace the army lost
at Cannae. Better yet, because Hannibal now possessed fewer than twenty
thousand troops and was not equipped for siege warfare, he still did not
march on the city.

The Battle of Cannae secured Hannibal's place as one of the greatest
generals in history. Legends of his brilliance abound. Hannibal had once
even outfoxed Fabius. Fabius had trapped Hannibal in a valley at Casil-
inum, because Hannibal's guide, misunderstanding his Carthaginian ac-
cent, had led him to the wrong place. Hannibal ordered the guide beaten
and crucified. There was only one pass out of the valley, and Fabius had
posted a detachment to block it. But Hannibal had used nightfall and a
clever ruse to mask his movements. The ruse had consisted of several thousand cattle with torches tied to their horns, which Hannibal stampeded in
the direction of Fabius's camp. Fooled by the sound of so many thundering
hooves and by the sight of so many flickering lights into believing that
Hannibal was hurling his whole army at Fabius, the detachment at the pass
had rushed to Fabius's aid, leaving the pass unguarded. Hannibal's army had
then slipped through the deserted pass.

The Loyalty of the Italian Allies
But Hannibal's impressive victories proved as futile as his pillaging of Italy.
The Romans displayed their usual determination to persevere, and most of

their well-treated Italian allies refused to join the Carthaginians. The Italians realized that they had little to gain and much to lose from a Carthaginian alliance. Except for the Gallic villages of northern Italy (which was not then considered part of Italy), only a few Italian cities joined the Carthaginians. (Rome put down these revolts between 211 and 209 BC. Fabius captured Tarentum and massacred its inhabitants; Marcellus seized Syracuse on a festival night but spared most of its inhabitants.) Naples even voluntarily contributed forty platters of gold to the Roman treasury.

The most remarkable and crucial fact about the Second Punic War was that the vast majority of Italians suffered death and destruction alongside the Romans for sixteen years rather than defect to the enemy. Their loyalty, combined with the gradual depletion of Hannibal's forces, undermined the Carthaginian war effort.

Scipio's Spanish Victories

Meanwhile, the Romans received good news from a different quarter. In 210 BC twenty-four-year-old Publius Cornelius Scipio was elected proconsul for Spain. The young man had fought his first battle at the age of seventeen. At the head of a troop of cavalry, Scipio had saved his wounded father from being surrounded. Scipio refused an award for his heroism, saying, "The action was one that rewarded itself." Having survived the rout at Cannae, Scipio had broken up a meeting of dejected officers who, believing Rome lost, were considering escaping overseas to serve as mercenaries for some king. As he was to do so many times, Scipio had reminded the officers of their duty and had inspired them with a new sense of confidence. After the Carthaginians defeated and killed Scipio's father in Spain, Scipio alone among the Romans volunteered to take the Spanish command.

Scipio then set about instilling confidence in the Roman people, the Roman soldiers in Spain, and the Spanish allies. His generosity soon secured the support of most of the Spanish tribes.

In 210 BC Scipio captured New Carthage, Carthage's greatest city and largest supply center in Spain. Overconfident after conquering nearly all of Spain, the Carthaginians had left the port city garrisoned by only one thousand men. Discovering from local fishermen that the sea ebbed dramatically in the late afternoon each day, Scipio told his soldiers that Neptune, the sea god, had come to him in a dream and promised aid. Scipio then assaulted the city from the usual approaches, attempting to scale its high walls. When this conventional approach failed, and the hour came for the tide to ebb, Scipio dispatched a special force to scale the eastern wall. The soldiers were astonished by the rate at which the ocean was receding, thereby allowing them to set up their ladders and scale the wall. Remembering Scipio's promise of help from the sea god, the soldiers were greatly encouraged. The Carthaginians had left the eastern wall virtually unmanned, since they had not expected an attack from that quarter.

Scipio then defeated Hasdrubal at Baecula, an inland city in southeastern Spain, in 208 BC. Doubting that Scipio would attack his strong position on a ridge, Hasdrubal had allowed his men to grow careless. Scipio used his heavy infantry to attack Hasdrubal's flanks, while his light infantry held the center. Hasdrubal lost one-third of his twenty-five thousand men.

Scipio then won another important victory at Ilipa in 206 BC. Near the end of each day, Scipio marched his soldiers out of their quarters in the same formation: his Roman legions were positioned in the center, the less reliable Spaniards on the wings. After staring across at each other for a while, each army would then return to its quarters. Then one day Scipio attacked the Carthaginian camp before dawn, with his Spaniards in the center and his Romans on the wings. The Carthaginians mustered in their customary formation, with the Carthaginians in the center and their Spanish allies on the wings. Thus, the Roman infantry and cavalry were able to fall on and rout the Carthaginians' Spanish allies. With their wings crushed, the Carthaginians were forced to retreat. The pursuing Romans slaughtered most of the fleeing Carthaginians. Out of the initial force of seventy thousand, only six thousand Carthaginians escaped. Unlike many generals, both ancient and modern, Scipio understood the importance of pursuit.

Scipio's victory at Ilipa drove the Carthaginians from Spain and caused the defection of King Masinissa of Numidia (eastern Algeria) to the Roman side. Scipio had been cultivating Masinissa, the brilliant commander of Carthage's Numidian cavalry, ever since the Battle of Baecula. After the battle, Scipio had released Masinissa's young nephew, who had been captured when thrown from his horse, and had dispatched him to his uncle on a charger, bearing a golden ring and draped in fine clothing as gifts of Scipio. When combined with Scipio's Spanish victories and Masinissa's disgruntlement with Carthage, Scipio's cultivation of Masinissa succeeded in securing an alliance that would pay huge dividends in North Africa. Because the Carthaginians did not treat their allies as well as the Romans did, they proved far less loyal.

The Death of Hasdrubal

Forced from Spain, Hasdrubal moved to aid Hannibal in Italy. But in 207 BC the Romans, having intercepted a dispatch from Hasdrubal to Hannibal that revealed his destination, surprised and routed Hasdrubal at Metauros in northern Italy. Out of thirty thousand Carthaginians, ten thousand were killed, including Hasdrubal himself, to only two thousand Romans. Another ten thousand Carthaginians were taken prisoner. Hannibal would get few reinforcements. His first inkling of the disaster came when the Romans flung his brother's head on the ground in front of his outpost.

The North African Campaign

The Romans were now prepared to strike their first direct blow at Carthage. The Senate granted Scipio, fresh from his conquest of Spain, its reluctant permission to land a force in North Africa. The cautious (and perhaps envious) Fabius opposed the daring expedition so vehemently he would not allow funds to be voted for it. Scipio had to pay for the expedition out of his own income. Furthermore, the Senate assigned Scipio minimal forces. Aside from Scipio's own recruits, the Senate granted him only the discredited remnants of the Fifth and Sixth Legions, legions that had been decimated by Hannibal in the shameful defeat at Cannae.

But Scipio, who was fully aware that the rout at Cannae had been the fault of the imbecilic Varro and not the result of any cowardice on the part of the soldiers, was delighted to command these battle-hardened veterans. A master at instilling confidence in troops, Scipio now took full advantage of the intense desire of his soldiers to avenge their fallen comrades, to wipe away the personal humiliation and stigma of Cannae, and to reward Scipio's own faith in them. With his own recruits, Scipio filled these neglected legions to full strength for the first time in over a decade, a move that further restored morale and the esprit de corps of the resurrected legions.

After a year of training and preparation, Scipio's army landed in North Africa in 204 BC. Using a peace conference to spy out the Carthaginian camp at Utica, he discovered that the soldiers' huts were wooden structures built close together. Therefore, Scipio attacked the camp at night, setting its buildings ablaze and slaughtering the bewildered soldiers, who often emerged from their huts unarmed, thinking that the fire was an accident. When another Carthaginian army rushed in to help put out the fires, it, too, was ambushed and slaughtered.

Scipio then defeated another Carthaginian army on the plains before Carthage. The Carthaginians became so confused and panic-stricken that they surrendered Tunis, only fifteen miles from Carthage, without a fight. After sixteen years of brilliant victories but no knockout blow, Hannibal was forced to return home to face the dire threat posed by Scipio's army.

The Battle of Zama

In 202 BC Hannibal faced off against Scipio's legions at Zama, eighty miles southwest of Carthage. Both had about forty thousand troops, though Scipio's force was greatly superior in cavalry. The fact that Hannibal had never been defeated as a commander did not intimidate Scipio, perhaps because neither had he. In fact, when Carthaginian spies were caught lurking about his camp, Scipio ordered an officer to give them a personal tour of the place and send them back, an act of bravado that impressed Hannibal.

Hannibal planned to use his eighty elephants to launch the opening assault, hoping that their charge would disrupt the Roman lines. While his Carthaginian and Numidian cavalry held off that of the Romans and Masinissa, the Roman infantry would wear themselves out on the mercenaries and Carthaginian civilians Hannibal placed in the front lines. (Since the Carthaginians, unlike the Romans, did not require military service of their civilians, the Carthaginian civilians now pressed into service were poor fighters.) When the Roman infantry was exhausted from the sheer energy required to kill all of these worthless masses of troops, he would then unleash his trained veterans on them.

But Hannibal's cunning and ruthless plan was thwarted by a clever stratagem of Scipio. Recalling that the Carthaginians' elephants at Ilipa had become so confused at one point in the battle that they had charged into the Carthaginian center, Scipio ordered a tremendous blare of trumpets along the front lines as Hannibal's elephants charged to begin the Battle of Zama. Frightened by the trumpets, some of the elephants wheeled around and collided with Hannibal's Numidian cavalry. The other elephants followed the path of least resistance, the semicircular line that Scipio had purposely left open for them where they were urged along by Roman darts and javelins, only to emerge and crash into the Carthaginian cavalry on the opposite side. Instead of wreaking havoc on the enemy, the elephants had scattered both wings of Hannibal's cavalry. Taking advantage of the chaos, Scipio's cavalry charged Hannibal's disoriented cavalry, driving the horsemen from the field and pursuing to ensure that they would not return.

Meanwhile, the rest of the battle proceeded as Hannibal planned. The Roman soldiers tired themselves killing mercenaries and Carthaginian civilians. Indeed, the civilians proved so cowardly, leaving the mercenaries to bear the brunt of the Roman attack, that the mercenaries finally turned on the civilians and struck many of them down. There were so many bodies and severed limbs, and there was so much gore on the ground, that the Romans had great difficulty maintaining their footing, much less advancing. When they were finally able to advance, Hannibal struck them with his well-rested veterans.

The Carthaginians then had the better of the battle, and victory seemed at hand, when Scipio's cavalry returned. Surrounded by Roman veterans and

Numidian horsemen, the Carthaginian infantry was beaten to a pulp. Twenty thousand Carthaginians were killed, and almost as many captured, compared with the Romans' 1,500. The Battle of Zama was the decisive battle of the Punic Wars, the crucial victory that led to Roman supremacy over western Europe and the Mediterranean world.

The Peace
Under the terms of the treaty of 201 BC, 500 out of the 510 ships of the Carthaginian fleet were towed out to sea and set ablaze in what might be called the funeral pyre of the Carthaginian Empire. The Romans also forced the Carthaginians to pay a huge indemnity of ten thousand talents, to relinquish their war elephants, and to cede Spain and southern France to the Romans. Henceforth, Carthage could not wage war outside of Africa and could not wage war within Africa without Roman consent. Yet, such was the weakness of the Carthaginian position that Hannibal physically pulled an astonished Carthaginian senator from the podium when the senator proposed rejecting the treaty terms. Hannibal was amazed that the Romans did not kill or enslave every Carthaginian in retribution for his destruction of Italy.

The Deaths of Hannibal and Scipio
Hannibal set about reducing corruption in the Carthaginian government and placing the city's finances on a sounder basis. Angered by his attacks on them, corrupt politicians and judges in Carthage joined with Roman senators led by Cato the Elder to accuse Hannibal of continuing to plot war against Rome. Against the protest of Scipio, Hannibal was called to Rome to stand trial on these charges. Hannibal fled to the Seleucid Empire, where he did indeed stir up opposition to the Romans. In 183 BC Hannibal poisoned himself when the king of Bithynia (in Asia Minor) surrounded his house with the purpose of killing him in order to win favor with Rome.

Once Hannibal ceased to be a threat to Rome, his legend fascinated Roman historians. While the Greek historian Polybius praised his intelligence and his ability to unite a motley group of Carthaginians, Numidians, Spaniards, Gauls, Italians, and Greeks into one of the greatest armies in history, Livy praised him for requiring little sleep and for dressing no differently than his soldiers.

Scipio was given the title "Africanus" in honor of his North African victories. Some people wanted to make him a perpetual consul and dictator, but he rebuked them. He even refused to allow statues of himself to be erected.

After helping to defeat the Seleucid king Antiochus III at Magnesia, Scipio was later tried on the preposterous charge of giving Antiochus favorable peace terms in exchange for a bribe, an accusation made by his implacable foe Cato the Elder. On the first day of his trial, which ironically fell on the anniversary of the Battle of Zama, Scipio stood, and with all eyes fixed on him, credited the gods for his famous victory. He then declared that he was going to the Capitol to sacrifice to the gods in order to "give them thanks for having, on this day, and at many other times, endowed me with both the will and ability to perform extraordinary services to the commonwealth." He added, "Such of you also, Romans, who choose, come with me and beseech the gods that you may have commanders like myself." The entire audience followed Scipio, leaving his accusers alone in a deserted Forum. Scipio refused to attend the rest of the trial, and the charges were dropped. He remained at his estate at Liternum, never visiting Rome again. Scipio left instructions that his body should be buried on his estate, where he died in 183 BC—ironically, the same year as Hannibal, his erstwhile foe and fellow enemy of Cato.

Shamelessly vindictive, Cato then succeeded in having Scipio's brother Lucius convicted of the same charge of accepting a bribe from Antiochus. When the praetor attempted to collect the imposed fine, which was equal to the alleged bribe, he discovered that the value of Lucius's entire estate did not equal the fine—strong proof of the brothers' innocence.

Problems with the Historians' Accounts

Much of Livy's patriotic account of early Rome, in particular his highly influential tales of the very earliest Roman heroes, was mythological in nature. He tended to downplay the crucial influence of the Etruscans and Greeks on Roman civilization and to attribute Roman success to the native qualities of the Roman people.

Furthermore, contrary to Polybius's equally influential analysis of Roman success, it is highly questionable whether Rome ever possessed a true mixed government. Although political power was certainly more balanced than it had been before the initiation of the republican reforms discussed earlier, the few still possessed more power than the many. Since the Senate still controlled the treasury, it could refuse to fund any measure passed by the popular assemblies. The patricians were also able to use their control of most Roman land to pressure many plebeians, including their own clients (various dependents, including tenant farmers, who worked patrician land in exchange for part of the crop), to vote the way they demanded. The patricians gave their clients jobs, protection, and legal aid (when called before the patrician-dominated juries) in exchange for their loyalty. Since most plebeians could not afford to hold office because officials did not receive salaries, the patricians controlled most offices. Even the tribunes were hardly immune from their influence. The fact that tribunes and many other officeholders knew that they would automatically become members of the Senate after they left office often led them to support aristocratic interests. Similarly, the consuls, who were almost always patricians, who shared in the economic interests of that class, and who generally had relatives in the Senate, can hardly be considered to have served as an effective counterweight to that body. In addition, the balances between the consuls and the people were of unequal weight. A consul's fear that he might have a treaty rejected hardly balanced plebeian terror at the thought of opposing someone who, as a military leader, would have the power of life and death over them. Indeed, the imbalance between the patricians and plebeians was increasing at the very time that Polybius and Cicero were writing their odes to the Roman republic, as we shall see in the next chapter.

The Lesson

VIRTUE

Nevertheless, the Founding Fathers learned the crucial importance of virtue in a republic from Livy, Polybius, and Plutarch's lives of Publius, Camillus, Pyrrhus, Fabius Maximus, and Marcellus. They learned that virtue was the backbone of a republic, as surely as vice was its cancer.

Alexander Hamilton was particularly fond of Roman republican pseudonyms. It was probably his idea to use "Publius" as the pseudonym for the *Federalist* essays, since he had already written essays under that name nearly a decade earlier. The choice was particularly apt, since Hamilton, James Madison, and John Jay were attempting to establish a new republic in the United States after the expulsion of George III's armies, just as Publius had helped established one in Rome after the expulsion of Tarquin. Hamilton also employed other pseudonyms from early Rome, such as "Horatius," "Camillus," and "Titus Manlius." Similarly, John Dickinson used the name "Fabius" for a series of essays endorsing the U.S. Constitution.

The founders also greatly admired Lucius Junius Brutus, who had helped expel Tarquin from Rome. In 1771 Samuel Adams praised "the independent spirit of [Lucius] Brutus, who, to his immortal honor, expelled the proud Tarquin of Rome." In 1777 John Adams contrasted Lucius Brutus's sincere republicanism with John Hancock's secret ambition. Denouncing Hancock's well-publicized donation of 150 cords of wood to the poor of Boston, Adams wrote, "Did [Lucius] Brutus in the Infancy of the Commonwealth and before the Army of Tarquin was Subdued, acquire Fame and Popularity by Largesses? No! These arts were reserved for Caesar in the Dotage and the last expiring Moments of the Republic." Ironically, Hancock's generosity, so great that it eventually exhausted his vast fortune, was an attempt to prove himself a genuine classical republican, willing to sacrifice his wealth for the good of the republic.

One of the founders' greatest heroes was Cincinnatus. In 1776 John Adams expressed his desire to emulate the Roman hero by resigning his worldly powers and cares. He wrote, "When a few mighty matters are accomplished here, I [will] retreat like Cincinnatus . . . and farewell Politicks." In 1780 Samuel Adams emphasized the need for Americans to elect capable and selfless men like Cincinnatus, noting,

> How different was [the sixth century BC Athenian dictator] Pisistratus from that Roman Hero and Patriot Lucius Quinctius Cincinnatus, who, tho vested with the Authority of Dictator, was so moderate in his Desires of a Continuance of Power, that, having in six weeks fulfill'd the Purposes of his Appointment, he resign'd the dangerous office, which he might have held till the expiration of six Months. When we formerly had weak and wicked Governors & Magistrates, it was our Misfortune; but for the future, while we enjoy and exercise the inestimable right of chusing them ourselves, it will be our Disgrace.

In opposition to the stronger federal government proposed by the U.S. Constitution, Patrick Henry contended that it was not "federal ideas" that had led to American victory in the Revolutionary War but rather "sons of Cincinnatus, without splendid magnificence or parade, going, with the genius of their just progenitor, Cincinnatus, to the plough; men who served their country without ruining it—men who had served it to the destruction of their private patrimony—their country owing them amazing amounts, for the payment of which no adequate provision was then made." John Adams probably had Cincinnatus in mind again in 1794, when he wrote to Thomas Jefferson, who had resigned as secretary of state a year earlier and had left Philadelphia, then the national capital. Adams declared, "If I had your Plantation and your Laborers I should be tempted to follow your Example and get out of the Fumum et Opes Strepitumque Romae [the smoke, the wealth, and the din of Rome], which I abominate."

George Washington not only took notice of the fact that people compared him with Cincinnatus but also worked consciously to promote the analogy. The comparison captured the imagination of numerous domestic and foreign artists. Horatio Greenough's twelve-ton statue of Washington for the Capitol Rotunda, based on Phidias's *Zeus* but altered to fit the Cincinnatus analogy, depicted the Virginian in classical dress. Washington's right arm was raised, index finger pointing heavenward, his left arm offering his sword, handle outward. Antonio Canova's statue of Washington depicted him in Roman military garb, with his sword laid down and his left hand clutching the Farewell Address, symbols of his two great surrenders of power. Giuseppe Ceracchi's bust portrayed the Virginian with Roman curls. Both John Trumbull and Charles Wilson Peale painted Washington as Cincinnatus. John J. Barralet's engraving *George Washington's Resignation* depicted Washington surrendering power to Columbia, while in the background, oxen, a plow, and Mount Vernon awaited. Similarly, a Fourth of July toast offered at Wilmington, Delaware, in 1788, declared, "Farmer Washington—may he, like a second Cincinnatus, be called from the plow to rule a great people." Lord Byron concurred wholeheartedly. His "Ode to Napoleon" contained these lines:

> Where may the wearied eye repose
> When gazing on the Great;
> Where neither guilty glory glows
> Nor despicable state?
> Yes—one—the first—the best:
> The Cincinnatus of the West
> Whom envy dared not hate,
> Bequeath'd the name of Washington
> To make men blush there was but one.

An astonished Western world agreed with the unintended praise of George III. Unable to believe that any military leader would voluntarily surrender such power, the king scoffed that, if Washington resigned his commission after the war, "He will be the greatest man in the world." The king's confusion epitomized his inability, throughout the Revolutionary conflict, to comprehend the enormous emotional power that classical republican ideals wielded over American minds.

Fully conscious of the Cincinnatus image and determined to nurture it, Washington recognized that his appeal lay not in military victories, of which he had precious few, but in the republican virtue revealed in his surrender of power. As Garry Wills has put it, "People did not admire a conquering Caesar in him, but a Cincinnatus resigning." Hence, Washington never offered to resign as commander of the Continental Army, even after the worst defeats, because he did not wish to spoil, by anticipation, the offer of resignation that he planned once he had, like Cincinnatus, defeated the enemy. Soon after that day arrived in 1783, Washington withdrew completely from public life, even going to the extreme of resigning from his local vestry. In his letters of 1784 Washington referred to Mount Vernon as his "villa," a term he had never before employed in allusion to his estate. Sounding like the Roman poet Horace, he referred to himself as "a private citizen of America, on the banks of the Patowmac . . . under my Vine and my own Fig-tree, free from the bustle of a camp and the intrigues of a court." Indeed, the Cincinnatus analogy benefited from a fact so obvious to every schoolboy it was rarely mentioned: "George" derives from the Greek *georgos*, meaning "farmer." Proud of his position as the first president of the Society of the Cincinnati, an association of Revolutionary War veterans, Washington demanded reforms when popular fears of the organization threatened to destroy the image associated with its name.

As head of Congress' Board of War during the Revolutionary War, John Adams found military models in Fabius and Scipio Africanus. In 1775 he confessed that although Fabius's patient policy of attrition against the Carthaginians had been "wise and brave," Adams himself was too impatient for such a strategy. He declared, "Zeal and Fire and Activity and Enterprise Strike my Imagination too much. I am obliged to be constantly on my Guard. Yet the Heat within will burst forth at Times." This last statement was certainly true, for in 1776 and 1777 Adams repeatedly complained that American strategy was too cautious. In 1776 he concluded, in a letter to General Henry Knox, "The Policy of Rome in carrying their arms to Carthage, while Hannibal was at the Gates of their Capital, was wise and justified by the Event, and would deserve Imitation if We could march into the Country of our Enemies." Adams understood that British control of the seas prohibited a reenactment of Scipio's amphibious assault on Carthage but still felt that some offensive action was in order. In this, he anticipated John Paul Jones's daring raids on British commerce.

Alexander Hamilton called George Washington "the American Fabius" because, like Fabius, Washington had wisely and steadfastly avoided engaging the better-trained British enemy in the early part of the war, waiting for more opportune moments to attack. In his (in)famous biography of Washington, the biography that originated the mythical cherry tree story, Parson Weems made the same comparison, declaring that Washington was as "prudent as Fabius."

Thomas Jefferson frequently compared the British commercialism he detested with that of the Carthaginians, thereby implying an analogy between the United States and the frugal Roman republic. In 1810 he scoffed at the suggestion that an alliance be made with Great Britain, connecting it with the Roman charge that the Carthaginians frequently violated their treaties: "The faith of a nation of merchants! The *Punica fides* of modern Carthage."

Later that year, after predicting a mutiny in the British navy, Jefferson further claimed that, if the mutineers were unable to establish a military dictator- ship, they would become individual pirates, and "the modern Carthage will end as the old one has done"—a reference to the Barbary pirates of North Africa. In 1815, a few months after the end of the War of 1812, Jefferson turned from predictions of doom to threats of violence. If the modern Carthage, Great Britain, did not stop injuring the United States, she would force the nation into yet another war, and "some Scipio Americanus will leave to posterity the problem of conjecturing where stood once the ancient and splendid city of London."

The conflicts of the Revolutionary and Constitutional periods increased the founders' sense of kinship with the ancients. Proud of America's firm resistance to the Intolerable Acts, Samuel Adams declared in 1774, "I think our Countrymen discover the Spirit of Rome or Sparta." In a 1776 letter to George Wythe, John Adams exulted, "You and I, my dear Friend, have been sent into life at a time when the greatest lawgivers of antiquity would have wished to have lived." In the same year, shortly after the Dec- laration of Independence was signed, Charles Lee told Patrick Henry, "I us'd to regret not being thrown into the world in the glamorous fourth cen- tury [BC] of the Romans; but now I am thoroughly reconcil'd to my lot." Edmund Pendleton cherished the memory of the Virginia Constitutional Convention of 1776, recalling, "The young boasted that they were tread- ing upon the Republican ground of Greece and Rome." In 1777 George Washington replied to British general John Burgoyne's peace offers, "The associated armies in America act from the noblest motives, liberty. The same principles actuated the arms of Rome in the days of her glory; and the same object was the reward of Roman valour."

Imagine the founders' excitement at the opportunity to match their an- cient heroes' struggles against tyranny and their sage construction of durable republics—to rival the noble deeds that had filled their youth. The founders were thrilled by the belief that they were beginning anew the work of the ancient republicans, only this time with an unprecedented chance of success. While the valiant Roman republicans had ultimately lost the first round of combat against tyranny, the founders, starting afresh in a virgin country with limitless resources, could pack the punch necessary to win the second and decisive round.

~

CHAPTER SEVEN

The Fall of the Roman Republic and the Need for Vigilance

The period of ancient history that most enthralled the Founding Fathers was the era that witnessed the decline and fall of the Roman republic. Since the founders equated "Rome" with the Roman republic, they considered the *real* decline and fall of Rome to have occurred in the second and first centuries BC, not half a millennium later when the empire collapsed. The founders' intense scrutiny of the late Roman republic resembled an autopsy. The purpose of this autopsy was to save the life of the American body politic by uncovering the cancerous growths that had caused the demise of its greatest ideological ancestor. Their study of the writings of Plutarch, Sallust, and Cicero not only reinforced their belief in the importance of virtue to a republic but also convinced them of the need for vigilance against ambitious individuals who might threaten the republic.

Roman Expansion, 200–133 BC

The Conquest of Illyria and Greece

The destruction of Carthaginian military power during and after the Second Punic War opened the Mediterranean world to Roman expansion. When King Philip V of Macedon allied himself with the Carthaginians during that war, even sending four thousand Macedonians to fight with Hannibal at Zama, the Romans defeated him and, in the process, conquered Illyria (Yugoslavia). After the war, the Romans responded enthusiastically to the call of Pergamum and Rhodes for aid against Philip. As we have seen, the Romans gained control of Greece by defeating the Macedonians in 197 BC, the Seleucids in 190 BC, and the Macedonians again in 168 BC. In 148 BC, when anti-Roman sentiment in Greece flared as a result of the Senate's policy of supporting oligarchies there, the Romans burned Corinth and converted all of Greece into a collection of provinces governed by a Roman proconsul.

The Third Punic War (149–146 BC)

Although the Romans had stripped Carthage of most of her armed forces and empire after the Second Punic War, some Romans remained obsessed by the fear that Carthage would threaten Rome again one day. Hence, in the mid-second century BC, when Carthage revived economically, Roman extremists demanded the complete destruction of the city.

The leader of the anti-Carthaginian faction was the austere Cato the Elder. "Cato" was not the Roman's original name but rather an epithet meaning "wise" or "experienced." The red-haired, grey-eyed Cato was an old-fashioned Roman. Despising weakness and luxury, Cato ate and worked beside his own slaves. His hero was Manius Curius, who had led the Romans to victory against the Samnites and against Pyrrhus but who had tilled his little farm with his own hands and whose diet had consisted mainly of boiled turnips. Cato admired simple Fabius and detested flamboyant Scipio. Equating simplicity with virtue and extravagance with vice, Cato was alarmed at the growing influence of Greek culture in Rome. When addressing an Athenian audience in Latin, he was appalled at the number of words his Greek translator required to express the same sentiments. He concluded that the Greeks were mere bladders of wind—cunning talkers, rather than pragmatic doers. (While it is true that a florid rhetorical style was then in vogue among the Hellenistic Greeks, Cato probably also had a poor translator.)

Having become censor in 184 BC, Cato set about purifying Roman society of "the extreme luxury and degeneracy of the age," even expelling Scipio's brother from the Senate for holding drinking parties. He expelled another senator for embracing his wife in the presence of his daughter, placed stiff taxes on luxury items, severed the pipes by which people diverted the public water supply free of charge, and demolished houses that encroached on public land.

A relentless enemy of Carthage, Cato completed every Senate speech, no matter the topic, with the refrain, "Carthage must be destroyed!" He once brought a basket of large North African figs into the senate chamber to show the senators what the literal fruits of a Roman victory over the Carthaginians would look like.

In 149 BC Cato received his wish. Rome presented a series of outrageous demands to Carthage, including one that all Carthaginians leave the city and settle at least ten miles inland, a move that would destroy the Carthaginian economy. When the Carthaginians refused, the Romans, under Scipio Aemilianus, besieged the city. Though often on the verge of starvation, the Carthaginians fought heroically and held out for three years.

When the Romans took the city in 146 BC, they killed every male Carthaginian and sold every woman and child into slavery. The Romans then reduced all of the buildings to rubble. Although the popular legend that the Romans plowed up the city and poured salt into the ground so that nothing would grow there for many years is probably false, the Romans did forbid the resettlement of Carthage for a quarter of a century. Rome then annexed the remaining Carthaginian territory. Ironically, Cato the Elder had died in the first year of the Third Punic War. He did not live to see the enemy crushed.

The Acquisition of Pergamum
In 133 BC, when Attalus III, the king of Pergamum, died without an heir, he left his kingdom to Rome. Fearing a popular revolt when he died, he knew that the Romans would maintain law and order and would continue to follow his policy of favoring the aristocrats over the masses. The Romans now controlled most of the Mediterranean basin.

The Effects of the New Roman Expansion

By making apparent the tremendous importance of the plebeians to the army, the first phase of Roman expansion, and the gradual conquest of Italy, had helped produce a republican form of government. By contrast, the Romans' rapid conquest of the Mediterranean basin helped destroy the same republic. By further increasing the already vast inequalities of wealth between the rich and the poor, the new Roman expansion generated class warfare, which, in turn, produced the chaos and violence that paved the way for the emperors.

The Decline of Popular Assemblies
The new Roman expansion strengthened the position of the wealthy and undermined that of the poor. The sudden and extensive expansion of Roman territory transformed Rome from a village into an imperial center, housing a host of domestic and foreign supplicants. It is estimated that the city possessed nearly 750,000 people by the mid-second century BC. Under such

conditions, the average Roman found it difficult to participate in government, even to the small extent that he had before. The popular assemblies became far too large to make the swift decisions required of an empire. Hence, both the Senate and the aristocratic proconsuls whom they appointed to govern the provinces wielded the power. The aristocrats had always held the upper hand, of course, but the commoners were now losing the little power they had once possessed.

Inequalities

Ever-increasing numbers of commoners lost their land and became the clients of the aristocrats. Moving to Rome, they were forced to support their masters' political interests in order to earn a living. Between 233 and 133 BC, a mere twenty-six noble families furnished three-quarters of the consuls; no more than ten families furnished half. Some aristocrats possessed armies of client-bodyguards.

How were the commoners driven off their farms and into clientage in Rome? First, long-term military service overseas had forced many soldiers to neglect their farms. Second, Hannibal's soldiers had destroyed many farms. Third, the commoners could not compete with the massive amounts of produce grown on the aristocrats' plantations (the *latifundia*). The Senate sold aristocrats these plantations in the conquered territories, as well as a slave labor force consisting mostly of prisoners of war, at a relatively low price. The Senate sold the land in large blocks, so that only the wealthy could afford it. The Senate also "rented" some of the land to aristocrats, and when the wealthy renters began to consider the land their own—building homes and family tombs on it and using it for dowries—the Senate did nothing to resist such claims. Some owners of the latifundia took advantage of new farming techniques to grow grapes and olives, while others continued to cultivate grain and to raise sheep and cattle. Small farmers could not compete with this large-scale production, which depressed prices. The potent combination of neglect, property damage, and depressed prices forced many veterans to sell their farms to aristocrats, move to Rome, and become their clients. Those whom the overseas wars had enriched exploited those whom they had impoverished.

The "Punic Curse"

Rome suffered a general moral decline that observers like Sallust attributed to the "Punic Curse," since the incredible wealth that had helped produce the decline was the indirect result of the Roman conquest of Carthage. New-found luxury undermined the traditional Roman values of frugality, discipline, honesty, and respect for law, the values on which the republic rested. Aristocrats sought profit with a ruthless abandon. Vote buying and ballot box stuffing proliferated. The crushing poverty and slum environment of the commoners rendered them equally cruel and lazy. The new class of merchants, moneylenders, tax collectors, and government contractors spawned by the rapid growth of the empire proved equally corrupt. The low-born wealthy were called *equites*, members of the equestrian order, because they could afford to maintain a horse and serve in the cavalry.

Roman provincial governors and tax collectors plundered their provinces shamelessly, both for Rome and for themselves. Far from the prying eyes of the Senate, and largely ignorant of local cultures, the underpaid and overworked proconsuls extorted as much wealth as possible from the helpless inhabitants of their provinces. One governor explained that he needed to extract three fortunes from his province—one to pay the debts incurred in bribing senators to obtain the position, another to bribe the jury at his trial for corruption, and a third fortune to last the rest of his life.

The Romans also treated their slaves harshly. As a result, there were slave revolts in 139, 134–131, and 104–101 BC. The largest slave rebellion occurred in 73–71 BC, when the Thracian gladiator Spartacus led seventy thousand slaves in revolt. The slave army defeated five separate Roman forces and plundered much of Italy before the rebels were finally overwhelmed at Lucania, their leader killed in battle. The Romans crucified six thousand of the rebels and lined the Appian Way, Rome's main highway, with their rotting corpses.

The Agrarian Reform Movement of the Gracchi

Tiberius Gracchus

In 133 BC, at the age of twenty-nine, Tiberius Sempronius Gracchus, a grandson of Scipio Africanus, was elected tribune. Tiberius recognized that growing inequalities between the rich and the poor threatened traditional Roman values and the republic itself. He decided that the way to return Rome to its old values was to restore the backbone of the Roman republic, the small farmer. Accordingly, Tiberius proposed that the *comitia tributa*, one of Rome's three popular assemblies, reenact a law of 367 BC (that had never been enforced) limiting the size of estates in the public lands (land rented out by the state) to roughly three hundred acres per person. (In ancient times, due to primitive technology, three hundred acres was considered a vast estate. Most farmers possessed only a few acres.) Although this three-hundred-acre plot would then become the renter's permanent property, the surplus land would be confiscated and allotted to the landless, who would pay a small rent to the state. Tiberius's moderate proposal even included compensation for the excess land that the patricians would have to surrender, though the land was not really theirs. Tiberius declared,

> The wild beasts that roam over Italy have their dens and holes to lurk in, but the men who fight and die for our country enjoy the common air and light and nothing else. It is their lot to wander with their wives and children, houseless and homeless, over the face of the earth. . . . The truth is that they fight and die to protect the wealth and luxury of others, and though they are called masters of the world, they have not a single clod of earth that is their own.

Slogans scrawled on nearly every portico, monument, and wall in the city urged Tiberius to proceed with land redistribution.

The comitia tributa passed the law, but the Senate bribed the tribune Marcus Octavian (an ancestor of Augustus) into vetoing it. Corrupted from its original purpose of blocking the aristocratic acts of the Senate, the tribunal veto power was now being used to block the popular will.

Infuriated, Tiberius responded by pushing through a second law that lacked a compensation provision. He pleaded with Octavian to either change his position or resign for the sake of justice and the republic. Octavian seemed moved but refused. Tiberius then persuaded the comitia tributa to impeach Octavian and pass the bill again. The impeachment of a tribune was unprecedented, but Tiberius argued that the people could remove from office any official they elected. However, the Senate, which controlled the treasury, refused to allocate sufficient funds for the enforcement of the land redistribution act. Intent on ensuring the enforcement of the new act, Tiberius attempted to bypass the Senate by using funds Attalus III of Pergamum had bequeathed to Rome.

Violating an almost sacred custom against consecutive terms, Tiberius ran for reelection as tribune. He spoke of the need to reduce the term of military service (it was nearly thirty years) and to give the people the authority to hear appeals from the aristocratic juries.

On election day near the end of 132 BC, fearing that Tiberius intended to make himself a king, a crowd of senators and their clients marched on Tiberius and clubbed him and three hundred of his followers to death. The senators threw all of the bodies into the Tiber River, thereby denying them a proper burial. Others were banished or executed without trial. The traditional Roman reverence for law was giving way to corrupt, unconstitutional, and violent acts.

Gaius Gracchus

Gaius Sempronius Gracchus, Tiberius's younger brother by nine years, was elected tribune for the year 123 BC. So many people poured into Rome from the rest of Italy to support Gaius that there was not enough shelter for them. Gaius was a passionate orator, in sharp contrast to Tiberius, who had possessed an almost Olympian calm. In fact, Gaius ordered one of his slaves to strike a soft tone on an instrument whenever Gaius's passion overcame him during a speech. After hearing the tone, Gaius would become aware of himself and regain his composure.

As tribune, Gaius pledged to secure the enforcement of Tiberius's agrarian law so that Roman colonies could be established at Tarentum, Capua, and Carthage, areas the Romans had depopulated. Gaius cultivated equestrian support by appointing equites to special juries that tried proconsuls for corruption and by issuing contracts to their tax collection companies. These private companies, which collected taxes for Rome in the provinces, were allowed to collect surplus taxes as profit. (It is no wonder tax collectors were the most hated figures of the New Testament.) Gaius also prevented food riots in times of famine by persuading the comitia tributa to purchase grain and store it in warehouses. The food would then be sold to the poor of Rome at cost, slightly below its market value. (Politicians later turned this price stabilization measure into a dole, which they manipulated for personal advantage.) Aristocrats hated the measure, fearing that it would undermine the dependence of the poor on them for food and, with it, the master-client relationship. Gaius also pleased the poor and angered the aristocrats by offering free seats at the gladiatorial contests. (The aristocrats rented seats to the poor.) Gaius persuaded the comitia tributa to insist that no one under the age of seventeen be conscripted into the army and that soldiers be issued free clothing. He supported the construction of roads, to the benefit of country farmers.

But Gaius lost the support of poor Romans by advocating the extension of full citizenship to Rome's Latin allies and the "Latin right" for her other Italian allies. The first step toward citizenship for all inhabitants, the Latin right included the granting of citizenship to the leaders of a foreign people. Fearing that they would lose control of the comitia tributa to non-Romans, the poor citizens of Rome guarded their privilege of citizenship. Due to a loss of support among the poor, combined with electoral fraud, Gaius suffered a defeat in his bid for a third term at the end of 122 BC.

Gaius's defeat led to some minor skirmishing between factions, which provided the Senate with the pretext to declare martial law at the beginning of 121 BC. The Senate ordered the Italian allies who supported Gaius to leave the city and called for the murder of Gaius himself. His supporters proved cowardly: rather than aiding him in evading the assassins that pursued him, Gaius's followers merely shouted at him to run faster. Knowing that the consul Opimius had agreed to reward Gaius's murderer with the weight of his head in gold, the assassin cleverly emptied the brain and filled the skull with molten lead, thereby increasing its weight to nearly eighteen pounds. Three thousand of Gaius's followers were also arrested and executed. The bodies of the victims were hurled into the Tiber, their property was confiscated, and their wives were even forbidden to mourn publicly.

The Romans' failure to enact Gaius's citizenship law, combined with Rome's growing harshness toward its Italian allies, eventually led the Italians to revolt (90–88 BC). Having loyally endured the horrors and hardships of two centuries of constant warfare on behalf of Rome, many Italians were furious at the Romans' unwillingness to grant them full citizenship. The Italians feared that, without voting rights, they might be dispossessed of their land to make room for Roman veterans. After this "Social War" (so-called because the Latin term for the Italian allies was *socii*), Rome was forced to grant citizenship to all Italians south of the Po River. Those to the north of the Po, mostly Gauls, were granted the Latin right.

The First Roman Civil War: Marius versus Sulla

Rome was increasingly divided between two factions, the Optimates, who favored the aristocrats, and the Populares, who favored the poor. (Even the leaders of the Populares were generally wealthy.) This schism led to three bloody civil wars in Rome.

Marius

In 107 BC Rome faced a grave crisis. A violent and corrupt Numidian king named Jugurtha (the grandson of Masinissa) was waging war against his brother for complete control of Numidia, in contradiction to the settlement the Romans had imposed. Partly because Jugurtha bribed some of the senators, the Senate was reluctant to act against him at first.

Furious at the Senate, the comitia tributa ordered the consul Gaius Marius, an eques, to proceed to North Africa and crush Jugurtha. It was the first time the assembly had ever insisted on assigning a general to a command, a power traditionally reserved for the Senate. A hard-bitten soldier from the country town of Arpinum, Marius declared regarding the aristocrats, "They call me vulgar and unpolished, because I do not know how to put on an elegant dinner and do not have actors at my table or keep a cook who has cost me more than my farm overseer. All this, my fellow citizens, I am proud to admit." He also expressed pride at not having studied Greek literature.

In 106 BC Marius destroyed Jugurtha's army. Having captured and imprisoned the Numidian through the treachery of an ally soon after, the Romans starved him to death. In 102 and 101 BC Marius followed this triumph with a successful defense of Italy against two large Germanic tribes, one of which had routed a Roman army and inflicted eighty thousand casualties a few years earlier.

Marius's army was composed of landless citizens (he disregarded the small property qualification for service in the army) whom he personally equipped with javelins that broke on impact so that the enemy could not throw them back. Marius also made the army more mobile by having soldiers carry their own entrenching tools and other equipment rather than relying on vulnerable baggage trains. Marius transformed the Roman army from a militia equipped by, and loyal to, Rome, into a professional army equipped by, and loyal to, its commander. He used the threat of armed force to overcome senate opposition to the distribution of land in North Africa to his troops—a tactic unheard of during the early days of the republic. But at least Marius did not yet take the opportunity to seize Rome. He contented himself with being elected consul six years in a row between 105 and 100 BC, though Roman law prohibited consuls from holding office for two consecutive terms.

Sulla

In 88 BC King Mithridates VI of Pontus (northeastern Asia Minor) led Greece and Asia Minor, both severely oppressed by corrupt proconsuls, tax collectors, and moneylenders, into revolt against Rome. Mithridates slaughtered eighty thousand Italian men, women, and children living in his territory. Both the Senate and the comitia tributa claimed supreme authority to put down the revolt, and each selected its own general. While the comitia tributa chose Marius, the Senate selected Lucius Cornelius Sulla, who had once served as Marius's quaestor but was now his rival.

After failing to find and kill Marius, who fled to North Africa, Sulla set sail for the East. Marius then returned to Rome in Sulla's absence, allowing his troops to loot and murder opponents, including a consul. Having put down Mithridates' revolt in 86–85 BC, Sulla then returned to Rome to rout Marius's army, which had been weakened by the leader's death from pleurisy.

Thousands of Romans died in the civil war, including many senators; the Senate had been reduced from its usual 300 members to about 150.

In 82 BC the Senate appointed the victorious Sulla dictator for an unlimited term, another unconstitutional act, and assigned him the task of revising the Roman political system. Sulla transferred almost all government functions to the Senate, leaving the popular assemblies and the tribunes virtually powerless. He removed equites from juries, returning nearly all judicial power to the Senate. To hobble popular leaders, he prohibited men from holding the same office twice within a ten-year period. To weaken the position of tribune by depriving it of ambitious leaders, he prohibited former tribunes from running for higher offices and restricted the tribune's veto power.

Worst of all, Sulla "proscribed" (listed for execution) his own enemies and the enemies of his friends. His soldiers killed thirty to fifty thousand people, so many that even the Senate begged him to stop. The victims included forty senators (Populares) and 1,600 equites, whose property Sulla confiscated and distributed among his 120,000 troops. Indeed, some Romans might have been killed purely for their property. Sulla expanded the Senate from 150 to 600 members, packing it with his own supporters.

But Sulla was not personally ambitious. He wanted only to "cleanse" Rome by restoring the Senate to a dominant position. In 81 BC he voluntarily surrendered power. After serving as consul in 80–79 BC, he returned to his rural estate and died peacefully in 78 BC. If Rome had escaped permanent dictatorship, it was due solely to the fact that Marius and Sulla still possessed a few scruples about openly assuming such power. Rome would not be so fortunate in the future.

The Second Roman Civil War: Pompey versus Caesar

Pompey's Conquests

The First Civil War accelerated the trend toward factionalism and personal ambition. In 70 BC, and again in 67 BC, Pompey (Gnaeus Pompeius) and Marcus Licinius Crassus were elected consul (partly through vote buying), though Pompey was below the legal age for that position. Though they had supported Sulla during his dictatorship, Pompey and Crassus won the favor of the masses by repealing nearly all of Sulla's laws. They reduced the senatorial representation in juries to one-third and restored the tribunician power.

In 67 BC, over senate objections, the comitia tributa gave Pompey temporary dictatorial power to clear the Mediterranean of the pirates who had proliferated as a result of the Senate's neglect of the navy. With a fleet of nearly one thousand ships, the pirates had captured or looted nearly four hundred towns. Proceeding methodically, Pompey cleared the sea of pirates in three months, thereby ending the threat to Rome's grain supplies.

As part of an effort to put down yet another revolt led by Mithridates, Pompey then spent four years conquering the remaining part of the Seleucid Empire, which included Syria, Armenia, Phoenicia, Pontus, and Cilicia (southeastern Asia Minor). He also conquered Judea (Israel), an independent kingdom that had successfully revolted against the Seleucids a century earlier. Thousands of Jews threw themselves to the ground before Pompey and begged him not to desecrate the Great Temple of Jerusalem by entering it, since it was a place forbidden to Gentiles. This display only convinced Pompey that the temple must contain great riches, so he barged in, even marching into the Holy of Holies, its innermost sanctum. Tacitus later wrote, "It is a fact well known that he found no image, no statue, no symbolical representation of the Deity; the whole presented a naked dome; the sanctuary was unadorned and simple." When the dumbfounded Pompey emerged from the temple, he exclaimed in wonder, "It is empty; there is nothing there but darkness!" Pompey's reaction typified Roman confusion concerning the Jews and their worship of an invisible, omnipotent God. Nevertheless, Pompey's conquests greatly added to the wealth and power of both Rome and himself.

Catiline's Conspiracy

While Pompey was away, in 63 BC, a corrupt, debt-ridden aristocrat named Catiline (Lucius Sergius Catilina), who had just lost a second consecutive election for the consulship, conspired to kill the consuls, seize power, and win popular support through the cancellation of debts and the redistribution of land. But one of the consuls, Cicero, an ardent defender of the republic, acted quickly to thwart Catiline's plan. Catiline fled north to Etruria, while Cicero denounced him in a series of famous speeches. In 62 BC a Roman army defeated and killed Catiline at Pistoria. Catiline's coconspirators in Rome were executed.

The First Triumvirate

When Pompey returned to Rome in 62 BC, the Senate refused to grant his soldiers the land he requested for them. Pompey had made the mistake of disbanding his army too quickly, leaving him with no leverage over the Senate. In frustration Pompey then formed what historians call the First Triumvirate, an alliance between Pompey, Crassus, and Julius Caesar, in 60 BC. Cicero, whose oratorical ability was highly prized, was asked to join the alliance but refused.

Famous for squelching Spartacus's slave rebellion, with a little help from Pompey, Crassus was the second wealthiest man in Rome. (Pompey was the wealthiest after he returned from his eastern conquests.) Crassus had amassed his vast fortune partly by purchasing the estates of Sulla's victims at a discount and partly by buying other houses at an even greater discount during the periodic fires that plagued the wooden city. Whenever a fire erupted, Crassus's slaves negotiated with the neighbors of the fire victims. As the fire spread closer to their homes, the desperate neighbors sold their homes for next to nothing. Once Crassus's agents had purchased the houses for him, his specially trained fire brigades, standing nearby, would then begin to extinguish the fires. Public fire departments did not yet exist.

Though a member of one of the oldest aristocratic families in Rome, Julius Caesar established himself as a champion of the masses. (Nearly proscribed by Sulla as a young man, Caesar was the nephew of Marius by marriage and had subsequently married the daughter of one of Marius's allies.) Tall, fair, thin, and epileptic, Caesar had a broad face and lively, dark brown eyes. Though he was bald, he tried to cover it up by combing his thin strands of hair forward (a gambit that has never worked in any era). He valued luxury and developed a reputation as a womanizer, even having affairs with the wives of his fellow triumvirs. His enemies also accused him of having had an affair with King Nicodemes of Bithynia in order to secure his patronage. One political opponent called Caesar "the Queen of Bithynia . . . who once wanted to sleep with a monarch, but now wants to be one." Once, when Caesar was listing his obligations to Nicodemes before the Senate, Cicero interrupted, saying, "Enough of that, if you please! We all know what he gave you, and what you gave him in return." Caesar first became associated with Crassus in 65 BC, when Caesar borrowed large sums of money from him, money that Caesar then used to curry favor with the masses by funding lavish gladiatorial games.

The triumvirate secured Caesar's election as consul in 59 BC. When Caesar's colleague proved uncooperative, Caesar threatened him so fiercely he stayed home the rest of the year, leaving Caesar, in effect, as sole consul. Caesar also once had Cato the Younger forcibly removed from the Senate House to stop a filibuster. Caesar also repaid his fellow triumvirs for their support by securing legislation that remitted taxes to Crassus's equestrian supporters and granted land to Pompey's veterans. Caesar then requested and received the proconsulship of Cisalpine Gaul (northern Italy), Transalpine Gaul (southern France), and Illyria, while Crassus secured command of the army in the East, and Pompey received an absentee command in Spain that allowed him to remain in Rome.

In 53 BC Crassus was killed while attempting to conquer Parthia, a new Persian Empire east of the Euphrates River. Crassus had foolishly advanced into open country east of the Euphrates, where the Parthians, under Suren, surrounded the Romans and pummeled them with arrows supplied steadily by a train of one thousand camels. Unwilling to risk a night attack on the enemy, Crassus then abandoned four thousand wounded soldiers, fleeing to Carrhae under cover of night. Lacking adequate supplies, Crassus was forced to negotiate. The Parthians killed him treacherously, under a flag of truce. Ten thousand of his soldiers were taken prisoner. Fortunately for the Roman position in Syria, Orodes, the king of Parthia, then had Suren killed as a potential rival.

Caesar's Conquests

Caesar, who had wept as a young man because he had accomplished nothing at the same age at which Alexander the Great had conquered a vast empire, now spent nine years subduing the rest of Gaul (what is now France, Belgium, southern Holland, Germany west of the Rhine, and most of Switzerland). One of the greatest generals in history, Caesar always made a careful reconnaissance, and in a hard-fought battle always sent all of the horses away, including his own, so that his soldiers would know that without victory there was no chance of escape. He inlaid his soldiers' weapons with silver and gold, which gave them such pride in their arms that they were especially careful not to be disarmed in battle. Ordinarily lax, he insisted on strict discipline whenever the enemy was in the vicinity. He made a point of becoming acquainted with all of his centurions, of heeding their advice, and of rewarding loyal service. Caesar himself was so loyal to his troops that he once disguised himself as a Gaul in order to reach them when the enemy had surrounded them. Caesar's intense loyalty to his soldiers, whom he called "comrades," was matched only by their fidelity to him. Caesar's legions never mutinied throughout the Gallic War, a record of loyalty unmatched by any other army of the period.

In 57 BC Caesar annihilated the Helvetii near Bibracte, routed the Germanic Ariovistus in Alsace, and destroyed the Nervii on the Sabis River. In 55 BC, and again the following year, Caesar's attempts to invade what is now Great Britain, also inhabited by Celtic tribes, were thwarted by storms, which prevented him from receiving vital supplies and cavalry units. Caesar then put down several revolts among the Gallic tribes in France.

Caesar's greatest victory in the Gallic War came at Alesia (near modern Dijon) in 52 BC, a victory that broke the back of Gallic resistance. While besieging an impregnable Gallic town situated atop a hill and manned by eighty thousand Gauls, Caesar was himself surrounded by an even larger force. He instructed his soldiers to construct a double ring of siege works, the inner ring extending ten miles. Caesar himself occupied a good observation post, from which he could follow the action in each part of the battlefield and dispatch reinforcements wherever they were needed. The brilliantly conceived siege works allowed Caesar to maintain the siege of Alesia while warding off the large Celtic army that surrounded his own. The shortage of food in Alesia became so severe that one Gallic leader even seriously suggested eating those too young and too old to fight. When the Gauls on each side of the Romans launched a simultaneous night attack, many of them fell into camouflaged pits and impaled themselves on sharpened stakes. Nevertheless, by attacking the Romans at their weakest point, the Gauls nearly succeeded. Only Caesar's timely dispatch of reinforcements prevented them from breaching the Roman line. Caesar then made a sortie and routed the larger force, sending the survivors scrambling to their individual homes and forcing the surrender of the smaller force in Alesia. Plutarch estimated that Caesar's legions killed as many as one million people and enslaved another million during the course of the Gallic War.

In conquering Gaul, Caesar acquired a fortune in plunder, which he used to bribe Roman officials and to curry favor with the Roman people. In preparation for another campaign for the consulship, Caesar kept his name before the Roman public by publishing his *Commentaries on the Gallic War*, a memoir in which Caesar wrote of himself in the third person to present the illusion of objectivity. Caesar's *Commentaries*, one of our most important sources concerning the Gallic and Germanic tribes, was so skillfully written it is still used as a Latin primer. Its simple but nonrepetitive prose is as free of colloquialisms as it is of pedantry. Even Cicero, whose style was far more florid, admired Caesar's lucid, graceful writing, remarking of his sentences, "They are like nude figures, upright and beautiful, stripped of all ornament and style as if they had removed a garment." Cicero also considered Caesar a great orator, calling his rhetorical style "elegant as well as clear, even grand and in a sense noble."

Civil War

But Pompey and the Senate had grown jealous of Caesar's victories. The death of Julia, Caesar's daughter and Pompey's beloved wife, in 54 BC, combined with the death of their common ally Crassus the following year, had removed powerful motives for cooperation between the former triumvirs.

In 49 BC two enemies of Caesar were elected consul with Pompey's tacit consent. The Senate then ordered Caesar to disband his army and return to

Rome. A tribune vetoed the order but was physically removed from the Senate chamber, a violation of the sanctity of tribunes. When Caesar balked at the Senate's order, the Senate retreated, voting overwhelmingly (370-22) in favor of a compromise proposal that both Caesar and Pompey disband their armies, but the proposal was vetoed by a different tribune. In fact, Caesar even proposed surrendering all but two legions and relinquishing command of Cisalpine Gaul and Illyria. Pompey was willing to accept this compromise, but the consuls refused.

Fearing for his life should he disband his army, his sole protection against his enemies, Caesar crossed the Rubicon River with his army. He understood that this act was tantamount to a declaration of war against the Senate (hence the phrase "crossing the Rubicon" to signify the performance of an act that cannot be reversed). Indeed, Caesar hesitated at the river but then declared, "Let the die be cast!" and plunged the republic into another civil war.

Pompey and most of the Senate fled eastward. After defeating the large armies of Pompey's legates in Spain, Caesar crossed the Adriatic Sea to face Pompey himself. Caesar besieged Pompey's army at Dyrrachium (in Epirus), but Pompey's force broke through and slaughtered one thousand of Caesar's men. Caesar thought Pompey could have won the civil war had he pursued and annihilated Caesar's army after the battle. But, fearing an ambush, Pompey allowed Caesar to retreat eastward.

The Battle of Pharsalus

Caesar was able to reorganize his troops, restore their morale, and make a decisive stand at Pharsalus in Thessaly in 48 BC. According to Caesar's account, Pompey's overconfident officers "were already starting to squabble openly among themselves about rewards and priesthoods and were assigning the consulships for years to come, while some were claiming the houses and property of people in Caesar's camp. . . . They were thinking not of how to win but of how to exploit the victory."

If so, Pompey's officers greatly underestimated Caesar's legions. Though outnumbered more than two to one (forty-seven thousand to twenty-two thousand), Caesar's troops were more experienced and more loyal than Pompey's. Many offered to serve without pay; none deserted, though Caesar allowed any centurion who wished to join Pompey to do so. When deprived of food and supplies at one point, Caesar's stalwarts had eaten grass, prompting Pompey to exclaim, "I am fighting wild beasts!"

When Pompey attacked with his left wing, composed of cavalry and archers, Caesar dispatched fresh, carefully selected reinforcements to face them. They managed to encircle and massacre Pompey's left wing, thereby turning his flank and initiating a rout of his whole army. Caesar had instructed his infantrymen to thrust their lances at the faces of Pompey's cavalrymen rather than hurling them. As Caesar expected, the handsome, inexperienced young cavalrymen shrank from facial disfigurement. Six thousand of Pompey's troops were killed in the battle; the rest surrendered. Generally magnanimous, Caesar did not allow the slaughter of any soldier who surrendered, shouting to his army, "Spare your fellow Romans!" Surveying the Optimate dead, Caesar cried, "They would have it thus!"

Pompey fled to Egypt. Wishing to please Caesar, Egyptian officials used treachery to assassinate him and sent his head to Caesar. But Caesar wept at the sight and ordered the murderers put to death. He then dallied with Cleopatra VII, the Macedonian queen of Egypt, who, on their first meeting, had herself smuggled to him in a carpet, from which she emerged nude.

Caesar did not defeat the last of Pompey's scattered forces until 45 BC. When defeat was certain for his republican army in North Africa, Cato the Younger fell on his sword at Utica. After putting down a revolt in Pontus, Caesar celebrated a triumph. One of the decorated wagons in the triumphal procession bore a banner that declared, "I came, I saw, I conquered."

Caesar's Assassination

From 48 BC to 44 BC Julius Caesar was first the unofficial, and then official, dictator of Rome. Caesar's arrogance and vanity offended some aristocrats. With the consent of a fearful Senate, he placed statues of himself among those of the ancient kings. He wore semiregal dress, sat on a golden throne in the Senate House, and allowed the Senate to rename the month of Quintilis July, after himself. One statue depicted him with a globe beneath his feet. When the senators came to him bringing honors, he remained seated, like a patron receiving clients. Finally, one of Caesar's underlings Mark Antony (Marcus Antonius) attempted to crown Caesar at a festival. Although Caesar refused the crown three times, the incident further alarmed some senators, who perceived Caesar as testing the waters for a return to monarchy.

Although the Senate agreed to extend Caesar's dictatorship from the initial ten years to life in February 44 BC, some senators began plotting his assassination. One month later, a group of conspirators, led by Marcus Junius Brutus and his brother-in-law Gaius Cassius Longinus, stabbed Caesar to death with daggers—ironically, in Pompey's Theater, where Caesar had called a meeting of the Senate. The senators attacked Caesar with such frenzy that they wounded each other and drenched themselves with his blood. Brutus supposedly stabbed him in the groin. Caesar fell dead at the foot of Pompey's statue, his body riddled with wounds.

Caesar had often refused a bodyguard, saying it was better to die than to live in constant fear of death. Clutched in Caesar's dying hand was a detailed warning of the assassination plot given him by an acquaintance of Brutus and his friends. Caesar had attempted to read the note several times but had been interrupted by supplicants each time. He was fifty-five years old and was planning a campaign against the Parthians when he died.

Cassius was a praetor who had distinguished himself by repelling a Parthian invasion of Syria in 51 BC. Brutus was a descendant of the legendary Lucius Brutus, who had expelled King Tarquin from Rome (and who had supposedly killed his own sons for conspiring to restore Tarquin). Brutus idolized his uncle, the republican martyr Cato the Younger, even marrying his daughter Porcia. Though Brutus had taken Pompey's side in the civil war, despite the fact that Pompey had executed his father, because he considered Pompey more likely to restore the republic, the victorious Caesar had befriended Brutus. One rumor even claimed that Brutus was really Caesar's son, though this was probably untrue. (When Brutus was born, Caesar was barely fifteen. However, Caesar did have an affair with Brutus's mother, Servilia, when Brutus was twenty-two. This misunderstanding probably accounts for Seutonius's claim that Caesar's last words were, "And you, son?" Shakespeare later substituted the more plausible, "Et tu, Brute?")

It was said that Brutus, the Stoic republican, had acted because he hated dictatorship, the fiery Cassius because he hated the dictator. While Caesar's supporters had placed crowns on his statues to encourage the people to make him king, Brutus's fellow republicans had scrawled messages on his praetorial desk every day reminding him of his ancestral duty to oppose monarchy. Nothing so moved a Roman as an appeal to family tradition.

The Third Roman Civil War: Antony versus Octavian

The Assassins' Mistakes

The assassins of Julius Caesar made two mistakes. First, on the insistence of Brutus, they spared the life of Caesar's chief lieutenant Mark Antony. Although some Romans despised Antony for his excessive drinking (he once vomited at a senate meeting after partying the whole night) and womanizing, his soldiers loved him because he ate and slept alongside them. He had commanded Caesar's left wing with distinction at Pharsalus. Cicero complained regarding the assassination of Caesar, "That affair was handled with the courage of men and the policy of children. Anyone could see that an heir to the throne was left behind."

Second, the assassins allowed Caesar a public funeral, at which Antony read his will. The people were moved to tears on learning that Caesar had bequeathed to each Roman seventy-five drachmas and the use of one of his gardens. Driven to a frenzy by grief when Caesar's bloodstained body was carried through the Forum, the mob even tore to pieces a man named Cinna, mistaking him for an assassin of Caesar who bore the same name. The mob then attempted to burn the houses of Brutus and Cassius. The assassins were forced to flee Rome. Many believed that a comet, which shone for seven days, was Caesar's soul.

The Second Triumvirate

Caesar's chief supporters, Antony, Marcus Aemilius Lepidus, and Octavian, eventually settled their differences and formed the Second Triumvirate. Lepidus was the proconsul of Spain. Octavian, newly arrived from military training in Illyria, was Caesar's grandnephew and (as the will revealed) adopted son. Caesar had no legitimate son of his own, and his only daughter had died childless. With his usual shrewdness, Caesar had seen more promise in the eighteen-year-old Octavian than Antony did; Antony sneered that he was a "mere boy, owing everything to a name."

The triumvirs slaughtered all opponents, including three hundred senators and two thousand equites, confiscated their property, and redistributed it among their supporters. In fact, it has been estimated that one-fourth of all Italian land changed hands as a result of the Second Triumvirate's proscriptions and evictions. One of their victims was Cicero, who was executed in 43 BC. Antony ordered Cicero's head and hands nailed above the rostrum in the Forum, where Cicero had spoken out against him in fourteen speeches popularly called the *Philippics* after Demosthenes' famous speeches against Philip II of Macedon. According to Plutarch, horrified Romans saw in the putrefying remains "not so much the face of Cicero as the soul of Antony." Octavian acquiesced in the murder but later, as the emperor Augustus, called Cicero "a learned man and a lover of his country."

The Battle of Philippi

In 42 BC the two largest armies in Roman history faced each other. The army of the Second Triumvirate defeated the republican army of Brutus and Cassius in two battles at Philippi in Macedon. In the first battle Brutus routed Antony's force, while Octavian's army (Octavian himself was too ill to be present) routed Cassius's force. Unaware of Brutus's success and thinking that all was lost, Cassius committed suicide. He fell on the same sword with which he had stabbed Caesar. Brutus called Cassius "the last of the Romans." In this first battle the triumvirate lost twice as many troops as their opponents (sixteen thousand to eight thousand).

But in the second battle Cassius's soldiers, demoralized by the death of their fiery leader, were easily routed, thereby bringing defeat on Brutus's troops as well. When one of Brutus's aides implored him not to take his own life, pleading tearfully, "We must escape," the Stoic replied, "Yes, we must escape, but this time with our hands, not our feet." He ordered one of his servants to hold his sword while he plunged himself into it. His wife Porcia suffocated herself.

Brutus was shrewd enough to predict that Octavian and Antony would soon be fighting each other. The Senate declared Julius Caesar a god, thereby granting added prestige to his adopted son Octavian, who had already curried favor with the Roman people by supervising the distribution of the funds Caesar had willed them.

Civil War

The triumvirs ruled the Roman Empire as virtual dictators. In 40 BC they formally divided the empire between them. Octavian received the western empire, except for North Africa, which went to Lepidus, and Mark Antony received the eastern empire. At the same time Antony married Octavian's sister Octavia to cement the alliance between them. Octavian evicted Lepidus from the triumvirate in 36 BC, after Lepidus's attempt to seize Sicily from Octavian failed when most of his troops deserted to Octavian.

At first glance, it appeared that Antony held the upper hand against Octavian, since he controlled Egypt, Rome's most important province. But Octavian's control of Italy allowed him to impress the most important men of Rome with his administrative talents.

Antony then sealed his own fate by falling in love with Cleopatra. Though not particularly beautiful, Cleopatra was extremely intelligent, knowledgeable (having mastered numerous languages), and charming. The couple entertained themselves by going about Alexandria dressed as slaves and ridiculing people. (Since most citizens never imagined that this pair could be the rulers of Egypt, Antony was beaten several times.) The couple held lavish parties at which Cleopatra dressed as Isis, Antony as Bacchus.

When Antony dispatched formal letters of divorce to Octavia, who was a kind and virtuous woman beloved by the Roman people, Octavian used the act as a pretext for waging war against Antony. He seized Antony's will from the Vestal Virgins and publicly revealed its contents. In the will

Antony made his sons by Cleopatra his heirs, even declaring that they would inherit Parthia, which had not been conquered. Romans were outraged at the eventual prospect of being ruled by men who were only half Roman. The people also discovered that Antony's will ceded control of three Roman territories to Cleopatra. Finally, the will declared that if Antony died in Rome, his body must be sent back to Cleopatra in Alexandria. Octavian cleverly used Roman xenophobia to attract broad support, claiming that Antony would transfer the capital of the empire to Alexandria. For propaganda purposes, Octavian declared war on Cleopatra, not Antony, claiming that Antony was acting under some sort of spell cast by this wicked, eastern woman. Nevertheless, Octavian's brazen act of seizing a will from the Vestal Virgins antagonized some Romans; one-third of the senators and both consuls bet their lives on Antony.

The Battle of Actium
In 31 BC Octavian's navy, under the leadership of Marcus Vipsanius Agrippa—a brilliant admiral of low birth who had built and trained a fleet from scratch—destroyed or captured three-quarters of Antony's fleet at Actium in Greece. Although Octavian possessed only four hundred ships to Antony's five hundred, Octavian's ships were more maneuverable and manned by better rowers. At a crucial point in the battle, Antony's center and left, perhaps alarmed by an enemy maneuver, began to retreat, forcing Antony to signal Cleopatra to escape with the war chest. Antony joined her squadron with forty ships of his own, leaving the remainder of his fleet to be destroyed or captured.

When Agrippa captured Antony's bases in the Peloponnesus, thereby severing the supply line to Antony's army in Greece, his 130,000 malaria-ridden soldiers, abandoned by their commander, surrendered. Octavian then cornered Antony in Egypt. When Antony heard a false rumor that Cleopatra had committed suicide, the fifty-three-year-old soldier stabbed himself through the stomach.

The thirty-nine-year-old Cleopatra, the last of the Ptolemaic rulers of Egypt, committed suicide after Octavian captured her and the city of Alexandria in 30 BC. According to Plutarch, Cleopatra chose to die from the bite of an asp, because the numerous experiments she had conducted on condemned prisoners convinced her that it was the least painful form of death. There may be some truth to this story, but it is also true that the asp was the representative of the Egyptian sun god, and its effigy encircled the crown of Egypt to protect the royal line. Cleopatra may have chosen the asp to represent the sun god rescuing his daughter Isis from humiliation. In any case, the asp was smuggled to her under a basket of figs.

Octavian approved the completion of the mausoleum Antony and Cleopatra had begun and allowed their burial together in the same tomb. Octavia, ever virtuous, took it upon herself to raise the three children produced by her philandering husband and Cleopatra, as well as the children from Antony's previous marriage. But Octavian killed Caesarion, Cleopatra's young son by Julius Caesar, whose potential claim as Caesar's heir made him a dangerous rival.

Octavian then annexed Egypt and placed it under his personal control, the first such arrangement in Roman history. Mopping up operations against Antony's allies continued until 27 BC. Octavian returned to Rome with so much gold that interest rates immediately plunged from 12 to 4 percent.

After a full century of chaos and violence, in which the Roman republic had proved incapable of maintaining any semblance of order or peace, Rome was now thoroughly prepared for the rule of an emperor.

Problems with the Historians' Accounts

The Founding Fathers learned the story of the decline and fall of the Roman republic from Plutarch's lives of Marius, Sulla, Crassus, Pompey, Caesar, and Cicero, from Sallust's *The Jugurthan War* and *The Conspiracy of Catiline*, and from the letters, speeches, and other writings of Cicero. These aristocratic sources romanticized the early Roman republic because it was a system that granted the predominant power to the aristocratic class. (Even Sallust, despite his association with Julius Caesar and the Populares, idealized the early republic and depicted the late republic as a society in moral decline. In fact, Sallust even married Cicero's ex-wife and praised the conservative republican in his account of Catiline's conspiracy.) Hence, these historians viewed the decline and fall of the republic as an enormous tragedy. They tended to portray the republicans Cicero, Cato the Younger, Brutus, and Cassius in a heroic light, while presenting the destroyers of the republic, especially Caesar and Catiline, in a highly negative light. Sallust even accused Catiline of killing his own son to placate a woman he loved who would not marry him because she was afraid of the son.

Yet the truth was far more complicated. The republic was hardly a utopia for the impoverished majority of Romans. If they had not considered themselves oppressed by the aristocrats, they would not have rallied to the banner of Caesar and the other demagogues.

Furthermore, as dictator, Caesar ruled magnanimously and accomplished much for Rome. Indeed, he was more magnanimous than was wise, even appointing some of his former opponents to high offices. Caesar also put down the street gangs that had paralyzed the city. He reduced Rome's debt through more efficient administration. He rebuilt much of the city. Caesar reduced the number of the unemployed from 320,000 to 150,000 through a public works program and through the decree that at least one-third of the laborers in the latifundia must be free men. He established both Italian and provincial colonies for his veterans and for eighty thousand poor Romans, the fulfillment of the Gracchi's dream. Caesar also canceled all interest on debts incurred during the recent civil war, an inflationary period. He planned a public library. As pontifex maximus (chief priest), he introduced the "Julian calendar" of 365¼ days, the calendar employed in Europe until Pope Gregory XIII modified it (removing one leap day every two centuries) in 1582. Caesar also restored order in the provinces. He removed many incompetent and corrupt proconsuls from office and ejected them from the Senate. In a momentous move Caesar extended Roman citizenship to numerous non-Italians for the first time, especially to the people of Cisalpine Gaul and to the chieftains of Transalpine Gaul. He even admitted some Gauls into the Senate, thereby accelerating the assimilation of Gaul. Rome was beginning to conceive of the empire more as a community and less as a field of exploitation.

In addition, the Roman republican heroes were hardly candidates for sainthood. Cato was a stubborn aristocrat whose overreaching on behalf of the Optimates had as much to do with Caesar's crossing of the Rubicon as the latter's ambition. Cicero was extremely vain and, at least in his early career, frequently behaved in a cowardly fashion, as when Pompey's positioning of his soldiers intimidated him into refusing to deliver a speech he had written in defense of a legal client. Brutus was a greedy man who had once ordered a representative to forcibly collect a 48 percent loan from the people of Salamis in Cyprus, though the maximum interest rate allowed in the province was 12 percent. Cassius was as much influenced by his personal hatred of Caesar as by republican sentiment.

The Lesson

Nevertheless, the founders learned from Plutarch, Sallust, and Cicero that if republics wished to survive, they must exercise eternal vigilance against cunning, ambitious individuals who would seek to advance their own power at the expense of the republic. Conversely, republics must also encourage the patriotic spirit of self-sacrifice. Therefore, like the ancient historians, the founders admired Cato the Younger, Cicero, Brutus, and Cassius and despised Catiline and Caesar.

A great fan of Joseph Addison's *Cato*, an enormously popular play based closely on Plutarch's lives of Cato and Caesar, George Washington often drew upon the play. In 1775 he prevented the resignation of General John Thomas, who was angered by an unjust demotion, by paraphrasing Cato's line: "Surely every post ought to be deemed honorable in which a man can serve his country." Despite congressional resolutions in 1774 and 1778 prohibiting all public officials from attending plays, Washington ordered *Cato* performed at Valley Forge. He hoped to improve the soldiers' morale by inspiring them with the example of Cato's men, who had demonstrated extreme selflessness in the struggle for liberty. During these difficult times, Washington often repeated another line from *Cato*: "'Tis not in mortals to command success." Perhaps it was Cato's willingness to sacrifice his property on behalf of the republic that led Washington to reproach his overseer for placating British troops with grain. Washington declared that the overseer should allow Mount Vernon to be leveled before giving any aid to the enemy.

In 1783 Washington turned to *Cato* when his officers, furious over Congress' perpetual inability to pay them, mutinied at Newburgh, New York. The rebels planned to threaten the states with a coup d'état unless they yielded more power to Congress. Although Washington considered the strengthening of the weak Congress vital to national survival, he perceived even the threat of a military coup as dangerous and dishonorable. In his speech to the officers he used the same three tactics Cato employed to face down his mutineers in Act III, Scene 5 of Addison's play. First, Washington rebuked the anonymous author of a circular letter that urged mutiny, just as Cato had lambasted his rebels. Second, like Cato, Washington pleaded with his officers not to tarnish the republican honor they had won by turning against the republic. Third, like Cato, Washington appealed to the sympathy and respect his past service had earned him. Washington even paraphrased lines from *Cato* in his own speech.

Other founders utilized Addison's *Cato*. The two most famous lines of the American Revolution, Patrick Henry's "Give me liberty or give me death" and Nathan Hale's "I regret that I have but one life to give for my country" were paraphrases of lines from the play. Noah Webster included a scene from the play in his enormously popular reader for schoolchildren, the first in North America.

Benjamin Franklin admired Cato. As early as 1728 Franklin wrote,

He that is acquainted with Cato, as I am, cannot help thinking as I do now, and will acknowledge that he deserves the Name [of 'great man'] without being honour'd by it. Cato is a Man whom Fortune has plac'd in the most obscure Part of the Country. His circumstances are such as only put him above Necessity, without affording him any Superfluities. Yet, who is greater than Cato? . . . In fine, his Consummate Virtue makes him justly deserve to be esteem'd the Glory of his Country.

In 1741 Franklin gave this advice on acquiring virtue: "Think Cato sees thee"—an interesting substitute for "Think God sees thee."

Benjamin Rush idolized Cato as well. In 1776, while in Congress, Rush wrote to his wife,

I hope, my dear, we shall see many happy days in Philadelphia together, notwithstanding we have precluded ourselves from the society of a few tory families. 'I should have blushed,' says Cato, 'if Cato's house had stood secure and flourished in a civil war.' I should have blushed much more to have heard it said that I shook hands or drank Madeira with men who would have sacrificed their country to ambition or avarice.

A month later, having spoken in Congress for the first time, Rush identified the assembly as another Roman Senate, explaining, "I felt that I was not thundering like Cato in the Utica of our [local] committee of inspection. The audience [in Congress] is truly respectable." Similarly, in the same year, Thomas Paine responded to William Smith's rebuttal of *Common Sense* by questioning Smith's right to use "Cato" as a pseudonym: "What pretensions the writer . . . can have to the signature, the public will best determine; while, on my part, I prophetically content myself with contemplating the similarity of their exits."

While Washington derived a sense of identity and purpose from his emulation of Cato, John Adams derived the same benefits from his lifelong identification with Cicero. In the autumn of 1758 Adams gloried in the fact that law, his chosen profession, was "a Field in which Demosthenes, Cicero, and others of immortal Fame have exulted before me!" That winter he confessed to his diary the pleasure he derived from reading Cicero's orations aloud: "The Sweetness and Grandeur of his sounds, and the Harmony of his Numbers give Pleasure enough to reward the Reading if one understood none of his meaning. Besides, I find it a noble Exercise. It exercises my Lungs, raises my Spirits, opens my Porrs, quickens the Circulation, and so contributes to

[my] Health." Indeed, after a family quarrel a few days later, Adams "quitted the Room, and took up Tully to compose myself." In 1774 Adams urged an aspiring politician to adopt Cicero as his model. He wrote regarding Cicero's proconsulship of Lilybaeum in Sicily: "He did not receive this office as Persons do now a days, as a Gift, or a Farm, but as a public Trust, and considered it as a Theatre, in which the Eyes of the World were upon him." Adams added that when Rome was short of grain, Cicero managed to feed the city without treating his own province unfairly.

When Adams, one of the greatest orators of his day, rose before the Continental Congress on July 1, 1776, to rebut John Dickinson's contention that American independence would be premature, the New Englander thought of Cicero. He recorded in his diary, "I began by saying that this was the first time of my Life that I had ever wished for the Talents and Eloquence of the ancient Orators of Greece and Rome, for I was very sure that none of them had ever had before him a question of more importance to his Country and to the World."

Adams's admiration for Cicero outlived the American Revolution. He spent the summer of 1796, several months before assuming the presidency, reading the Roman statesman's essays. In 1803 Adams quoted Cicero regarding the true public servant: "Such a man will devote himself entirely to the republic, nor will he covet power or riches. . . . He will adhere closely to justice and equity, that, provided he can preserve these virtues, although he may give offence and create enemies by them, he will set death itself at defiance, rather than abandon his principles." No one followed this ethic better than Adams. In the 1760s he had refused the lucrative and prestigious position of admiralty court judge because he considered the juryless British courts unconstitutional. In 1770 he had sacrificed his popularity to defend the British soldiers accused of murder in the "Boston Massacre." As president, in 1799–1800 he had made peace with Napoleonic France, leaving Thomas Jefferson the glory of the Louisiana Purchase three years later, at the expense of his own reelection. While no other founder yearned so much for popularity, none so continually sacrificed it to a strict code of ethics. It is not fanciful to suppose that, when making such painful decisions, Adams found consolation in contemplating the Roman statesman's sacrifices and the eternal glory they had earned him.

Adams continued to express admiration for Cicero in the correspondence of his twilight years. In 1805 Adams wrote,

> The period in the history of the world the best understood is that of Rome from the time of Marius to the death of Cicero, and this distinction is entirely

owing to Cicero's letters and orations. There we see the true character of the times and the passions of all the actors on the stage. Cicero, Cato, and Brutus were the only three in whom I can discern any real patriotism. . . . Cicero had the most capacity and the most constant, as well as the wisest and most persevering attachment to the republic.

In 1809 Adams poured out his heart in another letter:

Panegyrical romances will never be written, nor flattering orations spoken, to transmit me to posterity in brilliant colors. No, nor in true colors. All but the last I loathe. Yet, I will not die wholly unlamented. Cicero was libeled, slandered, insulted by all parties—by Caesar's party, Catiline's crew, Clodius's myrmidions, aye, and by Pompey and the Senate too. He was persecuted and tormented by turns by all parties and all factions, and that for his most virtuous and glorious actions. In his anguish at times and in the consciousness of his own merit and integrity, he was driven to those assertions of his own actions which have been denominated vanity. Instead of reproaching him with vanity, I think them the most infallible demonstration of his innocence and purity. He declares that all honors are indifferent to him because he knows that it is not in the power of his country to reward him in any proportion to his services.

Pushed and injured and provoked as I am, I blush not to imitate the Roman.

Adams was all too successful in his lifelong attempt to emulate Cicero. Adams's integrity, which found its greatest expression in his unwillingness to endorse party favoritism, led to unpopularity in both parties, and his responses to critics were often marked by the same petulance and vanity as the Roman's. The only difference between Cicero and Adams was that Cicero, uninfluenced by Christian notions of humility, had found nothing shameful in vanity. Not only would it have never occurred to Cicero to deny the charge of vanity; it would never have occurred to his contemporaries to make it.

Other founders also idolized Cicero. James Wilson cited the Roman statesman more often than any other author in his 1790 lectures to law students at the College of Philadelphia (now the University of Pennsylvania). Wilson exulted, "The jurisprudence of Rome was adorned and enriched by the exquisite genius of Cicero, which, like the touch of Midas, converts every object to gold." He called Cicero's *On Duties* "a work which does honour to human understanding and the human heart." Similarly, John Marshall, who patterned his portrayal of George Washington, in his famous five-volume biography of the first president, on Cicero, told his grandsons that *On Duties* was "among the most valuable treatises in the Latin language, a salutary discourse on the duties and qualities proper to a republican gentleman." Benjamin Rush and Thomas Paine quoted Cicero repeatedly concerning natural law. Benjamin Franklin cited Cicero often on the importance of hard work and virtue.

The founders also revered Caesar's assassins Brutus and Cassius. During the Stamp Act crisis in 1765 John Adams declared optimistically,

> Let us take it for granted that the same great spirit which once gave Caesar so warm a reception . . . [and] which first seated the great grandfather of his present most gracious Majesty on the throne of Britain is still alive and active and warm in England; and that the same spirit in America, instead of provoking the inhabitants of that country, will endear us to them forever and secure their good will.

In 1767 he quoted Shakespeare: "Cassius from Bondage shall deliver Cassius." In 1790 James Wilson quoted Cicero in praise of Brutus: "Even those against whom he made decisions he sent away unruffled and placated." Benjamin Rush liked to quote Brutus: "I early devoted myself to my country, and I have ever since lived a life of liberty and glory."

The flip side of the founders' reverence for Cato, Cicero, Brutus, and Cassius was their distaste for Sulla, Catiline, Mark Antony, and Julius Caesar, whose corruption of the Roman republic had resulted in the rise of the emperors. In 1777 John Adams compared British general William Howe's peace proposals with Sulla's favorite tactic of bribing his rivals' troops. In his *Vindication of the Conduct of the House of Representatives* (1762) James Otis, the first leader of the Boston patriots, quoted Cicero's rebuke of Catiline in denunciation of the loyalist Martin Howard for advancing the doctrine of virtual representation: "Do you dare to show yourself in the light?" In 1766 John Dickinson insisted that opposition to oppression was not equivalent to disloyalty to the king. Dickinson wrote, "Should he complain, would it not be the complaint of Catiline, that the senator he attempted to assassinate was so disrespectful to him, he would not receive the sword in his body?" In 1779 Christopher Gadsden, the patriot leader from South Carolina, claimed, "Catiline's Gang was not more atrocious than such as are daily deluded over to the Enemy from our back [western] parts." In 1806, as Thomas Jefferson's suspicion of Aaron Burr's alleged conspiracy progressed, Jefferson compared Burr with Catiline. In addition, both Jefferson and John Adams accused the Hamiltonian Federalists of using public grief over George Washington's death (in 1799) for political purposes, as Mark Antony had used Julius Caesar's demise, though Jefferson believed that the publication of Washington's papers would prevent "the high priests of federalism" from using them to support their own views as Mark Antony had utilized Caesar's secret papers. In 1804 Adams copied this statement of Lord Bolingbroke: "The citizens of Rome placed the images of their ancestors in the vestibules in their houses; so that . . . these venerable bustoes met their eyes and recalled the glorious actions of the dead." Adams retorted,

> The images of the Gracchi were made as well as those of Scipio, and the images of Caesar, Antony, and Augustus as well as those of Cicero, Pompey, Brutus, and Cassius. Statues, paintings, panegyrics, in short all the fine arts, even music and dancing, promote virtue while virtue is in fashion. After that they produce luxury, effeminacy, corruption, prostitution, and every species of abandoned depravity.

The founders' greatest villain was Julius Caesar. In 1764 James Otis called Caesar "the destroyer of the Roman glory and grandeur, at a time when but for him and his adherents both might have been rendered immortal." In a famous part of Patrick Henry's Stamp Act Speech of 1765, Henry even compared George III with Caesar, declaring, "Caesar had his Brutus, Charles the First his Cromwell, and George III [cries of 'Treason!'] may profit by their example." In 1771 John Adams compared Massachusetts' new royal governor, the loyalist Thomas Hutchinson, with Caesar: "Caesar, by destroying the Roman Republic, made himself a perpetual Dictator; Hutchinson, by countenancing and supporting a System of Corruption and Tyranny, has made himself Governor." Christopher Gadsden and Josiah Quincy summed up patriot sentiment when both claimed that Great Britain was to America "what Caesar was to Rome," a corrupting influence. In 1779, when opposing Congress' inflationary measures, Rush wrote, "None of you can be unacquainted with the depravity of morals and manners that preceded the overthrow of the Commonwealth of Rome. The effects of universal vice are the same whether produced by plentiful emissions of money or by the artful designs of a Marius or Sylla. Are we sure we have no Caesars nor Cromwells in this country?"

Both John Adams and Thomas Jefferson compared Alexander Hamilton with Caesar. Adams wrote, "When Burr shot Hamilton, it was not Brutus killing Caesar in the Senate-House, but it was killing him before he passed the Rubicon." Adams compared Caesar's and Augustus's exploitation of the First and Second Triumvirates with Hamilton's tactics, noting that "their intrigues and cabals have analogy enough with Hamilton's schemes to get rid of Washington, Adams, Jay, and Jefferson and monopolize all power to himself." In 1811 Jefferson told the story that at a party Jefferson had hosted while secretary of state in 1791, Hamilton had inquired into the identity of the three men portrayed in Jefferson's wall paintings. When Jefferson replied that they were "the three greatest men the world had ever produced," Isaac Newton, Francis Bacon, and John Locke, there had been a pause. Hamilton had then declared that "the greatest man that ever lived was Julius Caesar." Jefferson considered the story highly significant: while Jefferson, a true republican, modeled himself after men of learning, Hamilton, a secret monarchist, modeled himself after a military figure who had done more than anyone else to corrupt and overturn the illustrious Roman republic. The evidence indicates, however, that either Jefferson misunderstood Hamilton, or Hamilton was playing a joke on the humorless Virginian. All of Hamilton's references to Caesar in his correspondence were negative, with the sole exception of a neutral reference to his military skill.

Indeed, although Hamilton was well aware that detractors compared him with Caesar, he considered his opponents more deserving of the infamous name. As early as 1779, after remarking to his friend John Laurens that Henry Lee was "an officer of great capacity" but had "a little of the Julius Caesar or Cromwell in him," Hamilton declared in a postscript to the letter, "Apropos—Speaking of a Caesar & a Cromwell . . . the Cabal have reported that I declared in a public house in Philadelphia 'that it was high time for the people to rise, join General Washington, & turn Congress out of doors.' . . . But you who know my sentiments will know how to join me in despising these miserable detractors." In a 1792 letter to George Washington defending his plan for funding the national debt at face value, Hamilton declared, "It has aptly been observed that Cato was the Tory— Caesar the whig of his day. The former frequently resisted—the latter always flattered the follies of the people. Yet the former perished with the Republic, [while] the latter destroyed it. No popular Government was ever without its Catalines & its Caesars. These are its true enemies." In the next month Hamilton publicized the charge in the Philadelphia *Gazette of the United States*, calling the Democratic-Republicans "the Catalines and Caesars of the community (a description of men to be found in every republic) who, leading the dance to the tune of liberty without law, endeavor to intoxicate the people with delicious, but poisonous draughts, to render them the easier victims of their rapacious ambition."

Hamilton left no doubt regarding the particular Democratic-Republicans to whom he referred. In the same essay he concluded regarding Jefferson,

But there is always a first time, when characters studious of artful disguises are unveiled; when the vizor of stoicism is plucked from the brow of the Epicurean;

when the plain garb of Quaker simplicity is stripped from the concealed voluptuary; when Caesar coyly refusing the proffered diadem is seen to be Caesar rejecting the trappings, but tenaciously grasping the substance of imperial domination.

Three days earlier Hamilton had declared, "In a word, if we have an embryo-Caesar in the United States, 'tis [Aaron] Burr."

Most of the founders attributed the downfall of the Roman republic to ambitious individuals like Caesar. Only rarely did anyone attribute it to social institutions like slavery. One exception was George Mason. As early as 1765 Mason wrote regarding the Roman republic, "One of the first signs of the decay and perhaps the primary cause of the destruction of the most flourishing government that ever existed was the introduction of great number of slaves, an evil very pathetically described by Roman historians." On August 22, 1787, during the important debate over the importation of slaves at the Constitutional Convention, when Mason charged that slavery was an immoral and dangerous institution, Charles Pinckney replied that slavery was justified by the example of Greece and Rome. Siding with Mason, John Dickinson retorted, "Greece and Rome were made unhappy by their slaves."

Thomas Jefferson, who favored the emancipation and colonization of slaves in Africa, nevertheless disagreed with Mason's and Dickinson's implicit analogy between Roman and American slavery. Jefferson argued that Roman slavery was hardly analogous to American slavery since, whereas Africans were intellectually inferior to whites and, therefore, had never produced any great philosophers or poets, Roman slaves like the Stoic Epictetus and the comic playwright Terence had achieved prominence in spite of their lowly condition.

Needless to say, Jefferson's conclusion was dubious at best. While American slaves were often denied education by law, Epictetus, Terence, and numerous other Roman slaves were so well educated that they served as tutors to their masters' children. But, since the politically minded ancient historians whom the founders read and admired never attributed the fall of the Roman republic to slavery or to any other social institution, but focused their analyses on the threat posed by politically ambitious individuals instead, the founders largely did the same.

The founders' immersion in the history of the late Roman republic had a profound effect on their style of thought. They developed from the classics a suspicious cast of mind. They learned to fear conspiracies against liberty. Steeped in a literature whose perpetual theme was the steady encroachment of tyranny on liberty, the founders became virtually obsessed with spotting its approach, so that they might avoid the fate of their Roman heroes. In 1767 John Adams declared regarding the "spirit of liberty", "Principiis Obsta ['resist the beginnings' of tyranny] is her motto and maxim, knowing her enemies are secret and cunning, making the earliest advances slowly, silently, and softly." The following year his cousin Samuel used the Latin motto "Principiis Obsta" as a pseudonym for an essay warning against a British military dictatorship over America. John Dickinson echoed the sentiment, quoting Cicero: "Even though the ruler may not, at the time, be troublesome, it is a sad fact that he can be so, if he takes the fancy." Dickinson added that the smaller the illegitimate tax the greater the danger, since the more easily it would be accepted by the incautious, thereby establishing a precedent for greater encroachments. Dickinson concluded, "Nations, in general, are not apt to think until they feel. . . . Therefore, nations in general have lost their liberty."

So prevalent was the founders' fear of conspiracies against liberty, a fear derived largely from their lifelong immersion in classical political horror stories, that they could seriously equate one another—their recent partners in the struggle against British tyranny—with Caesar and Catiline. The presence of these irrational analogies in private letters and diaries suggests that they were fervent beliefs, not mere rhetorical devices. Rufus King noted that the Antifederalists seemed more afraid of the Federalists than of the Constitution itself, fearing that "some injury is plotted against them." The classics had taught the Antifederalists that tyrants generally proceeded by small degrees. Did not the Federalists seek to enslave the nation through the same insidious expansion of federal power? Likewise, the Federalists genuinely believed that their opponents were Caesars and Catilines, demagogues prepared to reduce the nation to anarchy in order to seize dictatorial power. Had not the Roman emperors secured their power in such a fashion? George Washington wrote concerning the Antifederalist opposition to the Constitution, "Whilst many ostensible reasons are assigned, the real ones are concealed behind the Curtains, because they are not of a nature to appear in open day." The Federalists perceived the marginal increase in federal power they proposed as an antidote to the absolute power that, ancient history taught, must follow anarchy. If federal power were insufficient to maintain law and order, disintegration must lead to interstate warfare, which must eventuate in the dictatorship of a Caesar or Catiline. The Federalists intended their booster shot to the federal arm of government as an inoculation against the full-fledged disease of dictatorship. Ancient history taught two diametrically opposed lessons regarding how tyrants acquired their power—sometimes through the gradual accretion of authority, but at other times through the fomentation of anarchy via the annihilation of legitimate government power. Federalists and Antifederalists each clung to their favorite classical lesson. The common denominator was the fear of conspiracy. The same conspiracy theories soon infected the Federalist and Democratic-Republican parties, as evidenced by the seriousness with which Jefferson and Hamilton compared each other with Julius Caesar.

The same visceral fear of conspiracies that instilled in the founders a passionate love of liberty and a proper recognition of its fragility also fueled the tendency to see a conspiracy behind every well-intentioned blunder, a conspirator in every opponent. There was a dark side to the sense of identity and purpose that the classical authors bequeathed the founders. It required fresh threats of tyranny for sustenance. Where such threats did not exist, they must be created.

CHAPTER EIGHT

The Roman Emperors and the Preciousness of Liberty

The Founding Fathers learned the story of the Roman emperors from Tacitus's *Annals of Rome* and Suetonius's *Lives of the Twelve Caesars*. From these historians' accounts of the worst emperors, Tiberius, Caligula, and Nero, they learned the preciousness of liberty. Tyranny was the worst fate, not merely because it deprived one of liberty but also because it deprived one of virtue.

Tiberius (AD 14–37)

Having accepted the title of Augustus (Consecrated One), a title previously reserved for the gods, Octavian ruled Rome for over forty years. When he died in AD 14, there was no question as to his successor. All but one of his male relatives had passed away, some rather mysteriously, and a reluctant Augustus had been forced to adopt his stepson Tiberius, the son of his third wife Livia Drusilla by a previous marriage, as his own son and successor. Indeed, Tacitus speculated that Livia had engaged in a long sequence of poisonings designed to secure the succession of her son. Among the heirs of Augustus who died unexpectedly were his nephew Marcellus (23 BC), his favorite general and son-in-law Marcus Agrippa (12 BC), and his grandsons Lucius (AD 2) and Gaius (AD 4). Tacitus even hinted that Livia poisoned Augustus himself, in order to prevent reconciliation between the emperor and Agrippa Postumus, his last remaining grandson, whom Augustus had exiled, a reconciliation that might have thwarted Tiberius's succession. If Livia did use poison to secure the throne for her son, it did her little good.

After Tiberius became emperor, complaining that his mother was trying to rule as coemperor, he nullified titles the Senate conferred on her, absented himself from her funeral, and vetoed her deification.

Fifty-five years old on assuming the throne, Tiberius had distinguished himself both as a general and as an administrator while serving in the Near East, Germany, and the Balkans. He began as a mild and capable ruler, much like Augustus. He appointed efficient governors for the provinces and balanced the budget. Whenever he received a New Years' gift, he made it a practice to reciprocate with a present four times its value—until his house was flooded with gifts, at which point he discontinued the practice.

But Tiberius was dour, melancholy, and insecure. Plagued by a skin disease that covered his face with sores, he became increasingly paranoid concerning plots against himself. In fact, Tiberius once declared that occupying the position of emperor was like "holding a wolf by the ears"—it was neither safe to hold it nor to let it go (a phrase Thomas Jefferson later employed regarding American slavery).

Tiberius's paranoia grew so great that he spent the last eleven years of his reign at Capraea (Capri), an island that had only one landing beach, the rest of the coast being sheer cliffs surrounded by deep water. One day a proud fisherman, hoping to win the emperor's favor, scaled a cliff in order to present Tiberius with the giant mullet he had caught that day. When the fisherman emerged up the cliff and strode toward Tiberius, the emperor panicked, and then, in anger, ordered his guards to rub the fisherman's face with the mullet, which skinned it raw. When the man shouted in agony, "Thank heaven I did not bring Caesar that huge crab I also caught!" Tiberius sent for the crab and had it applied in the same way.

While Tiberius was hiding from potential assassins (and molesting little boys, by one account) at Capraea, his administration languished under the cruel and arrogant direction of Lucius Aelius Sejanus, prefect of the Praetorian Guard (the palace guard). Sejanus concentrated the guardsmen, whom Augustus had wisely dispersed around various Italian towns, in a single base in Rome.

In 31, when Tiberius became suspicious of Sejanus (who was, indeed, plotting against the emperor), he ordered Macro, one of Sejanus's subordinates, to arrest him for treason. Sejanus was strangled to death in prison, his body was torn to pieces by a mob, and Macro assumed his post. Sejanus's family and supporters were put to death as well.

His paranoia now heightened by Sejanus's plot, Tiberius executed other citizens, including children. Since Roman tradition prohibited the strangling of virgins, executioners violated little girls before killing them. Informers were rewarded with one-quarter of the confiscated estates of the persons on whom they informed, and an informer's word was almost always believed. Many victims committed suicide rather than go through the charade of one of Tiberius's show trials. No one was allowed to mourn for the victims (an old lady was executed for grieving publicly for her son), and victims were denied decent burials, their corpses dragged down to the Tiber by hooks and tossed into the river. Two minor poets were executed for their attacks on Tiberius. One historian was executed for calling Brutus and Cassius "the last of the Romans," a reference Tiberius interpreted as an invitation to regicide, and his history was publicly burned.

Some Romans remarked that Tiberius's cruelty continued even after his death. On the day that Tiberius passed away, in 37, certain individuals were scheduled to be executed. Even after the news of Tiberius's death had arrived, none of his timid and terrified officials dared take the responsibility for revoking the orders of execution. Hence, the executions went forward. The people were so furious they attempted to seize the emperor's body and hurl it into the river, shouting, "Tiberius to the Tiber!" But the Praetorian Guard protected his body, which was cremated and given the proper honors.

Caligula (37–41)

Romans rejoiced when Tiberius's grandnephew and adopted son, Gaius, succeeded him. Gaius's biological father (Tiberius's nephew) Germanicus, a handsome, courageous, kind-hearted, and pious general, had been the most beloved man in Rome. It was Germanicus's soldiers who had given little Gaius his nickname Caligula (Little Boot), since, as a small boy traveling with his father and the army, Gaius had worn a miniature version of the soldier's uniform. (Unfortunately, the soldiers spoiled the child rotten, perhaps contributing to his egomania.) The Roman people were overjoyed at the prospect of being ruled by "a son of Germanicus."

At first, their confidence seemed justified. Not yet twenty-five when he took the throne, Caligula released Tiberius's political prisoners and gave financial aid to those whose houses had been damaged by fire.

But then, perhaps as the result of a severe fever six months into his reign, Caligula appears to have gone insane. He began to insist that Romans worship him as a god. (The Senate had formally recognized Caesar and Augustus as gods but only after their deaths.) Caligula was heard conversing loudly with Jupiter, the greatest of the Roman gods, and even ordering him about. He decapitated all of the statues of the gods and goddesses in Rome and replaced their heads with his own. He married one sister and had incestuous relations with all three at parties. At such gatherings he also examined every man's wife carefully and selected one for sex, returning afterward to comment in detail on her performance. He made top officials run for miles, dressed in their togas, alongside his chariot. For his amusement he pitted decrepit old men against equally decrepit wild animals, or people with disabilities against one another, at gladiatorial contests. When butcher meat for the wild animals proved too expensive, he fed them criminals. When a crowd at the races cheered for the team he opposed, he cried, "I wish all you Romans had only one neck!" Once, at a banquet, he suddenly erupted in peals of laughter. When the two consuls seated beside him asked politely if he would share the joke, he replied, "It occurred to me that I have only to give one nod and both your throats will be cut on the spot!" He gave his favorite horse a jeweled collar, a furnished house, slaves, a marble stable that outshone the nearby Senate building, and troops to maintain absolute silence around the stable while the horse slept. He even planned to make the horse a consul. A balding man, he became enraged at the sight of handsome men with full heads of hair and would often order the backs of their scalps shaved. He often dressed as a woman (sometimes as Venus) and practiced horrible grimaces before a mirror. He once summoned three senators, half dead with fear, to the palace at midnight. They were escorted to a stage, where Caligula suddenly burst out, dressed in an unusual outfit, began to sing and dance to the accompaniment of flutes, and then departed, leaving the senators more baffled and appalled than when they had arrived. He once prepared to invade Britain in order to accomplish what Julius Caesar had not, but lacking the courage required in a military operation, he halted the soldiers on the French coast and ordered them to gather seashells, which he then returned to Rome as "plunder from the ocean."

Disdaining the long hours of administrative work his office required, labor he considered beneath a god, Caligula devoted his time to lavish entertainment. Having exhausted the vast treasury left by the frugal Tiberius on palaces and other grand (often ludicrous) projects, Caligula forced many aristocrats to declare him their heir and then killed them. He pressured others into bidding ridiculous amounts they could not afford at palace furniture auctions. Everyone and everything was taxed. Caligula also established a state brothel at which even boys and married women were required to work.

Some Romans began to suspect that Tiberius had been killed by Macro, prefect of the Praetorian Guard, with Caligula's approval. According to one account, after Tiberius had fainted, Caligula falsely assumed he was dead. Caligula then removed the imperial ring from Tiberius's finger and accepted the congratulations of a group of senatorial sycophants. When someone announced that the emperor had revived, the sycophants scattered in panic and Caligula stood paralyzed with fear. At this point, Macro saved the day for Caligula by smothering Tiberius with a pillow. By this act, Macro won Caligula's gratitude, though no one ever possessed it long; Caligula later ordered Macro's execution. If this account of Tiberius's death is accurate, the manner of his demise may have constituted poetic justice, since the bitter Tiberius had allegedly made Caligula his heir as a kind of cruel joke on the Rome he had grown to hate, sneering, "I am nursing a viper for the Roman people."

In AD 41 officers of Caligula's own Praetorian Guard killed him. In an off-hand remark he had accused two of its commanders of plotting against him. Fearful, the commanders had begun to plot in earnest. One of the officers (ironically, a descendant of Cassius, Caesar's assassin) was all the more anxious to kill the emperor because Caligula had repeatedly humiliated him by giving him passwords that made him look ridiculous. The commanders and their fellow assassins killed Caligula as he left the Palatine Games at about noon. They stabbed him thirty-one times, eight more wounds than Caesar had received. Arriving late, Caligula's fiercely loyal German guards killed several assassins and a few innocent senators. Searching the palace, they then found Claudius, Caligula's fifty-year-old uncle (Germanicus's brother) and one of the few surviving members of the imperial family, trembling behind drapes. They proclaimed him emperor.

Claudius (41–54)

Because of a speech impediment, a tendency to drool, a facial tic, and a limp, Claudius had long been considered an idiot. (Like many other peoples, the Romans equated physical disabilities with mental incompetence and associated both with a divine curse. The Romans greatly valued physical toughness in males.) Even the kindly old Augustus would not sit next to Claudius at the games. Caligula had kept his Uncle Claudius around the palace to serve as the butt of his jokes and had once ordered him thrown into the Rhine fully clothed. Ironically, the widespread perception of Claudius as an idiot may have saved him from the numerous executions and assassinations that had claimed the rest of the Julio-Claudian males, thereby allowing him to become emperor by default.

After Caligula's assassination, the Praetorian Guard proclaimed Claudius emperor against the wishes of many senators, who wanted to restore the republic. Evidently, the senators were willing to be ruled by a madman but not by an idiot. The soldiers of the Praetorian Guard, who preferred their lucrative and comfortable lifestyle protecting emperors in Rome to fighting barbarians on the frontier, required an emperor to guard. The average guardsman received three times the pay of the average soldier in the army.

Nero (54–68)

Claudius's fourth wife Agrippina the Younger—who was also his niece, the daughter of Germanicus—poisoned his mushrooms in 54, so that Nero, her son by a previous marriage, would become emperor. Nero was Agrippina's son by Gnaeus Ahenobarbus. Ahenobarbus was allegedly so cruel he once deliberately whipped up his horses and ran over and killed a boy while passing through a village. He also gouged out the eye of an eques who criticized him in the Forum. But at least he was shrewd and honest: he once declared that any child born to himself and Agrippina was bound to have a detestable nature and become a public menace.

Claudius had adopted Nero, thereby placing him ahead of his own son Britannicus, who was almost four years younger, in the imperial succession. Like most emperors who did not murder an inordinate number of people, Claudius was later deified. Nero joked that mushrooms were "the food of the gods."

Only sixteen when he took the throne (is there anything more frightening than a teenage emperor?), Nero poisoned Britannicus within a year and buried him without ceremony. (There is probably no substance to the legend that when Nero first became emperor he was so softhearted he wept on having to sign a death warrant, saying, "I wish I had never learned to write.") Nero then tried to poison his overbearing mother three times, supposedly in retaliation for her opposition to his second marriage, but each time Agrippina learned of the attempt and took the antidote beforehand. Nero then rigged her bedroom ceiling to collapse, but she learned of that plot as well. He then had the ship aboard which she was cruising the Adriatic sabotaged so that it would fall apart at sea. Some of the crew drowned, but she swam ashore. Not realizing that the disaster was the result of a murder plot, one of Agrippina's panic-stricken friends cried out, "Help me! I'm Agrippina, mother of the emperor!" Hearing this, several sailors involved in the plot began to smash the woman in the head with a pole and with anything else immediately available, thereby killing her.

Finally, in 59, Nero took the direct approach with his mother. He accused her of treason and had her killed by two soldiers. One clubbed her in the head. When the other moved to stab her with a sword, she cried, "Here," pointing to the womb that had borne so ungrateful a son. Nero's only comment on seeing his dead mother was that she had a nice figure. Some Romans believed that there had been incest between the two, initiated by Agrippina for the purpose of maintaining her power over her growing son.

Nero also killed his aunt for her money, had his first wife executed on a false charge of adultery, kicked his second wife to death while she was pregnant for complaining when he came home late from the races, and killed his third wife's husband in order to marry her. He even drowned his stepson, a mere boy, for playing at being emperor.

But Nero was perhaps hated and feared most for his notorious concerts, at which he played the lyre and sang. Attendance at these concerts was mandatory, and no one was allowed to leave them for any reason before they were finished, though Nero sometimes sang for hours. At his first concert Nero even disregarded an earthquake that shook the whole theater, singing to the bitter end. Women gave birth in the concert halls at some of Nero's performances. Others feigned death in order to be carried out. Some men even jumped down from the rear walls, risking disability or death in their desperation to escape Nero's caterwauling. Not surprisingly, he was showered with all sorts of undeserved musical awards, yet remained so envious of all previous award winners he had their statues taken down and hurled into public lavatories, no doubt surprising those using the facilities. In Nero's defense, he did make one contribution to the arts that more than compensated for his crimes against music: he expelled all of the mimes from Rome.

Nero often prowled the streets of Rome at night, in disguise, attacking people and committing robberies. While in disguise, he was once almost beaten to death by a senator whose wife he had molested on one of these adventures. He once raped a Vestal Virgin. He had a youth castrated and took him for his bride at a marriage ceremony, prompting Romans to joke that the world would have been a better place had Nero's father taken such a bride. Nero never wore the same clothes twice and traveled with a vast train of carriages pulled by mules shod with silver.

In 64 two-thirds of Rome burned in a fire that lasted six days. Contrary to popular myth, Nero could not have been playing the fiddle while Rome burned, since that instrument was not invented until many centuries later. This legend probably arose from the equally dubious, contemporary rumor that he had been watching the flames from the Tower of Macenas while singing his own wretched poem, "The Sack of Troy." In truth, Nero was at Antium when the fire started. Rushing back to Rome, he provided temporary housing and low-cost food to victims of the fire. But Nero also falsely charged that Christians had started the fire and executed them in a grisly fashion.

Discontented with Augustus's modest abode, Nero then constructed a vast and gaudy palace called the Domus Aurea (Golden House). Adjoined by lakes and filled with gold, precious gems, and ivory, the palace featured a 120-foot statue of Nero, hidden perfume sprinklers, and a revolving dome that showered flowers on diners below. When the gigantic palace was completed, Nero deadpanned, "Good, at last I can begin to live like a human being!"

The ostentatious palace fueled rumors that Nero himself had ordered Rome burned so that he could rebuild it to his own glory and rename it "Neropolis." Some Romans alleged that, on the night of the fire, men who claimed to be acting on orders had been seen throwing torches and preventing others from extinguishing the fire.

The extravagance of Nero and his friends led to higher taxes, the devaluation of the coinage, and the quasijudicial fleecing of rich victims. Nero told one magistrate, "You know my needs! Let us see to it that nobody is left with anything." He even stripped temples and melted down their images.

When Nero began to hint that he intended to kill all of the senators, their fear finally got the better of their cowardice. By 65, the Senate, the Praetorian Guard, some military leaders, and even Nero's former tutor, the Stoic philosopher Seneca, were all conspiring against the emperor. Discovering the plot, Nero forced many of the conspirators, including Seneca, to commit suicide. Nero frequently added insult to injury by ridiculing the faces of his victims when their heads were brought to him. While holding the head of one victim in his hands and staring into his face, he said, "How could I have been afraid of a man with such a long nose?" Free speech was in such short supply during Nero's reign that Pliny the Elder decided to assemble a dictionary, since it was the only type of literary work he could conceive that would not get him executed.

In 67 Nero put aside his toy chariots, made of ivory, and decided to enter the Olympic chariot race, despite the fact that he was no athlete but rather an effeminate man with carefully coifed blond hair and sideburns. The Olympic Games were not scheduled for that year, but they were held anyway so that the emperor could compete. Although Nero fell from his chariot and never finished the race, the judges wisely awarded him the victory. For their unorthodox interpretation of the race rules the judges were rewarded with Roman citizenship and hard cash. Indeed, Nero won 1,808 first prizes at the Olympics that year, including several for competitions in which he did not compete.

By 68, Roman armies in Gaul, Spain, Armenia, Britain, and Judea were in revolt. (On hearing of the initial revolt in Gaul, Nero was upset only that the rebellious commander had called him a bad lyre player.) A multitude of troops now marched on Rome. Nero tried to recruit a loyal army, but no volunteers came forward. His maids even absconded with his bed linen. On one of the emperor's statues someone scrawled a reference to his phony victories in a host of musical and athletic contests: "This is a real contest for once, and you are going to lose!" After the Senate condemned Nero to death by flogging, he sighed, "What a great artist the world is losing!" and stabbed himself in the throat.

Problems with the Historians' Accounts

Since Tacitus's *Annals* began with the death of Augustus, he glossed over the reign of the first emperor, who was one of the most capable rulers in Roman history. The reign of Augustus was one of unprecedented peace and prosperity. During his rule the doors to the temple of the god Janus, closed only in times of complete peace, were closed three times. The doors had been closed only twice in the centuries before Augustus.

When combined with the construction of durable roads throughout the empire, peace made extensive trade and travel possible. The increase in trade produced prosperity. Merchants even dispatched 120 ships per year to India via the Red Sea to trade their pots and other goods for Indian spices, jewels, and ivory and for Chinese silk. Augustus also increased prosperity by establishing an efficient monetary system, made possible by elaborate mining facilities and augmented by local small change.

During the few periods of war in Augustus's forty-one-year reign, his generals extended the empire's northeastern frontier to the Danube River. Augustus established a professional army of twenty-eight legions, stationed it on the frontiers, and largely succeeded in keeping it out of politics. The army proved a tremendous Romanizing influence. Towns sprouted around its camps (e.g., Cologne, Mainz, and Baden), as Roman soldiers intermarried with native women, settled down on their pensions, and became local dignitaries. After twenty-five years of service, foreigners who served in the auxiliaries were issued a pair of bronze tablets called a *diploma* (double tablets) that granted them full citizenship. Augustus also maintained fleets throughout the Mediterranean to transport troops and to suppress piracy.

Augustus reduced the number of the senators from nine hundred to six hundred, making the Senate more efficient. He appointed honest and efficient legati to govern the outer provinces. Respecting local cultures to a large extent, the legati emphasized provincial autonomy and local self-government. This pluralism was one of Rome's wisest policies. It enabled the Romans to hold together a vast empire of innumerable ethnic groups with a minimum of rebellion and to avoid an inefficient, centralized bureaucracy, thereby allowing them to maintain taxes at a tolerable level.

Augustus established a periodic census to monitor changes in the population, wealth, and resources of each province, thereby allowing him to shift the tax burden away from those provinces least able to pay. Most money raised in the provinces remained there, to cover the expense of local administration; few provinces provided a surplus for Rome. Augustus reduced the number of taxes collected by private tax collectors. He assigned equites, as well as aristocrats, to financial posts, to the governorship of small provinces, to the command of armies, and to the Praetorian Guard.

Augustus constructed another forum in Rome to relieve congestion in the original. It was narrower than he originally planned because he could not bring himself to evict the owners of the houses that would have to be demolished. He also cleared the Tiber of rubbish to improve navigation and to help prevent floods.

Augustus rebuilt eighty-two temples destroyed during the civil wars in a single year alone, revived old priesthoods, and restored religious festivals. Holding to traditional Roman frugality, he lived in a modest house on Palatine Hill (the word "palace" derives from the more lavish royal mansion later constructed there by the emperor Domitian), ate frugally, and dressed in simple clothes made by his female relatives. Concerned about the decline of traditional Roman values and fearing depopulation, he passed laws rewarding the production of legitimate children and penalizing adultery, bachelorhood, and childlessness. He even banished his own promiscuous daughter for adultery.

Augustus must rank as one of the most skillful and energetic administrators in history. In fact, he once expressed astonishment that Alexander the Great had devoted so much energy and attention to conquering an empire and so little to administering it properly.

Furthermore, most modern historians consider Tacitus's unrelentingly negative treatment of the other emperors excessively harsh. He almost always seemed to adopt the least favorable interpretation of an emperor's motives, and even when he complimented an emperor, he did so with palpable reluctance, and the compliment was almost always followed by a deflating postscript. From Tacitus's discussion of Claudius, which focuses on the emperor's lascivious wife Messalina and on Claudius's own eccentricities and foibles, the reader would never gather that Claudius was a capable emperor. Claudius improved Ostia, Rome's chief harbor, so that ships could better navigate it in winter, an improvement crucial to the city's grain supply. He built aqueducts and drained marshes near Rome. He extended the Latin right to many conquered peoples. He allowed many capable commoners (including his own freedmen) to rise in the Roman bureaucracy. Claudius also charged with murder those slaveholders who rid themselves of their sick slaves by killing them. In 43 he added much of what is now the southern portion of Great Britain to the Roman Empire. This conquest removed a thorn from the Roman side, since the Celts of Britain had provided a safe haven for rebellious Celts in Gaul.

It is true that Suetonius was more balanced than Tacitus, offering a more complete and more positive account of some of the emperors without ignoring their crimes. But Tacitus's condemnatory tone was one of the two principal reasons the founders preferred him to Suetonius. The other reason was that Suetonius's breezy style, more similar to that of a modern gossip columnist than to that of most other classical historians, accorded far less well with the founders' moralistic tendencies than Tacitus's somber, judgmental tone.

Furthermore, even the worst emperors largely confined their murders and other depredations to the aristocratic class of the city of Rome, from whose ambition they had most to fear. It was precisely for this reason that aristocratic historians like Tacitus so despised the emperors, whom he also criticized for elevating freedmen and others he regarded as inferiors to high positions he considered reserved for his own class and for other measures that modern historians now celebrate as social reforms. The ordinary provincial saw little difference between the administrations of a "good emperor" and a "bad emperor," since the imperial system remained largely the same regardless of who stood at the helm. In short, Tacitus's history, however fascinating, brilliantly written, and valid in some of its criticisms of the emperors, was an insular account aimed at a small, urban, aristocratic audience.

Finally, the fact that Tacitus was able to publish his scathing attacks on the early Roman emperors is a tribute to the freedom of speech allowed by the later emperors, as he himself acknowledged. The second century witnessed the rise of the so-called Five Good Emperors, Nerva, Trajan, Hadrian, Antoninus Pius, and Marcus Aurelius. These emperors brought the Roman Empire to its zenith of power and prosperity. They generally considered themselves the servants of Rome rather than its masters. Nerva (96–98) established the *alimenta*, a fund that provided aid to the poor children of forty Italian cities. Nerva funded the program with the interest from public land sales and loans to farmers. In this way he increased agricultural productivity and helped poor children simultaneously. The Roman Empire reached its greatest extent (3.5 million square miles and seventy-five million people) under Trajan (98–117). Trajan added fertile, gold-rich Dacia (what is now western Romania), Armenia, and Mesopotamia to the empire.

Trajan appointed aristocrats from the eastern portion of the empire to the Senate. He dispatched *curators* to advise cities in local self-government and to weed out corrupt local officials. One year Trajan set aside the entire imperial budget for the loans that financed the alimenta, thereby allowing him to dramatically expand the number of its beneficiaries. He was so proud of this achievement that he highlighted it on his coins and on his Arch of Beneventum. Trajan's generosity encouraged private citizens like Pliny the Younger to practice philanthropy as well. Hadrian (117–138) erected the Pantheon, a domed temple to "all of the gods." Hadrian also extended to many towns the "right of municipia," a middle step between the Latin right and full citizenship that granted a partial citizenship to the people of a town. By then, half of the Senate consisted of provincials. Antonius Pius (138–161) admitted North Africans into the Senate. He was humble, tolerant, hardworking, and, yes, pious. Of all the Roman emperors Antonius's nephew, son-in-law, adopted son, and successor, Marcus Aurelius (161–180), came the closest to Plato's ideal of the "philosopher-king" (though he considered Plato's *Republic* impractical). Marcus Aurelius was so magnanimous that when presented with evidence of a conspiracy against his life, he ordered the incriminating letters burned so that he could not learn the names of the conspirators and, therefore, have a reason to dislike them. He even sold some of his personal possessions to assist victims of famine and plague. Marcus Aurelius wrote the *Meditations* (in Greek), a personal, philosophical journal that is considered one of the greatest works of Stoicism.

For all of its horrible abuses, the system of imperial government established by Augustus created unprecedented security and prosperity throughout the Western world for over two centuries. In the process it saved the political, social, and cultural heritage of Greece and Rome, which had been threatened by the instability, chaos, and violence of the late Roman republic.

The Lesson

Nevertheless, the founders read and admired Tacitus's dark and brilliant *Annals of Rome*. At the same time, the founders mined Suetonius's *Lives of the Twelve Caesars* for negative information regarding the emperors, while largely ignoring his positive comments. Hence, the founders learned to regard one-man rule as an absolute horror to be avoided at all cost. Thomas Jefferson claimed that living under the thumb of the emperors had corrupted Rome to the extent that even high officials lacked political courage. Jefferson noted that even those who had opposed imperial rule had often chosen suicide over the "better remedy" of "a poignard in the breast of the tyrant." In 1821 Jefferson argued, "There are three epochs in history signalized by the total extinction of national morality. The first was of the successors of Alexander, not omitting himself: The next, the successors of the first Caesar. The third, our own day." Nonetheless, as he had explained in 1813, Jefferson preferred to read about Rome's corrupt periods than to read about his own era:

> I turn from the contemplation with loathing, and take refuge in the histories of other times, where, if they also furnish their Tarquins, their Catilines, and Caligulas, their stories are handed to us under the brand of a Livy, a Sallust, and a Tacitus, and we are comforted with the reflection that the condemnation of all succeeding generations has confirmed the censures of the historian, and consigned their memories to everlasting infamy, a solace which we cannot have with the Georges and Napoleons but by anticipation.

Similarly, John Adams wrote regarding Thucydides and Tacitus, "When I read them I seem to be only reading the History of my own Times and my own Life."

During the Revolutionary period, the founders compared the British parliament and the Tories with the Roman emperors and their minions. In his *Letters from a Pennsylvania Farmer*, John Dickinson wrote,

> Indeed we ought firmly to believe what is an undoubted truth, confirmed by the happy experience of many states heretofore free, that unless the most watchful attention be exerted, a new servitude may be slipped on us, under the sanction of the usual and respectable terms. Thus, the Caesars ruined Roman liberty, under the titles of tribunicial and dictatorial authorities, old and venerable dignities, known in the most flourishing times of freedom.

Likewise, under the Townshend Acts, parliament sought to hide "impositions for raising a revenue" under the venerable title of "regulation of trade." Samuel Adams compared a certain Tory with the multitude of informers whom Caligula and Nero had employed. Adams added, "The Stamp Act was like the sword that Nero wished for to have decollated the Roman Empire at a stroke." (As we have seen, it was Caligula who had made that remark.) In 1767 John Adams rather improbably compared the dull royal governor of Massachusetts, Francis Bernard, with Nero, Caligula, Attila the Hun, and Caesar. Adams compared the Tories' slander of William Pitt the Elder and Benjamin Franklin with Nero's murder of Seneca. Adams wrote, "Nero murdered Seneca that he might pull up virtue by the roots, and the same maxim governs the scribblers and speechifyers on the side of the minister."

These improbable analogies were not mere rhetorical flourishes. They represented the genuine fear of tyranny inherent in nearly all classical texts. Tyranny was an inexorable cancer that must be destroyed in its early stages. Unconstitutional taxes, however small, violated sacred principles of liberty as surely as mass executions. Indeed, if unchecked, the former would likely eventuate in the latter. The "slippery slope" was a quintessentially classical idea.

In a similarly serious vein during the constitutional debates, the Antifederalists compared the Federalists with Roman emperors. Responding to James Wilson's assurance that the federal government would not be able to dissolve the state legislatures under the new Constitution, since the legislatures would be needed to elect senators, the essayist "Centinel" argued that form might be maintained without substance:

> Augustus, by the aid of a great army, assumed despotic power, and not withstanding this, we find even under Tiberius, Caligula, and Nero, princes who disgraced human nature by their excesses, the shadows of the constitution held up to amuse the people. The senate sat as formerly; consuls, tribunes of the people, censors, and other officers were annually chosen as before, and the forms of republican government continued.

The Federalists were playing the same game, "Centinel" claimed. George Clinton, the governor of New York, applied the same argument to the constitutional clause guaranteeing republican government to the states. This was mere form, like the Roman emperors' use of republican symbols. The "Impartial Examiner" applied the analogy to the Federalists' appropriation of that name. He compared the adoption of that label to the emperors' clever avoidance of the title "king." He contended, "That which in any particular form has once produced much evil and discontent generally stamps a lasting impression on the mind, and is not contemplated but with extreme detestation; although evils of the same nature, when inflicted under a different appearance, are frequently submitted to without repining." Although the last Roman king was expelled in 509 BC, and "the name of King was ever odious to the Roman people" thereafter, the Romans at last concentrated even greater power in a single man named "emperor." In the same fashion the Federalists avoided revealing their true identity because they knew that the American people staunchly opposed the annihilation of state power.

Other Antifederalists also expressed the common hatred of the Roman emperors. Rejecting the Federalist claim that Americans should support the new Constitution simply because George Washington and other respected leaders endorsed it, "a Republican Federalist" asked impatiently,

> If the plan is properly before the States, is good, and will secure to them [the people] "peace, liberty, and safety," should it not be adopted, were they even sure that every member who subscribed [to] it was in principle a Caligula or Nero? And if the plan is bad and will entail slavery on the land, ought it not to be rejected should every subscriber excel in wisdom and integrity Lycurgus or Solon?

"Philadelphiensis" was more melodramatic. He wailed, "Ah, my friends, the days of a cruel Nero approach fast." He added that "the language of a monster, of a Caligula, could not be more imperious" than that of the "lordlings" of the Constitutional Convention and concluded by reviling old patriot soldiers who supported the document: "Curse on the villain who protects virgin innocence only with a view that he may himself become the ravisher." The near-hysterical nature of these unlikely comparisons was even more remarkable than those leveled against the British, since the Antifederalists had just fought beside the Federalists against British "tyranny." But anyone who dared introduce the cancer of tyranny into the vibrant American body politic, in however small a tumor, must be regarded as a cunning enemy of the ilk of Caligula or Nero.

The Antifederalists contended that the tyranny of imperial Rome lay in store for Americans if the Constitution were ratified. Fearing that the president possessed too much power, "Poplicola" wrote, "For my part, I do not believe that there is a man on earth to whom it would be safe for the people to entrust the powers of a despot. . . . Nero was said to be blest with a kind and affectionate heart; but the powers of a despot intoxicated his mind." "A Friend to the Rights of the People" pursued the Nero analogy, writing, "Nero was one of the best among the Roman Emperors at his first entering the Imperial throne, [but] in a short time, he proved a monster of iniquity." Nathaniel Barrell concurred. He told the Massachusetts ratification convention, "History tells us Rome was happy under Augustus, though wretched under Nero, who could have no greater power than Augustus; and yet this same Nero, when young in government, could shed tears on signing a death warrant, though afterwards he became [so] callous to the tender of feelings of humanity as to behold, with pleasure, Rome in flames."

Responding to the Federalist enticement that George Washington would be the first president, "A Farmer" argued that if the first president were a good one, he would only be opening the door wider for wicked ones. The mild administration of Augustus had "secured the power and gave full scope to the vices of Tiberious, Caligula, and Nero."

Such emperors would corrupt the Congress and the American people, "A Farmer" claimed, as Caligula and Nero had corrupted the Senate and the people of Rome. Regarding Caligula's corruption of the Senate he wrote, "A grave senate of Rome—the senate which twenty or indeed ten years before, had commanded the awe and veneration of mankind, solemnly proposed a law, as Suetonius informs us, to submit their wives and daughters to his embraces." Could not the U.S. Senate be corrupted by a powerful president then? Regarding Nero's corruption of the Roman people he added, "During the reign of Nero, fiddling—dancing—singing—burning cities—plundering States—perfidy and assassination were the manners of the age." He concluded,

> But can these things happen to Americans? . . . America is in great measure peopled by emigrants from the old countries, now enthralled in slavery—Does crossing the Atlantic alter the nature of these people?—Let our countrymen reflect on this awful truth, that nothing creates that wide distinction between them and the white slaves of the old world, or indeed their black slaves here, but their government.

Americans were as subject to corruption by a powerful executive as any other people.

Of course, the Federalists retorted that it was absurd to compare the limited power and term of the elected president with the unlimited power and lifetime term of the unelected emperor. But the fact that the Federalists succeeded in ratifying the new Constitution only by a very narrow margin reveals the serious and widespread nature of the concern that the creation of a powerful executive might lead to a revival of the tyranny of the Roman emperors.

The Founding Fathers, both the Federalists and the Antifederalists, learned from Tacitus and (to a lesser extent) Suetonius to fear tyranny not so much because it deprived citizens of their liberty as because it robbed them of their virtue. The corrupting effects of living in tyranny—the dehumanizing sycophancy and the degrading collaboration necessary to remain in the tyrant's good graces—were more abhorrent and disgusting than the oppression itself.

Perhaps more than any other argument, this fear had produced the desire for independence from Great Britain. If the cunning prime ministers of Britain could ever convince the American public to accept even the smallest unconstitutional tax, Americans would eventually lose, not only the power, but also the very will, to resist. Americans would then be no more than slaves, subject to the whims of distant masters. To stay within the British Empire would be to witness the recreation of that horrifying degradation and depravity Tacitus and Suetonius had so vividly described in Rome. But to leave the empire and start anew would be to embrace the exciting possibility of creating a society so elevated and virtuous as to inspire future Plutarchs to immortalize the nation. The fear of witnessing another Roman Empire was as essential to producing the revolution as the hope of creating another Roman republic. As Jefferson astutely noted in the Declaration of Independence, humans are not, by nature, rebels. Only genuine fear of the dire consequences of persisting in their current situation, coupled with real hope in the possibility of achieving a better fate, can inspire people to disrupt their lives and undertake the arduous sacrifices and hazard the frightful dangers characteristic of revolutions.

Conclusion

The Founding Fathers learned valuable lessons from the stirring stories of Greece and Rome, tales they first encountered as children. From the story of the Spartans they learned the importance of individual liberty to a republic. From the Persian Wars they learned that the inherent strengths of republican government made it possible for republics to defend themselves against strong, centralized monarchies like Persia or Great Britain. From the fall of Athens they learned that majority rule must be tempered by checks and balances if the instability and oppression of ochlocracy were to be averted. From the fall of Greece to Macedon and Rome they learned that a certain degree of centralization was necessary if a confederacy of republics were to avoid fragmentation and interstate warfare. From the early Roman republic they learned the importance of individual and societal virtue to the success of a republic. From the decline and fall of the Roman republic they learned to be wary of ambitious individuals, who might conspire to subvert the republic in order to expand their own power. Finally, from the Roman emperors they learned that just as vice led to tyranny, tyranny led to even greater vice, thereby producing the most degraded society imaginable.

One can question the validity of any of these lessons, and one can challenge the accuracy of some of the stories on which the lessons were based, but what is beyond question is the power these vivid stories wielded over the founders. The Greek and Roman classics gave the founders the courage to face the great challenges of their time. During the Revolutionary era, the classics provided an indispensable illusion of precedent for actions that were essentially unprecedented. In 1775 John Adams had been able to write regarding the popular sovereignty theory that underlay American resistance to British measures: "These are what are called revolution-principles. They are the principles of Aristotle and Plato, of Livy and Cicero, of Sidney, Harrington, and Lock.—The principles of nature and eternal reason." In an age in which rebellion was considered an act of the darkest villainy, and rebels were summarily hanged, ancient history (interwoven with British Whig and American colonial history) enabled the conservative American revolutionaries to argue that they were preserving past liberties rather than presumptuously tinkering with the natural order. Classical republican ideology enabled them to cast King George III as Nero or Caligula, George Washington and Thomas Jefferson as Cato and Cicero—in other words, to portray the king as the real rebel, the violator of that natural law that lawful patriots would die to defend. Without this illusion of precedent, it is unlikely that the founders could have persuaded themselves and many other Americans to rebel against the mother country. The American Revolution was a paradox: a revolution fueled by tradition.

The success of the Revolution raised other unprecedented questions: what form should the new federal government take, and how much power should it possess? The founders again turned to ancient history for answers. In seeking to emulate Rome, a republic possessing a dubious reputation for mixed government, the founders created something entirely new, a government truly mixed, though not by economic class. Furthermore, they strengthened the federal government in an effort to avoid the fate of the ancient Greek confederacies. Old stories had again served as the essential catalysts for the creation of a new reality.

Just as the Founding Fathers learned valuable lessons from ancient stories about their Greek and Roman heroes, Americans have traditionally learned important lessons about courage and self-sacrifice from their own tales concerning the founders. In the nineteenth century American orators turned repeatedly to stories about the founders for inspiration. Even at the turn of the twenty-first century, long after social critics had lost all hope that these inspirational tales about the founders would ever regain their place at the center of public consciousness, a place taken by the often superficial and cynical creations of television and film producers, books concerning the founders reached the top of the best-seller lists. Better yet, these books, such as Joseph J. Ellis's *Founding Brothers*, David McCullough's *John Adams*, and Ron Chernow's *Alexander Hamilton*, portrayed the founders in all of their complex glory, not in the simplistic and plastic terms of pseudohistorians like Parson Weems. These historians redefined heroism as it should be defined, not as perfection, but rather as the over-coming of imperfections to achieve great ends. Coming in the wake of a national revival of stories regarding the "greatest generation," the generation that saved the world from enslavement by the Axis powers, the popularity of these new histories of the founders bodes well.

As long as human society exists, there will be a need for stories. The only question is whether the stories provided will be rich enough and inspirational enough to serve societal needs. Perhaps it is now time for the American public not only to return to the founders—to explore the totality of their lives, its tragic as well as its heroic elements—but also to return to the great fountainhead of knowledge at which the founders filled their own buckets. Perhaps it is time to learn whatever lessons the ancients can teach the twenty-first century.

Selected Bibliography

General Works

Adair, Douglass. *Fame and the Founding Fathers*, edited by H. Trevor Colbourn. New York: W. W. Norton, 1974.

Agresto, John T. "Liberty, Virtue, and Republicanism, 1776–1787." *Review of Politics* 39 (October 1977): 473–504.

Appleby, Joyce O. *Capitalism and a New Social Order: The Republican Vision of the 1790s*. New York: New York University Press, 1984.

———. *Liberalism and Republicanism in the Historical Imagination*. Cambridge, Mass.: Harvard University Press, 1992.

Bailyn, Bernard. *The Ideological Origins of the American Revolution*. 2nd ed. Cambridge, Mass.: Harvard University Press, 1992.

———, ed. *Pamphlets of the American Revolution*. Cambridge, Mass.: Harvard University Press, 1965.

Banning, Lance. "Jeffersonian Ideology Revisited: Liberal and Classical Ideas in the New American Republic." *William and Mary Quarterly* 43 (January 1986): 3–19.

———. *The Jeffersonian Persuasion*. Ithaca, N.Y.: Cornell University Press, 1978.

Becker, Carl; J. M. Clark, and William E. Dodd, eds. *The Spirit of 1776 and Other Essays*. Washington, D.C.: Robert Brookings Graduate School of Economics and Government, 1927.

Berrigan, Joseph R. "The Impact of the Classics upon the South." *Classical Journal* 64 (Winter 1968–1969): 18–20.

Boorstin, Daniel. *The Lost World of Thomas Jefferson*. New York: Henry Holt, 1948.

Botein, Stephen. "Cicero as Role Model for Early American Lawyers: A Case Study in Classical 'Influence.'" *Classical Journal* 73 (Spring 1978): 313–21.

Bradford, M. E. "That Other Republic: Romanitas in Southern Literature." *Southern Humanities Review* 11 (1977): 4–13.

Bridenbaugh, Carl, and Jessica Bridenbaugh. *Rebels and Gentlemen: Philadelphia in the Age of Franklin.* New York: Reynal and Hitchcock, 1942. Reprint, Westport, Conn.: Greenwood Press, 1978.

Bruce, Dickson D., Jr. "The Conservative Use of History in Early National Virginia." *Southern Studies* 19 (Summer 1980): 128–46.

Burns, Edward M. "The Philosophy of History of the Founding Fathers." *The Historian* 16 (Spring 1954): 142–61.

Colbourn, H. Trevor. *The Lamp of Experience: Whig History and the Intellectual Origins of the American Revolution.* Chapel Hill: University of North Carolina Press, 1965.

Commager, Henry Steele. "The American Enlightenment and the Ancient World: A Study in Paradox." *Proceedings of the Massachusetts Historical Society* 83 (Winter 1971): 3–15.

——. "Leadership in Eighteenth-Century America and Today." *Daedalus* 90 (Fall 1961): 652–73.

Conkin, Paul K. *Self-Evident Truths.* Bloomington: Indiana University Press, 1974.

Curti, Merle. *The Growth of American Thought.* New York: Harper and Brothers, 1943.

Davis, Richard Beale. *Intellectual Life in Jefferson's Virginia, 1790–1830.* Chapel Hill: University of North Carolina Press, 1964.

Eadie, John W., ed. *Classical Traditions in Early America.* Ann Arbor, Mich.: Center for the Coordination of Ancient and Modern Studies, 1976.

Ellis, Joseph J. *Founding Brothers: The Revolutionary Generation.* New York: Prentice-Hall, 2000.

Gregg, Gary L. *Vital Remnants: America's Founding and the Western Tradition.* Wilmington, Del.: ISI, 1999.

Gribbin, William. "Rollin's Histories and American Republicanism." *William and Mary Quarterly*, 3rd ser., 29 (October 1972): 611–22.

Gummere, Richard M. *The American Colonial Mind and the Classical Tradition: Essays in Comparative Culture.* Cambridge, Mass.: Harvard University Press, 1963.

——. "The Heritage of the Classics in Colonial North America." *Proceedings of the American Philosophical Society* 99 (January 1955): 68–78.

——. *Seven Wise Men of Colonial America.* Cambridge, Mass.: Harvard University Press, 1967.

Haines, Charles Grove. *The Revival of Natural Law Concepts.* New York: Russell and Russell, 1965.

Hoffman, Richard J. "Classics in the Courts of the United States, 1790–1800." *American Journal of Legal History* 22 (January 1978): 55–84.

Horowitz, Maryanne Cline. "The Stoic Synthesis of the Idea of Natural Law in Man: Four Themes." *Journal of the History of Ideas* 35 (January–March 1974): 3–16.

Jones, Howard Mumford. *O Strange New World: American Culture, the Formative Years.* New York: Viking Press, 1952.

———. *Revolution and Romanticism.* Cambridge, Mass.: Harvard University Press, 1974.

Kerber, Linda K. *Federalists in Dissent: Imagery and Ideology in Jeffersonian America.* Ithaca, N.Y.: Cornell University Press, 1970.

———. *Women of the Republic: Intellect and Ideology in Revolutionary America.* Chapel Hill: University of North Carolina Press, 1980.

Ketcham, Ralph. *From Colony to Country: The Revolution in American Thought, 1750–1820.* New York: Macmillan, 1974.

———. *Presidents above Party: The First American Presidency, 1789–1829.* Chapel Hill: University of North Carolina Press, 1984.

Le Boutillier, Cornelia Greer. *American Democracy and Natural Law.* New York: Columbia University Press, 1950.

Litto, Frederick W. "Addison's *Cato* in the Colonies." *William and Mary Quarterly,* 3rd ser., 23 (July 1966): 431–49.

MacKendrick, Paul. "This Rich Source of Delight: The Classics and the Founding Fathers." *Classical Journal* 72 (Winter 1976): 97–106.

May, Henry F. *The Enlightenment in America.* New York: Oxford University Press, 1976.

McCoy, Drew R. *The Elusive Republic: Political Economy in Jeffersonian America.* Chapel Hill: University of North Carolina Press, 1980.

McDonald, Forrest. *Novus Ordo Seclorum.* Lawrence: University of Kansas Press, 1985.

Miles, Edwin A. "The Old South and the Classical World." *North Carolina Historical Review* 48 (1971): 258–75.

———. "The Young American Nation and the Classical World." *Journal of the History of Ideas* 35 (April–June 1974): 259–74.

Mullett, Charles F. "Ancient Historians and 'Enlightened' Reviewers." *Review of Politics* 21 (April 1959): 550–65.

———. "Classical Influences on the American Revolution." *Classical Journal* 35 (November 1939): 92–104.

———. *Fundamental Law and the American Revolution, 1760–1776.* New York: Octagon Books, 1966.

Pocock, J. G. A. *The Machiavellian Moment: Florentine Political Thought and the Atlantic Republican Tradition.* Princeton, N.J.: Princeton University Press, 1975.

Reinhold, Meyer. *Classica Americana: The Greek and Roman Heritage in the United States.* Detroit: Wayne State University Press, 1984.

———, ed. *The Classick Pages: Classical Reading of Eighteenth-Century Americans.* University Park, Pa.: American Philological Association, 1975.

Roberts, Jennifer Tolbert. *Athens on Trial: The Anti-Democratic Tradition in Western Thought.* Princeton, N.J.: Princeton University Press, 1994.

Rossiter, Clinton. *Seedtime of the Republic: The Origin of the American Tradition of Liberty.* New York: Harcourt, Brace, 1953.

Shavel, Eran. "Empire Transformed: Britain in the American Classical Imagination, 1758–1783." *Early American Studies* (Spring 2006): 112–46.

Stein, Peter. "The Attraction of the Civil Law in Post-Revolutionary America." *Virginia Law Review* 52 (1966): 403–34.

Wheeler, Joseph Towne. "Reading Interests of the Professional Classes in Colonial Maryland, 1700–1776." *Maryland Historical Magazine* 36 (September 1941): 184–201, 281–306.

Wiltshire, Susan Ford. "Aristotle in America." *Humanities* 8 (January–February 1987): 8–11.

———. *Greece, Rome, and the Bill of Rights*. Norman: University of Oklahoma Press, 1992.

———, ed. *The Usefulness of Classical Learning in the Eighteenth Century*. Washington, D.C.: American Philological Association, 1975.

Winterer, Caroline. *The Culture of Classicism: Ancient Greece and Rome in American Intellectual Life, 1780–1910*. Baltimore: Johns Hopkins University Press, 2002.

Wood, Gordon S. *The Creation of the American Republic, 1776–1787*. Chapel Hill: University of North Carolina Press, 1969.

———. *The Radicalism of the American Revolution*. New York: Alfred A. Knopf, 1992.

Wright, Benjamin Fletcher, Jr. *American Interpretations of Natural Law: A Study in the History of Political Thought*. New York: Russell and Russell, 1962.

Classical Education

Axtell, James. *The School upon a Hill: Education and Society in Colonial New England*. New Haven, Conn.: Yale University Press, 1974.

Bailyn, Bernard. *Education in the Formation of American Society*. Chapel Hill: University of North Carolina Press, 1960.

Benario, Herbert W. "The Classics in Southern Higher Education." *Southern Humanities Review* 11 (1977): 15–20.

Cohen, Sheldon S. *A History of Colonial Education, 1607–1776*. New York: John Wiley and Sons, 1974.

Coon, Charles L., ed. *The Beginnings of Public Education in North Carolina: A Documentary History, 1790–1840*. Raleigh, N.C.: Edwards and Broughton Printing Co., 1908.

Cremin, Lawrence A. *American Education: The Colonial Experience, 1607–1783*. New York: Harper and Row, 1970.

Hansen, Allen Oscar. *Liberalism and American Education*. New York: Macmillan, 1926.

Hardy, C. Dewitt, and Richard Hofstadter. *The Development and Scope of Higher Education in the United States*. New York: Columbia University Press, 1952.

Herbst, Jurgen. "The American Revolution and the American Univerity." *Perspectives in American History* 10 (1976): 279–354.

Hiden, Martha W. "Education and the Classics in the Life of Colonial Virginia." *Virginia Magazine of History and Biography* 49 (January 1941): 20–28.

Hofstadter, Richard, and Wilson Smith, eds. *American Higher Education: A Documentary History*. Chicago: University of Chicago Press, 1961.

Holmes, Pauline. *A Tercentenary History of the Boston Latin School, 1635–1935*. Cambridge, Mass.: Harvard University Press, 1935. Reprint, Westport, Conn.: Greenwood Press, 1970.

Knight, Edgar W., ed. *A Documentary History of Education in the South before 1860*. Chapel Hill: University of North Carolina Press, 1949–1953.

Marson, Philip. *Breeder of Democracy*. Cambridge, Mass.: Schenkman Publishing, 1970.

Middlekauff, Robert. *Ancients and Axioms: Secondary Education in Eighteenth-Century New England*. New Haven, Conn.: Yale University Press, 1963.

———. "A Persistent Tradition: The Classical Curriculum in Eighteenth-Century New England." *William and Mary Quarterly*, 3rd ser., 18 (January 1961): 54–67.

Morford, Mark. "Early American School Editions of Ovid." *Classical Journal* 78 (Winter 1982): 150–58.

Pomfret, John E. "Student Interests at Brown University, 1789–1790." *New England Quarterly* 5 (January 1932): 135–47.

Rexine, John E. "The Boston Latin School Curriculum in the Seventeenth and Eighteenth Centuries." *Classical Journal* 72 (Winter 1976): 261–66.

Rudolph, Frederick, ed. *Essays on Education in the Early Republic*. Cambridge, Mass.: Harvard University Press, 1965.

Smith, Wilson, ed. *Theories of Education in Early America, 1655–1819*. New York: Bobbs-Merrill, 1973.

Stone, Lawrence, ed. *The University in Society*. Princeton, N.J.: Princeton University Press, 1974.

Straub, Jean S. "Teaching in the Friends' Latin School in Philadelphia in the Eighteenth Century." *Pennsylvania Magazine of History and Biography* 91 (October 1967): 434–56.

Vine, Phyllis. "The Social Function of Eighteenth Century Higher Education." *History of Education Quarterly* 16 (Winter 1976): 409–24.

Yost, Mary A. "Classical Studies in American Colonial Schools, 1635–1776." *Classical Outlook* 54 (October 1976): 40–43.

The Constitution

Ames, R. A., and H. C. Montgomery. "The Influence of Rome on the American Constitution." *Classical Journal* 30 (1934–1935): 19–27.

Chinard, Gilbert. "Polybius and the American Constitution." *Journal of the History of Ideas* 1 (May 1940): 38–58.

Corwin, Edwin S. *The "Higher Law" Background of American Constitutional Law*. Ithaca, N.Y.: Cornell University Press, 1928.

Elliot, Jonathan, ed. *Debates in the Several State Conventions on the Adoption of the Federal Constitution*. Philadelphia: Lippincott, 1888. Reprint, New York: Burt Franklin, 1968.

Farrand, Max, ed. *The Records of the Federal Convention of 1787*. 3rd ed. New Haven, Conn.: Yale University Press, 1966.

Ford, Paul Leicester, ed. *Pamphlets on the Constitution of the United States: Published during Its Discussion by the People*. New York: Lenox Hill Publishing, 1888. Reprint, New York: Burt Franklin, 1971.

Gummere, Richard M. "The Classical Ancestry of the United States Constitution." *American Quarterly* 14 (Spring 1962): 3–18.

Hamilton, Alexander, John Jay, and James Madison. *The Federalist: A Commentary on the Constitution of the United States*. New York: Random House, 1941.

Lienesch, Michael. *New Order of the Ages: Time, the Constitution, and the Making of Modern American Political Thought*. Princeton, N.J.: Princeton University Press, 1988.

Madison, James. *Journal of the Federal Convention*, edited by E. H. Scott. Freeport, N.Y.: Books for Libraries Press, 1970.

Murphy, John P. "Rome at the Constitutional Convention." *Classical Outlook* 51 (December 1974): 112–14.

Storing, Herbert J., ed. *The Complete Antifederalist*. Chicago: University of Chicago Press, 1981.

Wills, Garry. *Explaining America: The Federalist*. New York: Penguin Books, 1981.

The Individual Founders

John Adams

Adair, Douglass, and John A. Schutz, eds. *The Spur of Fame: Dialogues of John Adams and Benjamin Rush, 1805–1813*. San Marino, Calif.: Huntington Library, 1966.

Adams, Charles Francis, ed. *The Life and Works of John Adams*. 10 vols. Boston: Little, Brown, 1850–1856.

Adams, John. *A Defence of the Constitutions of Government of the United States of America*. London, 1787–1788. Reprint, New York: Da Capo Press, 1971.

Butterfield, L. H., ed. *The Adams Family Correspondence*. Cambridge, Mass.: Harvard University Press, 1963–1973.

———, ed. *The Diary and Autobiography of John Adams*. Cambridge, Mass.: Harvard University Press, 1961.

———, ed. *The Earliest Diary of John Adams*. Cambridge, Mass.: Harvard University Press, 1966.

Cappon, Lester J., ed. *The Adams-Jefferson Letters: The Complete Correspondence between Thomas Jefferson and Abigail and John Adams*. Chapel Hill: University of North Carolina Press, 1959.

Chinard, Gilbert. *Honest John Adams*. Boston: Little, Brown, 1933.

Gummere, Richard M. "The Classical Politics of John Adams." *Boston Public Library Quarterly* 9 (October 1957): 167–82.

———. "John Adams, Togatus." *Philological Quarterly* 13 (April 1934): 203–10.

Haraszti, Zoltan. *John Adams and the Prophets of Progress*. Cambridge, Mass.: Harvard University Press, 1952.

Koch, Adrienne, and William Peden, eds. *The Selected Writings of John and John Quincy Adams*. New York: Alfred A. Knopf, 1946.

McCullough, David. *John Adams*. New York: Simon & Schuster, 2001.

Robathan, Dorothy M. "John Adams and the Classics." *New England Quarterly* 19 (March 1946): 91–98.

Shaw, Peter. *The Character of John Adams*. Chapel Hill: University of North Carolina Press, 1976.

Taylor, Robert J., ed. *The Papers of John Adams*. Cambridge, Mass.: Harvard University Press, 1977–.

Samuel Adams

Cushing, Harry Alonzo, ed. *The Writings of Samuel Adams*. New York: G. P. Putnam's Sons, 1908. Reprint, New York: Octagon Books, 1968.

Lewis, Paul. *The Grand Incendiary: A Biography of Samuel Adams*. New York: Dial Press, 1973.

Miller, John C. *Sam Adams: Pioneer in Propaganda*. Stanford, Calif.: Stanford University Press, 1936.

John Dickinson

Bradford, M. E. "A 'Better Guide than Reason': The Politics of John Dickinson." *Modern Age* 21 (Winter 1977): 39–49.

Flower, Milton E. *John Dickinson: Conservative Revolutionary*. Charlottesville: University Press of Virginia, 1983.

Ford, Paul Leicester, ed. *The Political Writings of John Dickinson, 1764–1774*. Philadelphia: Historical Society of Pennsylvania, 1895. Reprint, New York: Da Capo Press, 1970.

Gummere, Richard M. "John Dickinson, Classical Penman of the Revolution." *Classical Journal* 52 (November 1956): 81–88.

Benjamin Franklin

Best, John Hardin, ed. *Benjamin Franklin on Education*. New York: Teachers College of Columbia University, 1962.

Labaree, Leonard W., ed. *The Papers of Benjamin Franklin*. New Haven, Conn.: Yale University Press, 1959–.

Le May, J. A. Leo, ed. *The Writings of Benjamin Franklin*. New York: Library of America, 1987.

Lemisch, L. Jesse, ed. *Benjamin Franklin: The Autobiography and Other Writings*. New York: Penguin Books, 1961.

Schleiner, Winfried. "The Infant Hercules: Franklin's Design for a Medal Commemorating American Liberty." *Eighteenth Century Studies* 10 (Winter 1976): 235–44.

Woody, Thomas, ed. *Educational Views of Benjamin Franklin*. New York: McGraw-Hill, 1931.

Alexander Hamilton

Adair, Douglass. "A Note on Certain of Hamilton's Pseudonyms." *William and Mary Quarterly*, 3rd ser., 12 (April 1955): 282–97.

Chernow, Ron. *Alexander Hamilton*. New York: Penguin, 2004.

Flexner, James Thomas. *The Young Hamilton: A Biography*. Boston: Little, Brown, 1978.

Govan, Thomas P. "Alexander Hamilton and Julius Caesar: A Note on the Use of Historical Evidence." *William and Mary Quarterly*, 3rd ser., 32 (July 1975): 475–80.

McDonald, Forrest. *Alexander Hamilton: A Biography*. New York: W. W. Norton, 1979.

Mitchell, Broadus. *Alexander Hamilton: A Concise Biography*. New York: Oxford University Press, 1976.

Stourzh, Gerald. *Alexander Hamilton and the Idea of Republican Government*. Stanford, Calif.: Stanford University, 1970.

Syrett, Harold C., ed. *The Papers of Alexander Hamilton*. New York: Columbia University Press, 1961–1979.

Patrick Henry

Henry, William Wirt, ed. *Patrick Henry: Life, Correspondence, and Speeches*. New York: Burt Franklin, 1969.

Meade, Robert Douthat, ed. *Patrick Henry*. Philadelphia: J. B. Lippincott, 1957–1969.

Thomas Jefferson

Adams, Dickinson W., ed. *Jefferson's Extracts from the Gospels*. Princeton, N.J.: Princeton University Press, 1983.

Adams, William Howard. *Jefferson and the Arts: An Extended View*. Washington, D.C.: National Gallery of Art, 1976.

Bedini, Silvio A. *Thomas Jefferson: Statesman of Science*. New York: Macmillan, 1990.

Bergh, Albert Ellery, and Andrew A. Lipscomb, eds. *The Writings of Thomas Jefferson*. Washington, D.C.: Thomas Jefferson Memorial Association, 1903.

Berman, Eleanor Davidson. *Thomas Jefferson among the Arts: An Essay in Early American Esthetics*. New York: Philosophical Library, 1947.

Boyd, Julian P., ed. *The Papers of Thomas Jefferson*. Princeton, N.J.: Princeton University Press, 1950–.

Chinard, Gilbert, ed. *The Commonplace Book of Thomas Jefferson: A Repertory of His Ideas on Government*. Baltimore: Johns Hopkins Press, 1926.

———, ed. *The Literary Bible of Thomas Jefferson: His Commonplace Book of Philosophers and Poets*. Baltimore: Johns Hopkins Press, 1928. Reprint, New York: Greenwood Press, 1969.

———. "Thomas Jefferson as a Classical Scholar." *Johns Hopkins Alumni Magazine* 18 (1929–1930): 291–303.

Colbourn, H. Trevor. "Thomas Jefferson's Use of the Past." *William and Mary Quarterly*, 3rd ser., 15 (January 1958): 56–70.

Cunliffe, Marcus. "Thomas Jefferson and the Dangers of the Past." *Wilson Quarterly* 6 (Winter 1982): 96–107.

Dethloff, Henry C., ed. *Thomas Jefferson and American Democracy.* Lexington, Mass.: D. C. Heath, 1971.

Kimball, Fiske. *Thomas Jefferson, Architect.* Boston: Riverside Press, 1916.

Kimball, Marie. *Jefferson: The Road to Glory, 1743–1776.* New York: Coward-Mc-Cann, 1943.

Koch, Adrienne. *The Philosophy of Thomas Jefferson.* New York: Columbia University Press, 1943.

Lehmann, Karl. *Thomas Jefferson: American Humanist.* Chicago: University of Chicago Press, 1964.

Matthews, Richard K. *The Radical Politics of Thomas Jefferson: A Revisionist View.* Lawrence: University Press of Kansas, 1984.

Miller, John C. *The Wolf by the Ears: Thomas Jefferson and Slavery.* New York: Free Press, 1977.

Padover, Saul K., ed. *The Complete Jefferson: Containing His Major Writings, Published and Unpublished, Except His Letters.* New York: Duell, Sloan, and Pearce, 1943.

Peden, William, ed. *Notes on the State of Virginia.* Chapel Hill: University of North Carolina Press, 1955.

Peterson, Merrill D. *Thomas Jefferson and the New Nation: A Biography.* New York: Oxford University Press, 1970.

Wilson, Douglas L. "The American Agricola: Jefferson's Agrarianism and the Classical Tradition." *South Atlantic Quarterly* 80 (Summer 1981): 339–54.

———, ed. *Jefferson's Literary Commonplace Book.* Princeton, N.J.: Princeton University Press, 1989.

———. "What Jefferson and Lincoln Read." *The Atlantic* 267 (January 1991): 51–62.

Wiltshire, Susan Ford. "Jefferson, Calhoun, and the Slavery Debate." *Southern Humanities Review* 25 (Winter 1977): 33–40.

———. "Thomas Jefferson and John Adams on the Classics." *Arion* 6 (Spring 1967): 116–32.

Wright, Louis B. "Thomas Jefferson and the Classics." *Proceedings of the American Philosophical Society* 87 (1943–1944): 223–33.

James Madison

Brant, Irving. *James Madison.* New York: Bobbs-Merrill, 1941–1961.

Hunt, Gaillard, ed. *The Writings of James Madison.* New York: G. P. Putnam's Sons, 1901–1910.

Madison, James. *Letters and Other Writings of James Madison.* New York: R. Worthington, 1884.

Meyers, Marvin, ed. *The Mind of the Founder: Sources of the Political Thought of James Madison.* New York: Bobbs-Merrill, 1973.

Peterson, Merrill D., ed. *James Madison: A Biography in His Own Words*. New York: Harper and Row, 1974.
Rutland, Robert A., et al., eds. *The Papers of James Madison*. Chicago: University of Chicago Press, 1962–1977. Charlottesville: University Press of Virginia, 1977–.

George Mason
Rowland, Kate M., ed. *The Life and Correspondence of George Mason*. New York: Russell and Russell, 1964.
Rutland, Robert A., ed. *The Papers of George Mason*. Chapel Hill: University of North Carolina Press, 1970.

Thomas Paine
Aldridge, A. Owen. "Thomas Paine and the Classics." *Eighteenth Studies* 1 (Summer 1968): 370–80.
Conway, Moncure Daniel, ed. *The Writings of Thomas Paine*. New York: AMS Press, 1967.
Van der Weyde, William, ed. *The Life and Works of Thomas Paine*. New Rochelle, N.Y.: Thomas Paine National Historical Association, 1925–1927.

Benjamin Rush
Butterfield, L. H., ed. *Letters of Benjamin Rush*. Princeton, N.J.: Princeton University Press, 1951.
Corner, George W., ed. *The Autobiography of Benjamin Rush: His "Travels through Life" Together with His Commonplace Book for 1789–1813*. Princeton, N.J.: Princeton University Press, 1948.
Goodman, Nathan G. *Benjamin Rush: Physician and Citizen, 1746–1813*. Philadelphia: University of Pennsylvania Press, 1934.
Runes, Dagobert, ed. *The Selected Writings of Benjamin Rush*. New York: Philosophical Library, 1947.

George Washington
Craven, Wayne. "Horatio Greenough's Statue of Washington and Phidias's Olympian Zeus." *Art Quarterly* 26 (Winter 1963): 429–40.
Cunliffe, Marcus. *George Washington: Man and Monument*. Boston: Little, Brown, 1958.
Fitzpatrick, John C., ed. *The Writings of George Washington*. Washington, D.C.: Government Printing Office, 1931–1940.
Flexner, James Thomas. *George Washington*. Boston: Little, Brown, 1965–1969.
Ford, Paul Leicester. *Washington and the Theater*. New York: Benjamin Blom, 1899. Reprint, New York: Dunlap Society Publications, 1967.
Jackson, Donald, and Dorothy Twohig, eds. *The Diaries of George Washington*. Charlottesville: University Press of Virginia, 1976.
Montgomery, Henry C. "Addison's *Cato* and George Washington." *Classical Journal* 55 (February 1960): 210–12.

————. "Washington the Stoic." *Classical Journal* 31 (March 1936): 371–73.

Schroeder, John Frederick, ed. *Maxims of George Washington*. New York: D. Appleton, 1855.

Wills, Garry. *Cincinnatus: George Washington and the Enlightenment*. Garden City, N.Y.: Doubleday, 1984.

James Wilson

McCloskey, Robert Green, ed. *The Works of James Wilson*. Cambridge, Mass.: Harvard University Press, 1967.

Seed, Geoffrey. *James Wilson*. Milkwood, N.Y.: KTO Press, 1978.

Smith, Charles Page. *James Wilson: Founding Father, 1742–1798*. Chapel Hill: University of North Carolina Press, 1956.

Others

Barry, Richard. *Mr. Rutledge of South Carolina*. New York: Duell, Sloan, 1942.

Bernhard, Winfred E. *Fisher Ames: Federalist and Statesman, 1758–1808*. Chapel Hill: University of North Carolina Press, 1965.

Billias, George Athan. *Elbridge Gerry: Founding Father and Republican Statesman*. New York: McGraw-Hill, 1976.

Cary, John. *Joseph Warren: Physician, Politician, and Patriot*. Urbana: University of Illinois Press, 1961.

Dangerfield, George. *Robert R. Livingston of New York, 1746–1813*. New York: Harcourt, Brace, 1960.

Ernst, Robert. *Rufus King: American Federalist*. Chapel Hill: University of North Carolina Press, 1968.

Godbold, E. Stanley, and Robert H. Woody. *Christopher Gadsden and the American Revolution*. Knoxville: University of Tennessee Press, 1982.

Morris, Richard B., ed. *John Jay: The Making of a Revolutionary, Unpublished Papers, 1745–1780*. New York: Harper and Row, 1975.

Taylor, John. *An Inquiry into the Principles and Policy of the Government of the United States*. New Haven, Conn.: Yale University Press, 1950.

Walsh, Richard, ed. *The Writings of Christopher Gadsden, 1746–1805*. Columbia: University of South Carolina Press, 1966.

Zahniser, Martin R. *Charles Cotesworth Pinckney: Founding Father*. Chapel Hill: University of North Carolina Press, 1967.

~

Index of Translations
for Long Quotations

195

Index

~

About the Author

Carl J. Richard is professor of history at the University of Louisiana at Lafayette. He received his Ph.D. in American history from Vanderbilt University in 1988. His books include *The Founders and the Classics: Greece, Rome, and the American Enlightenment* (1994), *Twelve Greeks and Romans Who Changed the World* (2003), and *The Battle for the American Mind: A Brief History of a Nation's Thought* (2004).